The Future of
the American School System

Irving H. Buchen

ScarecrowEducation
Lanham, Maryland • Toronto • Oxford
2004

KH

Published in the United States of America
by ScarecrowEducation
An imprint of The Rowman & Littlefield Publishing Group, Inc.
4501 Forbes Boulevard, Suite 200, Lanham, Maryland 20706
www.scarecroweducation.com

PO Box 317
Oxford
OX2 9RU, UK

British Library Cataloguing in Publication Information Available

Library of Congress Cataloging-in-Publication Data

Buchen, Irving H., 1930–
    The future of the American school system / Irving H. Buchen.
        p. cm.
    Includes bibliographical references.
    ISBN 1-57886-135-7 (pbk. : alk. paper)
    1. Education—United States—Forecasting. 2. Educational change—United
States. 3. Educational leadership—United States. I. Title.
    LA217.2.B816 2004
    370'.973—dc22   2004000222

∞™ The paper used in this publication meets the minimum requirements of
American National Standard for Information Sciences—Permanence of
Paper for Printed Library Materials, ANSI/NISO Z39.48-1992.
Manufactured in the United States of America.

9/20/05

Contents

Preface

This book is ambitious—some may claim overly so. It attempts to describe and examine in detail the entire educational system of K–12. It addresses virtually all the major players: teachers, administrators, students, and parents. It seeks to identify the significant drivers of change and to estimate their impact on the system and players. And, finally, it projects the future direction of education for the next two decades, in the process offering some solutions to many current educational problems.

Why include so much? A great many studies are narrower, focusing on special aspects of education—curriculum or assessment—or restricting themselves to different educational levels—elementary or high school. They deal with one group—teachers or students—but not all groups. They seldom if ever speculate about the future, unless to sadly imply that education may lack one. Above all, they generally steer clear of recommending changes. They focus on problems rather than solutions.

But such approaches are, in the final analysis, deceptive. They pass off halves as wholes, pieces as complete parts. The system has to be viewed in its totality because many of of education's problems are in fact systemic. Similarly, the roles of various major players do not exist in isolation from each other. They constantly interact. If parents really want to know what is going on in schools with their kids, they also have to know what is going on with teachers and with principals. If it takes a community to raise a child, then it is important to know what everyone is contributing to the total educational process.

Then, too, education has changed. It no longer resembles what parents, teachers, and administrators experienced as children, any more than medicine today is the same as it was then. Moreover, education is in "future flux." The projected changes will transform schooling and learning so significantly that by the time a current kindergartener enters middle school it will have been altered dramatically. Profiling the major drivers of change thus generates the kind of timelines that mirror and parallel the developmental stages of current students. Finally, focusing on the future compels solutions. Problem solving cannot be avoided, dodged, or muted. Change requires changing.

Reducing the scope is thus not a meaningful option. The clarity of specific parts is too high a price to pay for fidelity to the whole. Only when the big picture is presented, no matter how difficult and generalized that may be, will it be possible to understand the scope and extent of the challenge and promise of education. Moreover, assuring the future of education may be bracing enough to manage education's current flux and oscillations. The value of identifying future prospects is to invite interventions that minimize the undesirable and optimize the aspirational. In short, far from being self-indulgent or escapist, forecasting is predicated on intervention and action now, and using the intervening years to position education for a desirable future equal to its public mission. Indeed, there is much evidence to point to a rich and varied future for education.

So much then for my rationale for being inclusive and trying to link all the critical parts. Finally, let me address or rather confess two biases. The first has to do with balancing different and often hotly contested points of view. If I have erred, it has been on the side of preserving the range of difference. The second problem—communication—may be unsolvable. I am a parent with six kids, a college professor, a teacher of teachers, a trainer of administrators, an educational consultant, and an educational researcher. All of these perspectives shape my thinking and prose. My goal was to write a book that everyone could read and find useful. So I straddled writing for the general reader and for the specialist, giving facts but also citing sources, dramatizing situations and plights while being objective and detached. Citations have been included unobtrusively in the text and full references placed at the end of the book. I have studiously tried to write in a nonacademic style, but certain habits die hard.

The reason I have labored so hard to be clear and concrete in describing and including so much is that I am convinced that collective action alone can give education back its future. We all have to become leaders. It cannot be left to any one group or constituency, because the really important and innovative changes are crossover solutions. They must be not just large and deep, but also systemic. They cannot happen unless all the parts and players are on the same page, really understand each others' self-interest, and see the big picture of collective action. What we need, then, is for every constituency to be knowledgeable and respectful of every other constituency until a breakthrough emerges as a shared purpose, larger than the sum of its parts. In short, I believe in the vision of the ancient Tao proverb: "When leaders lead well, the people believe they did it all themselves." As indeed they should.

Part I

THE PAST, THE PRESENT, AND THE FUTURE

CHAPTER 1

The Record of the Past

Although the confidence of the American people in the presidency, the Congress, the economy, the military, and so forth has varied over time, their confidence in education has remained firm for many generations. For example, a recent sampling poll of residents of Ohio found that 60 percent of respondents believed schools were headed in the right direction. But there was an important qualification. Almost 85 percent believed that schools cannot significantly improve unless they involve parents and residents. Thus, support for school renovation or construction went from a timid 47 percent to a strong 65 percent when respondents were told that the schools could include multipurpose facilities that could be used after school and year round. Finally, they were not in favor of large high schools of one thousand students or more. Instead, they favored smaller ones of four hundred students (*Education Week* 2003b).

This guarded "Yes, but" affirmation of schooling is typical of the new attitude toward education. The support is there but there are strings of participation and involvement attached. In addition, taxpayers are weary of having their tax levies used exclusively for the young. The schools should also be perceived as a community resource. In fact, a significant current trend is the development of community schools that share common space between classrooms for students and meeting places for members of the community. Finally, the public is savvy enough to recognize that bigger schools are not good places to learn. In short, this generation of parents and citizens is smart and vocal. They are not as obedient or accepting as their own parents and certainly their grandparents were.

When I was a kid, school was the kingdom of the future and my teacher the keeper of the holy grail. To my parents, teachers could do wrong. If there was ever a discipline problem or an issue raised about tests and answers, teachers were always right and I was always wrong. I was not that kind of parent when my kids were in school. I was very much like the residents of Ohio surveyed above—supportive but questioning, an advocate for teachers but a believer in higher standards. Above all, I openly acknowledged what public education had done for not only me but my entire generation. It is generally a splendid record.

Many professionals today were educated in the public school system, myself included. I attended public schools from kindergarten through twelfth grade. Many of my friends and contemporaries then went on to secure an equally superior education in public universities with little or no tuition. In a number of cases the graduates were the first members of their family to receive a college degree. And that process of acculturation is still going on for all new immigrants. Many high school and college commencements include a large proportion of new arrivals as well as mothers and even grandmothers. Moreover, 90 percent of all students today still attend the public schools. Such access honors the schools' public mission and social purpose.

Unfortunately, such records of achievement are often minimized or even trivialized. Indeed, it currently appears fashionable to engage in educational bashing as a form of being politically correct. Recently, the executive director of the Coalition for Evidence-Based Policy, in an article in *Education Week* (2002e), declared, "There's been no improvement in education in the last 30 years, despite a 90 percent increase in real public spending." That double whammy would be a real indictment if it were true. But it is not:

- In 1970 only about 57 percent of whites aged 25 or older had completed high school. In 2000, it was 88 percent.
- In 1970 less than 37 percent of all blacks aged 25 or older has completed high school. In 2000 it was nearly 79 percent.
- In 1970 only 15 percent of white males and less than 9 percent of white females had completed college. In 2000, it was 30 and 25 percent, respectively.

- In 1970 only about 6 percent of all blacks had completed college. In 2000, it was over 16 percent.
- The number of students taking tougher high school courses has increased fourfold. SAT verbal scores have increased six points since 1990, math scores thirteen points since 1990.
- National Association of Education Progress tests at fourth, eighth, and twelfth grades have shown a steady and often significant increase in both reading and math performance across the country and across urban, suburban, and rural schools.

Given such a record of accomplishment, it is not surprising that Reg Weaver, president of the National Education Association, urges that instead of crying, like Chicken Little, that the sky is falling, we count our blessings (*Education Week* 2003a). But that still leaves the nagging problem of unfavorable current public and professional perception—the "Yes, but" response. If so much has been achieved, why is there such an extreme indictment of the educational system?

The reasons, which are many and complex, will be discussed in detail in the rest of the book; however, there are at least three that can be quickly shared here.

1. WORK PREPAREDNESS

Feedback from employers who hire public school graduates has not been generally positive. Employers find graduates weak or inadequate. Many graduates cannot read, write, or calculate. In other words, the performance standards of schools are too low. Four-year and community colleges have had to offer remedial courses in English and math to bring incoming students up to speed. Some state universities offer Composition 0, a course for which students receive no credit. In other words, the qualitative record often does not match the quantitative record. The increase in numbers of white and black, male and female high school graduates does not mean the students are adequately prepared. Indeed, the high percentage of high school students who currently are failing state graduation exams, which were introduced as an across-the-board quality-control measure, confirms the above charge of inadequate preparation. The decision to postpone the implementation of such tests to a later date—California just chose 2006—or to allow seniors this year and for the next three to graduate without having to pass the tests does not inspire confidence in public education or its tactics.

Juggling the statistics offered by both sides of the debate will not take us to the truth. That requires combining the gains and the shortfalls of the educational system. To be persuasive and deep, scholastic achievement has to be both quantitative and qualitative. Unfortunately, the gap between the two areas has widened enough for both sides to be right. And conflicts between rights are harder to reconcile than conflicts between right and wrong. But the basic argument is that education has accepted levels of performance that are too low, has passed the buck to colleges and the workplace, and thus has failed to fulfill its mission of educating students to acceptable levels to go on and achieve the social goals of work, college, and citizenship.

2. BALANCED ACCESS

The other argument against education is based on unequal access. Improvements have been not only inadequate but also unevenly distributed. The complaints have taken two forms. The first, as noted above, is that education has stopped short of assuring not just exposure to but competence in the basics. The second complaint often takes the form of demographic advocacy for urban and rural schools. Studies have clearly documented that such schools have larger classes and a larger proportion of uncredentialized and/or inexperienced teachers and administrators than suburban schools. Administrative turnover has been so high that recently New York City and other municipalities began to offer incentive bonuses to principals who remain at least three years in poorly performing schools. In short, inequity of expenditure and commitment has resulted in the accusation that educational achievement has been accomplished at the expense of the disenfranchised. The inequities of distribution often have been disguised by the massaging of data to exclude lower-performing students. Hence, the recent federal mandate that seeks to redress the various sins of omission is appropriately titled "No Child Left Behind."

3. IRRELEVANT

The last complaint is in many ways the most serious and profound. Whether or not what is being done is enough, and fairly distributed to all, it is past oriented. It is not what is needed now and in the future. This goes way beyond the issue of competence in the three Rs. It also goes beyond incremental gains or the popular cry for relevance. It is a profound criticism of education not at the branches but at its root.

What is the point of endlessly tweaking the basics of education or even the delivery system if what is being provided fails to reflect the major changes of a global economy, electronic interconnectivity, and more demanding jobs (many of which did not exist before)? Lou Perelman argues that the great failing of education is that it has been insulated from the major forces that have been transforming society, the economy, work, and even aging. That disservice has not only removed education from the mainstream but also led to a general failure to incorporate those larger forces of change as defining and shaping agents to evolve a new kind of education, one that is needed now and more so in the future.

The projections are dramatic and, to many, alarming. A number of scientists believe that machine intelligence will match and even surpass human intelligence within the next two decades. Pharmacologists are altering plants genetically so that they can grow drugs. The world increasingly will become man made. Technology and nature will merge to a point at which they will fuse. The major technologies of the twentieth century were nuclear, biological, and chemical (NBC). The major technologies of the twenty-first century will be genetics, nanotechnology, and robotics (GNR). Even if only half of what is projected happens, the growth rate of new knowledge and inventions in the twenty-first century will be equivalent to ten thousand to twenty thousand years of progress by existing standards.

That or some variation of that world is what kids currently in school will inherit and live in. Nor will it be familiar or reassuring to their parents. How well are students being equipped to face the globality of GNR? Given such visions of change and discontinuity, schooling should be a lab of the future. Minimally it should be technological. In many schools it is not. Schools boards, departments of education, legislators, and school superintendents show little evidence of developing a vision of the future of education commensurate with the future of the world outside schools. Instead of envisioning education in cyber space and time, they are using limited resources to build new schools that may become obsolete before being completed. Working parents aware of the constant changes in their careers have a better sense of what is happening. Current students, who live with technology daily, would not regard such a future as science fiction. Why then are not educators as proactive as students and their parents?

Educators tend to talk to and write only for educators. Recently, when a midwest business coalition invited some hundred educational administrators to a corporate-education conference, they found that the educational participants were woefully ignorant of business in general and, more important, of all the changes businesses have to make to survive and grow. Of course, that has not stopped educators from displaying their ignorance as they criticize the application of business practices to education.

Typically administrators are exposed only to the literature of educational leadership and thus are generally unaware of the extensive literature of business leadership. In short, even if education alters its branch but leaves alone the root, and even if it includes every child, it may still fall short of engaging the challenging reality its graduates will face. Worse, the changes it contemplates are timid or shallow. They are one mile across and one inch deep. They are Band-Aids. They deal with symptoms, not causes.

Until educators understand why insurance companies export underwriting assignments to Ireland, and why Dell has shifted technical customer support and software development to India, education will be viewing the future through a rearview mirror. Offering better versions of the same old stuff is offering built-in obsolescence. The corrective strategy can be called "Operation Leapfrog": while we are catching up, let us also get ahead.

All megatrends already exist and even appear in realized or embryonic form in daily newspapers. Thus, perhaps the most important value of looking ahead is to dramatize the here and now and thus provide education with a chance to face a changing world. Calling on education to be more proactive and future directed provides a natural segue to the next chapter, which provides a description of forecasting as a rigorous and responsible process. This description is intended to impart greater credibility to the call for education to be more forward looking and offer a better understanding of the ways of a changing world.

CHAPTER 2

The Laws of the Future

Yogi Berra, that fount of wisdom, declared that it is difficult to predict, especially the future. Skepticism regularly greets forecasters, perhaps rightly so. To be sure, futurists in turn try to be reassuring. They claim that they do not dictate or predict the future; they merely offer projections. But clearly this sidesteps an issue that must be addressed, especially when audiences are often so beset by uncertainty that they grasp at straws and convert the tentative and limited into the gospel. For instance, when a news story appears reporting the curative value of broccoli, immediately, supermarket shelves are bare. But there are other forecasting professionals who approach the task of looking ahead more seriously, cautiously, and honestly.

Recently, a group of Minnesota futurists urged the group's members to be more candid and to define projections as at best a collective hunch. Another group argued that the only way futurists can secure credibility is to put their forecasts on trial, subject them to the third degree, judge harshly, and throw out those that exhibit fatal flaws under cross-examination. Because forecasting is allied to and often resembles science fiction, it may be both sobering and enlightening to recall the definition of science fiction offered by Isaac Asimov: "an escape to reality." That is reminiscent of the classic definition by Carson McCullers of poetry as an imaginary garden with a real toad. The most recent and popularized version of the paradox may be the bumper sticker that reads, "The future is where the rubber meets the sky."

What all the above have in common is the need to bridge the imagined and the real, future trends and the concrete present. Indeed, one way this book will seek to honor that convergence is by presenting scenarios of the projections offered. Scenarios are future scripts anchored in real life. They present scenes of the future in which real people, not ideas, face real situations, not imagined constructs. Scenarios are alive in the future. Persuasion thus rests not on ideology or authority but on verisimilitude.

But probably the most convincing arguments futurists have to offer is their knowledge of the ways the future works. In particular, they have found that the future regularly exhibits three laws: escalation, accessibility, and choice.

1. THE LAW OF ESCALATION

The first law of the future functions as an early warning system. Specifically, the future visits the present progressively in three versions: future stretch, future strain, and future shock. The three operate sequentially in escalation fashion.

In the first instance, the handwriting on the wall asks only for stretch—for a manageable and relatively easy series of adjustments to change. It is legitimate to expect people to be flexible. In fact, many organizations have incorporated stretch goals in their strategic plans and even the job descriptions and evaluations of their employees. But if the opportunity is not heeded, then the future ups the ante to the next stage.

Future strain is obviously more taxing and exacting. Draconian measures may begin to appear; medication is replaced by surgery; desperation drives downsizing. Although there are still some options available, they are fewer in number and often invite choosing the lesser of two evils.

But if future strain too is ignored, then the future unleashes the full wrath of discontinuity. Things are grim and ugly. Scapegoats are sought. Bosses become oppressive and punitive, justifying their behaviors by pointing to the times. Workers retaliate by secretly sabotaging products, using up all their sick days, and trying to find another job before the ax falls. Crisis management is paraded as the new norm, although all its martyred exponents fail to realize that it is a contradiction in terms.

The same three conditions can be used to define three kinds of organizations: future oriented, future directed, and future driven. The application is in reverse order. Future-driven organizations are routinely proactive and inhabit future stretch. The future is never an abstract notion or far-off time but a familiar companion. Management and rank and file are in a constant state of future readiness. Like the U.S. Coast Guard they are *semper paratus*—always prepared. Stretch is something they do routinely; their clocks and calendars are always doubly set on now and tomorrow.

Future-directed companies are unevenly futuristic. They move in fits and starts between being totally future directed and dropping back into the daily routine of business as usual. They are prime candidates for future strain. They hang inspiring pictures on the walls of corporate training centers exhorting planning and morale. They trade on the reassuring patterns of the past. They can never imagine not being needed or valued, or, worse of all, failing to exist.

Finally, future-oriented organizations are likely to skip all intermediate stages and go directly into future shock. Future shock is not unlike the cold water of reality experienced by high school seniors who fail the state-mandated graduation tests or do not secure good jobs. Future-oriented organizations traffic in token gestures, lip service, and cosmetic fixes. Many American companies regarded themselves as permanent fixtures and concluded that they were indispensable, only to find that they are noncompetitive and in some cases almost superfluous. Some have disappeared altogether or were transformed or broken up into parts, but all are lesser versions of their former glory.

Do the three categories apply to education? It varies by constituency. Generally teachers, parents, and students inhabit stretch; financial officers strain; and administrators, school boards, colleges of education, and federal and state departments of education straddle strain and shock. The reason for that last designation is that the crisis of education is increasingly a crisis of leadership.

Educational administration frequently lacks direction, vision, or decisiveness and is scattered in all directions seemingly without a common plan or purpose. Administrators increasingly occupy the bully pulpit and extol the virtues and verities of the past. They vacillate between eagerly accepting punitive policies like zero tolerance, and bribing teachers with incentives and bonuses. In short, educational leadership at all levels is in bad futures shape.

In contrast, teachers, parents, and students generally inhabit stretch, which is always defined by choice. Teachers have left traditional schools for charter schools, often giving up tenure. Many have despaired of reform happening and left the field altogether. A number have joined educational firms providing curricula or technological support to education. In contrast, educational administrators have generally remained where they are. A few have gone back into teaching, not all with success. A smaller number have become principals in for-profit management companies like Edison, but in general educational leaders have not had the flexibility and diverse choices of teachers (which may further explain why they find themselves stuck).

Parents generally resemble teachers in inhabiting stretch. Over a million households have elected homeschooling. Parents have also chosen to enroll their offspring in over two thousand charter schools. Community political action has led to community school boards and, more importantly, perhaps, to site-based management of schools. Parental fundraising has often made the difference between sparse and ample school budgets.

Students generally have fared equally well adjusting to different versions of schooling and learning: home, charter, and cyber. Their adaptability indeed has influenced a change even in the way we talk about education. "Learning" rather than "schooling" is the preferred term to signify that education is no longer limited to the school or classroom. Indeed, many students have elected to follow less traditional curricula. Service learning, which honors Dewey's focus on experiential learning, or learning by doing, is community based. Inquiry and project learning place great emphasis on independent and group learning, planning, and direction. In a number of cases students have given new or real meaning to the slogans schools often adopt proclaiming they are student centered. Student-led parent-teacher conferences, assumption of custodial and lunch supervision duties, community service and volunteering—all these are examples of an elastic school environment that is not just student centered but student driven.

The value of the first law of the future is thus its many applications. It not only describes how the future works and impacts us, but also provides an overlay for sorting out the major players and constituencies. The second law deals with the extent to which the future gives and withholds, cooperates and ultimately remains aloof.

2. THE LAW OF ACCESS

The future is available, but in a distributed way. The future is a mixture of the known, the unknown, and the unknowable. The known: we already know a great deal about the next twenty-five years. Public utilities project energy and water needs, school board buildings, global populations, land use, and so on. All is based on current demographics, extended or extrapolated.

The unknown is not unknowable. It is based on what seem to be emerging patterns. Trends are sought and identified. Experts in various fields may be assembled and employ the forecasting tool called Delphi (named after the famous Greek oracle). The specialists review the relevant trends and estimate the extent of their impact and their comparative durability. The trends projected to happen early, last long, and have the greatest impact enjoy the highest priority. In Naisbitt's terms they are megatrends.

The last member of the trinity is not only unknowable but also unavailable. That unavailability is how the future remains unpredictable—how it remains the future. In mythology, theology, and literature, such ultimate future knowledge is treated as a divine preserve. But regularly it invites the presumption of many overreachers, starting with Adam and Prometheus, and perhaps now including geneticists attempting to clone living things and offer immortality. But we should not despair at being denied total access to the future, since enough access for our purposes is available.

Combining the known and unknown provides forecasters and planners with about two-thirds of what they need to know about the future. And that is enough to move ahead with intelligence and foresight, especially in conjunction with the knowledge of future stretch, strain, and shock. There is one other law of futures that offers guidance and even a reality check.

3. THE LAW OF CHOICE

The third law involves identifying whether forecasts, or futures, are probable, possible, or preferred. A probable future enjoys the most creditability and a high likelihood of happening. It has been massaged by the experts and in effect given a seal of approval. In some cases it is able to survive the rigors of the Baldridge, ISO, or Six Sigma criteria, as well as the EPA methodology, by which it must record not only the initial, but also the secondary and tertiary, orders of impact. In short, it is the darling of all forecasts and is granted the greatest attention and acceptance.

A possible future is more of a stepchild. While a possible future cannot be ruled out completely, it is less likely to happen and is generally given a lower priority. Its value often is to make the highly probable look good. But because the future sometimes deals wild cards, the surprises inherent in possible futures cannot be overlooked. The possible always is a contingency; it is plan B.

A preferred future does not seem to fit the progression. It does not obviously relate back to the other two versions. Indeed, it appears to offer a departure from its more scientific partners. It appears willful and assertive, based more on vision and aspiration than methodology. It is driven by what a group or organization wants, regardless of what the trends say is likely to happen. It does not ignore the value of exploring and documenting the probable and the possible, but it proceeds from a less neutral and more explicitly values-centered basis. It essentially offers those contemplating the future the opportunity to design it.

It is always easier to ride with than to buck demographics and trends. The preferred future is placed over the probable and the possible to identify where it coincides and where it does not. The space between the preferred and the probable/possible defines the planning gap. The next step is to determine what it will take to close that gap and bring the three closer together. It may require an adjustment of time parameters or allocation of resources. It may even require going back to the drawing board. But if the values of the vision can remain intact and strong in the face of the probable, then the preferred future may find ways to close the planning gap, becoming not only more possible, but also more probable.

It is critical to encourage aspiration and accommodate dreams. But dreams need to be tasked by what is likely to happen. Recall Asimov— the escape is to reality. Although I believe the future needs education as much as education needs the future, the issue is whether education is receptive to that mutual task and whether education's current structure supports or opposes such forward-looking change.

CHAPTER 3

The System of Systems

Imagine a hub and a series of concentric circles surrounding it. The hub is the familiar individual school. It is staffed by teachers, counselors, and administrators who minister to students. There are a number of such hubs in a typical K–12 school district: traditionally, many elementary schools, fewer middle schools, and one or two high schools. The progression of size generally reflects the developmental levels of student independence.

The first ring that encircles that hub of all schools in the district is totally administrative. It consists of the superintendent, the staff of the central office, and the school board. The next outer ring is broader based. It includes the community members who elect the school board and whose taxes help to support the district; local businesses and chambers of commerce; teacher and administrator associations; and above all those most directly involved—parents.

To most citizens, the configuration of the hub and its two outer circles constitutes the basic educational system. It is clearly visible and accessible. Direct involvement by parents and parent associations is accommodated; citizens can attend and speak at board meetings and elect new members; referenda for new buildings and propositions on policy such as class size are voted on. The media provide reports on school board meetings and elections, the coming and going of superintendents, and school achievements and shortcomings. Except for occasional stories about the budget decisions of the state legislature, education has historically been a local community affair. Not so anymore.

Here is a summary of what can impact local education in a typical week:

- A statewide reduction in class size is implemented.
- More teachers are hired with no new funding.
- State plans are submitted to satisfy federal mandates.
- National reports find that education is failing.
- The PTA, through its foundation, raises funds for a new computer lab.
- Three new charter schools are approved.
- Two Catholic middle schools close.
- The state supreme court upholds vouchers.
- Almost 20 percent of high school seniors fail the graduation exam.
- The costs of special ed have doubled in five years.
- The school board recommends a longer day and year.
- A zero tolerance policy backfires; honors students are prohibited from attending their graduation ceremony.
- Bullying incidents increase dramatically.
- A new ethical decision-making program is introduced by Junior Achievement.
- Education buildings fail a fire code inspection.

The initially clear picture of the local school district and its schools begins to blur as other circles exert their clout. The most insistent and proximate are the all-important state departments of education, which regulate and oversee education; and the state legislatures, which appropriate the state's share of funds for schools and fund the departments of education.

But it does not stop there. Beyond that circle are a number of federal agencies in general and above all the national Department of Education. Occasionally, local schools may be caught in the political limelight when the president of the United States seeks to achieve visibility as an education president.

Finally, less official but no less influential are a whole host of more distant outer circles that exercise a clout out of proportion to their distance: all the colleges of education, and all the unions and professional associations of teachers, staff, administrators, parents, school boards, state officers, and so on. These are further amplified into other advocacy organizations on the one hand and neutral professional support organizations like ACSD, which run influential conferences and workshops, on the other. The last circle, one that is often omitted, is made up of a number of powerful, well-funded (sometimes, it seems, clandestinely so) national educational think tanks, which launch or staff various national commissions; public policy research consultants like the RAND Corporation and Resources for the Future, which produce influential white papers; and advocacy groups and lobbyists for all constituencies.

It is formidable. Worse, it is oppressive. When the question of why we cannot do something is asked, or a solution that seems obvious and plausible is proposed, the response of hemming and hawing is often seen as legitimate. "Well, it all depends; we have to take it step by step; we have to touch all the bases."

Elaborate systems are labyrinths. Everything is contingent. Approval follows the wedding cake model of ascending and consulting at every level. The layers on layers of rules and sign-offs seem endless. Just getting paid or reimbursed invokes a protracted process with such elaborate and repetitive consultations at each stage that one better understands why cases of educational embezzlement can happen and why they often take years to uncover.

But it can be argued bureaucracy always has been with us and is everywhere. Education, like every public sector, has developed step-by-step levels that sadly function to insulate jobs and impede change. Changing the rules and access of government agencies has been rightly compared to moving a graveyard. But education does not have a monopoly on systemic opacity and impeding flow. They operate in the private sector as well, if more quietly. The recent revelations and corporate meltdowns at Enron, Tyco, and other companies involved auditing cover-ups that took advantage of the system. The net result is a divergence between what constitutes the organization and what constitutes the business. Increasingly, they are not the same.

But still, the educational version of bureaucracy has become so powerful, complex, and invasive of late that it appears to be overwhelming the historical roles of local and communal participation and self-definition. Some claim the system has become a perfect storm—a colossal system of systems.

How did it happen? What has brought about so much greater centralization, on the one hand, and fragmented and even paralyzed individual, school, and community self-determination and self-direction, on the other hand?

Sometimes complex questions need to be first answered simply. Three major novel developments have changed the basic system of education: the federal government, accountability, and competition. Singly and together, they have subjected education to the new paradoxes of contraction and expansion, increased regulation and entrepreneurship, the slap and the caress. Although each of these three drivers of change will be discussed later and in greater detail, the extent to which they have transformed the microsystem of education into a macrosystem of systems can be quickly outlined.

1. THE NEW ROLE OF THE FEDERAL GOVERNMENT

The federal government always has played a significant role in education. Although its role has focused mostly on the financial allocations of Title 1, the federal government has used that leverage, for example, to specify the governance process of allocating such funds. In particular, it initially mandated community school boards and later mandated site-based management. Although the federal government took no part or position in the perennial debate about the lack of a national curriculum and accompanying standards, advocates for both cited the number of developed countries with national curricula that outscored us on international math and science tests. But the fear was that government would become Big Brother and compromise local and state school control. Then in 2001 No Child Left Behind (NCLB) legislation was passed.

Focusing only on its systemic impact, what does the legislation require? Most obviously, it mandates national standards, a process of meeting those standards, and a timetable. State education no longer can be self-defining. In fact, each state department of education has to submit its plans of compliance to the federal Department of Education for approval. Many states have had their plans returned for revision. In the process, states have had to identify all poorly performing or failing schools and provide detailed plans of remediation.

In the process, all state departments of education in effect have had to become agents of the federal Department of Education. They in turn have required every school district to align its educational goals and assessment processes with those of the state-federal plan. And following the chain of command, every superintendent of every school district has sent the same alignment message to all his or her principals, who in turn have relayed it to all their teachers. Never before in the history of local-based education in America has there been such massive, direct, and nonnegotiable control of the future of education. If that alone had happened, it would be sufficient to have created the system of systems. But there is more.

2. ACCOUNTABILITY

Long before NCLB was passed, state legislatures and often local school boards, concerned about annual increases in teacher salaries and the reports of failing schools and students, tied a string of accountability measures to allocations. Because adaptation was allowed to take many forms, local autonomy initially was preserved. To be sure, the sheer variety of the responses, coupled with the fact that many were only tokens, aggravated the situation. In state after state departments of education then upped the ante by adding teeth to the process across the board. State departments of education developed accountability systems. Educational researchers and consultants joined in. Then, unexpectedly, enterprising educational computer companies that specialized in data-tracking software that could monitor not only student, but also teacher, performance offered the kind of precision a serious accountability process requires. Shortly thereafter some districts developed incentive or bonus pay for teachers who raised student performance to certain levels. Soon after, a new norm of grading individual schools emerged. Schools that received failing grades in two consecutive statewide exams became subject to censure, state takeover, or the loss of students to a voucher system.

As momentum increased and school-based report cards created both satisfaction and condemnation, accountability became the new savior and villain. Charges and countercharges emerged. On the downside were the accusations of teaching to the test, stripping curricula to only what was being tested, massive switching of personnel to schools that had failed once and might fail the second time, and so on. Further, battle lines were drawn between teachers and administrators; between angry parents whose kids had failed the high school exit exam and school boards; and between local officials and state departments of education. All became increasingly involved in the blame game. The wars of accountability prepared the way for federal intervention in at least two ways. On the one hand, statewide accountability systems had laid the foundation and established the precedent for comprehensive assessment. On the other hand, the variability of assessment practices within and between states cried out for greater and often higher-level commonality and uniformity. Besides, the feds played their unique trump card: they became advocates across the board for all students, especially those in danger of being left behind.

3. COMPETITION

Initially, the business sector played a generally minor role in accountability. Later it expanded rapidly. Computer companies provided education with the data tracking it needed to respond adequately to the accountability pressures of NCLB. But in the process of becoming indispensable in a supportive role, computer companies also crossed the line and went into direct competition with what had been essentially the public monopoly on public education.

Nobel Enterprises created and marketed small private independent schools located all over the country in areas that had the right demographics of money and aspiration. Private and for-profit school management companies began to appear. Their claims were embarrassing. They offered to increase student scores, stay within budget, and even make a small profit. If they could do that, why couldn't public schools do the same? Then that claim was carried further by charter schools that sought to raise the accountability of the bottom line to a higher level than their public counterparts. If they went into the red, they closed down. Unlike under-performing public schools, which not only were subsidized but showered with resources, charter schools functioned as businesses. They epitomized and affirmed competition. Finally, homeschooling became increasingly attractive to many families, especially when boosted by technology. Although homeschooling, unlike charter schools, did not directly drain off per capita dollars, many districts lamented losing the cream of the crop. That they had became increasingly apparent when many homeschoolers won national merit scholarships and competitions. In short, for the first time in the history of U.S. education the monopoly of K–12 was challenged. And with competition came school choice, the ultimate sign and benefit of a free-market economy. What minimally is clear is the following:

- Federal legislation has become the dominant and dominating system.
- It is the system of systems.
- Accountability and assessment will become permanent norms of education.
- Testing may become an everyday experience.
- School choice will offer new options to parents and students, to investors, and unexpectedly to teachers as well.

Everyone involved in education will have to become smarter, more knowledgeable, and savvier about much more than just their hub school and reach beyond the narrow circle that used to define education. The scope is sometimes daunting. Explaining, negotiating, and navigating the complexity of the system of systems has to be joined to the new world of mandated accountability and choice. Moreover, somehow all these new realities have to converge and shape the leadership agenda of all constituencies. More than ever education needs the sharing of common cause and purpose. That has to become the ultimate accountability and choice of its advocates and supporters.

RESPONDING TO THE NEW NATIONAL MANDATE OF NCLB

All systems exhibit two distinguishing characteristics. The first is complexity. Education is a system within a system within a system ad infinitum. Situated at the center, the school is the target for all the rules, regulations, research, and reforms of the larger system. The barrage reaches down to the most basic level. Typically, the mailboxes of teachers and administrators are jammed full. Much of what sets the current situation of education apart from that of previous periods is the constant noise—the proliferation of invasive and unsolicited communications and implied criticisms, on the one hand, and the multiplication of the number of experts and blue-ribbon panels and their cures, on the other hand. In short, education is on overload. As a system, it also is overmanaged.

The second characteristic of systems is centralization, which entails a methodology and ideology of control and measurement. The hub, initially important by virtue of being at the center of things, appears smaller as it is dwarfed by the larger roles of the outer circles. Individual schools and their educators and students appear to be less in control of their own fate. In fact, they appear to be pawns. Above all, centralizing systems expose basic oppositions between parts and players.

Teachers value coordination, school districts control. Teachers talk in terms of student needs, districts in terms of data outcomes. Individual schools desire to create their own reform efforts; districts seek a single, across-the-board, uniform coherent effort that enables them to compare apples to apples. It is the classic opposition between the horizontal and the vertical, coordination and control, between being given choices and told what to do. In short, education increasingly is being micromanaged.

The system is thus not an abstract or removed player. It is terribly intrusive and present in every classroom. In Chicago, curricula were redesigned so as to be teacher-proof. Teachers were discouraged from being creative and departing from the standard process. Many wondered why certified teachers were even necessary. Such standardized material perhaps would be better taught by a machine. Given this trend toward top-down uniformity, the notion of teaching as an art increasingly may disappear. Golden Apple awards may have to be given to outstanding machines.

As the machinery of No Child Left Behind grinds its way through the states toward its various deadlines, high-stakes testing now dominates the scene to such an extent that it has become the new hub. Evaluation has replaced curriculum as a growth industry. Some districts have created and hired new administrators who are solely in charge of data tracking and assessment. Performance evaluation and testing have been joined at the hip, and the evaluation of both has been dropped in the laps of overworked principals. The net result is such a busy and clotted educational agenda that no one seems able to get through, let alone solve, it. Sticking one's head in the sand like an ostrich appears to be an intelligent strategy.

Unexpectedly, that applies not only here but abroad. England is expected to lose nearly one-third of its total teaching force in the next five years. The reasons given are work overload and class size, excessive external regulations and reporting, and increasingly unruly and even violent behavior on the part of students. In the United States, the same shortages are projected for both teachers and administrators, and pretty much for the same reasons. The way California just recently solved its teacher shortage problem, especially in math and science, was to attract and hire recently downsized engineers and computer programmers from failed Silicon Valley companies. But what happens when their industries revive? Will they remain, or happily scurry away from an embattled job to the relative security of a highly competitive environment?

Professionals vote with their feet. When conditions become oppressive and work is perennially devalued and criticized, people, who do not want to be associated with failure, leave. Or they plan to leave as soon as their pensions permit. Those who stay survive by putting everything on hold and doing the least possible work to get by. Thus, the next few decades, according to the projections of the Department of Labor, will require some ten thousand new administrators and double that number of teachers by 2010. Given the current crushing configuration of education, those estimates may be low.

Nor can education count on an influx of new graduates. In a perplexing and even perverse way, education stands apart from all other professions. One-half of all students who major in education never go on to teach. That does not apply to majors in business, engineering, or even the social services. It gets worse. An equal number leave teaching in the first year and then half that number in the next four years.

Education is thus the only profession that devours its young. It is also the only profession in which what is initially chosen does not remain primary. The employee displacement and disenchantment process is systemic. Addressing the teacher without attending to the system that envelopes and shapes educators is a piecemeal approach. Empowering teachers in an imprisoning system only increases demoralization. Liberalizing the system but attracting and retaining less than the most talented minimizes and even trivializes outcomes. Change has to be cojoined, branch and root, top and bottom, near and far.

Perhaps, the pill that is the hardest to swallow is the recognition that real, extensive, and respectable educational reform can happen only outside the system. A number of major businesses have learned this lesson. When a new division needs to be created or an innovative goal to be reached, organizations have found that housing it under existing structures is fatal. Instead, it must be located outside the current system and allowed to float free and evolve. Otherwise, the prevailing system would put its heavy-handed stamp on the fledging offspring and gradually bend it into being an obedient copy of the parent.

In short, systems are tyrannical. Although they may be necessary evils, when it comes to change they are often more evil than necessary. They are more interested in territorial preservation than improvement. Feeding and sustaining the organization of education may be starving and stifling the educational enterprise. The reason charter schools have gained ground and appear to be a breath of fresh air is the appearance or even the illusion of breaking free of the system. Indeed, many of the participants believe, not incorrectly, that no real, lasting, or meaningful change is possible within the system. Only by leaving that oppressive environment and creating a new way of managing and organizing learning can real change occur and the hub remain the hub. Only through the creative convergence of professionals and process can a new center be created. Only then can the root become the branch; the bottom, the top; the far, the near. In short, educators have yet to find creative and internal ways of responding to external forces imposing educational change. Indeed, one of the common themes of the profiles of the major players that follow is the alternative and innovative solutions each group has developed as antidotes to a crushingly invasive and centralized system. As always, people and their good ideas make the difference.

Part II

TEACHERS AS MAJOR PLAYERS

CHAPTER 4

Hiring Teachers

A good place, perhaps, to start this discussion is to examine typical advertisements for new teachers. What are schools and districts looking for? Putting aside cheerleading prose and local public relations, at least eight qualifications routinely are listed.

1. *Subject-Matter or Grade-Level Competence.* This is always is at the top of the list, partly because it is required and because it is easily verifiable by a certificate or credential.
2. *Classroom Management.* Although acquired more from experience than instruction in college courses, this skill has become increasingly important, as noted by the exiting teachers in England. In many schools, sadly, it has become the prime prerequisite, because students in general have become increasingly unruly. Violent behavior is not uncommon and in a number of cases has led to direct assaults on teachers. In some schools classroom management consumes so much time and energy that subject matter competence waits in the wings for an occasional entrance. In fact, more than anything else this factor demoralizes teachers who do not see their roles as correctional officers or wardens. Workshops offered teachers now routinely include dealing with difficult students and finding alternatives to detention and expulsion. Alternative schools were created by districts as a way of getting rid of the bad apples before they affected the good apples. But they are basically holding pens. The halls are patrolled not by hired security guards but by regular local police officers. Little if any learning takes place there.

3. *Student Centered.* This requirement has to do with teaching the student, not just the subject. Teachers are expected to tap into the developmental patterns of Piaget and Erikson, and now also Gardner's multiple intelligences and all the brain and cognitive research associated with learning. In some schools and districts, the relative priority of certain student-centered curricula constitutes a subspecialty of competence that teachers need to acquire.

4. *Inspirational Role Models.* Teachers are expected especially to inspire student performance on mandated tests. Indeed, it may rank as high as, if not higher than, subject-matter competence and classroom management because of high-stakes testing.

5. *Knowledge of Evaluation and Data Assessment Systems.* As evaluation attains an importance equal to or greater than that of curricula development, teachers also are expected to comprehend, use, and apply the latest data-tracking systems that measure not only general and grade-level performance, but also individual student performance and even teacher performance. Indeed, such monitoring is necessary in order to determine who receives incentive bonuses and how much.

6. *Differentiated and Diversity Applications.* Because of the commitment to different strokes for different folks, or differentiated education and NCLB, teachers are expected to develop and apply rubric matrices or aggregations of learning skills and goals to both group and individual learners.

7. *Good Character.* Current teachers, like those of old, have to exhibit good character and model acceptable behaviors. They are also expected to be familiar with the curricula of character education as well as be aware of certain legal restraints concerning speech or political positions.

8. *Computer Literate.* Teachers are required to be knowledgeable about educational technology in general and the use of instructional-skills and test-prep software in particular.

This is an impressive job description, especially for a job that on average pays ten to twenty thousand dollars less than other entry-level professional positions. It is routinely multitasked. Differentiation compels it also to be multitracked. If the class is large, individualization is more often than not hurried. If there are behavioral problems, instruction time may be compromised. Covering the curriculum is increasingly a problem when the ante is upped to meet new state and federal standards and expectations. Teaching to the test is accepted as a norm. Finally, poor performance of schools is determined by test scores. In Florida if schools receive failing grades for two consecutive years, all the students are given state vouchers to facilitate school choice. That includes attending parochial or private schools.

How demoralizing and cynical that process of judgment and later of choice must be. Imagine what teachers of failing schools must feel like, and how that stigma must cling even to the students when they are applying to another school. Teachers feel battered and abused, and justly so. Teachers are being held accountable for a hand dealt to them from a loaded demographic deck. Then, too, who are the basic beneficiaries of vouchers? Largely, parochial schools, because the voucher amount is far below the tuition of private schools, which are probably not interested in welcoming students from failing schools in the first place. So we also break down the constitutional separation of church and state by using public money to subsidize religious education. But most lamentable of all, vouchers subject teachers to a morale-destroying, destructive competition and to substituting solid understanding for test performance.

It is a wonder that any teachers remain in such a system, let alone accomplish anything. It is also understandable, although lamentable, that so many others hunker down and do the minimum as they inch their way to retirement. "See Spot run." He is lucky if he can walk.

But surely that picture fails to do justice to all the superb teachers who achieve much. What about all the Golden Apple winners, and those who secure national board certification? While many come from schools and districts in which the demographics are friendly and supportive, these teachers would be remarkable in any school and in anything they attempted.

They are like their overachieving students. They always exceed the norm. They are not just teachers but learning managers, naturally curious classroom researchers, and stirring coaches; they are constantly questioning students, staying abreast of new developments, and compiling best practices. They are the cream of the crop.

They do not just teach but administer learning. They do not just evaluate but turn evaluation back on itself so that it begets more learning. They can survive and keep out all the bad stuff because they are able to remain connected to and nourished by the vital center of teaching—learning—and because they have the strength of will and personality to keep all the noise and nonsense at bay so that they can remain professionals. Their self-respect extends to their work; one is the mirror of and passage to the other. National board certification only confirms their strong self-image. If every teacher were like them, then even all the stuff thrown at education by the system would either not get through or be declawed. And of course there would be no crisis in education.

Well, if that is so the answer is clear. Get rid of as much of the deadwood as possible, hire the best, and get out of their way. But it is precisely at this point that sensible problem solving encounters the systemic structure and values of education.

There are at least two approaches to the prospect of increasing the number of outstanding teachers (and perhaps administrators as well): maximize and optimize. The maximizing solution is quantitative. Increase the number of outstanding teachers by increasing salaries to the level of effectively competing with other professions. But that assumes that the principal obstacle to becoming a teacher is financial.

Those who want to become doctors and lawyers, just like teachers themselves, choose what involves and absorbs their interests. They do not want to be teachers, no matter how high the salaries are or how prestigious the field may be. And those who are lured primarily by salary may have to sublimate their different passion or talent, which will prevent them from being outstanding teachers anyhow. Outstanding teachers have a natural gift for teaching and a special ability to sustain the double achievement of individual and group growth. In other words, money won't and hasn't worked.

If the goal is to attract outstanding candidates who have not committed to other fields or are currently employed and are contemplating switching fields, then the entire recruiting process has to be altered. The current process is essentially inimical to finding and attracting quality.

The key strategy is to optimize. Put outstanding teachers solely in charge of hiring. They alone possess and can communicate the template. Talent responds to talent. Besides, the level and language of exchange has to be generic to cut across different fields and still be engaging. The typical broad-based hiring committee of representative teachers, token parents, and the principal as the titular head would favor the lowest common denominator and fail as badly as the financial approach. But with outstanding teachers in charge not only would quality rule and override everything else, but those hired would belong to that corps of teachers who hired them for at least the first three years. The hirers alone would serve as the new teachers' mentors and coaches, preside over their ritual passage, buffer bureaucratic intrusions, screen out invasive irrelevancies, and raise their sights constantly. The hiring teachers, not the principal, would be the prime evaluators and determine retention and tenure. In fact, two of the conditions for tenure would be eligibility for completing national board certification and serving as a recruiting and mentoring member of the corps of learning managers.

Will it work? It already has in business and industry. A number of organizations, especially manufacturing plants, have turned over the interviewing and selection of future employees to workers. The results have been a dramatic drop in turnover and a significant increase in productivity. The reasons are not hard to find. Only workers really know the job. And they have to live with any mistakes they make. Can this kind of system be carried over and happen in education? It probably cannot.

The educational hierarchy will not yield and permit principals to stand aside, especially since they are the embodiment and supporters of hierarchy. Administrators prefer to hire and handle more docile and obedient types. Indeed, administrators often appoint such teachers to hiring committees, who prefer teachers like themselves and do not take kindly to those who offer sharp contrasts. Is it then not surprising that most of the new teachers or principals hired fit in and are just like all those already there—and that mediocrity is perpetuated?

The basic problem is that education is so labor intensive and requires so many hands that the bell curve rules. As a result, 95 percent of everything is not first rate. If the system does not permit or encourage expanding the base of top talent, then the only other alternative is to optimize the talent available by changing the structure of instruction to tap that talent.

If the number of outstanding teachers is limited and the prospects of increasing that number dim, then perhaps what needs to be done is to make better use of those teachers through reconfiguration. Outstanding teachers are invariably excellent managers of learning. They know not only how to organize but also how to structure learning. They also tend to be experimental and use a variety of ways to deliver learning. Suppose, then, that instead of wasting such valuable resources by limiting them to a single classroom or specialization, schools developed a new structure.

It would involve a student cohort of about 100–150 students, either all at one grade level or at a mixture of grade levels. In the latter case it would be a miniature of the whole. Instruction would be the responsibility not of a set of single, uncoordinated teachers but of a learning team. At its head would be our outstanding master teacher, functioning as the learning manager.

The team would consist of other teachers, aides, tutors, part-time specialists, and volunteers (parents, retired professionals, etc.). The total budget for the team would not exceed the per-capita allowance for 100–150 students or the total of what it would cost to hire the teachers for that group of students. The team would function as a school within a school, a boon to big and depersonalized high schools of two to five thousand students. Students and teachers within the cohort would regularly interact and come to know one another well. No Child Left Behind would also become No Child Left Unknown (*Education Week* 2003b). If multiple grade levels were involved, crossover based on competence, not age, could occur more often and more easily and naturally. The performance level of the other teachers on the team would likely be enhanced by the practice of the learning manager, who, in the final analysis, would exemplify the master teacher. Above all, outstanding teachers would not be lost but remain in the classroom; their interaction with students would increase; and a mix of students would gradually become an interdependent learning community.

The difference between the approaches of maximizing and optimizing is both instructive and predictive. To be effective, problem solving minimally has to be doable, durable, and cost effective. It also should recycle existing personnel and resources already in house or allocated. Importing new hires or requesting additional funding would not be an option. Above all, the solution proposed must be subjected to future pressures and circumstances lest it turn out to be a problem later on.

On virtually all grounds, the approach of maximizing fails. The present hiring structure opens the process to the most negative intrusions of the bureaucratic system and perpetuates the instructional and administrative status quo. In fact, historically, the gates were more open and relaxed only when desperation transcended exclusion. Major shortages in the late 1950s and 1960s resulted in significant numbers of liberal arts graduates being accepted into teaching without education certificates. Surveys later found that those teachers for the most part out-performed certified teachers; and this laid the basis for later research on subject-matter knowledge as being more important than teacher methodology.

Maximizing additionally consumes scarce resources and sends a negative message to the rank and file. The winners get all the attention, not those who labor daily in the trenches. No teacher wants to be told that he or she is not first rate. And remember that these teachers constitute the bulk. But the basic reason maximizing fails is that it is a mechanism, not a model. It seeks to achieve its ends through manipulation of the existing parts rather than putting them together in a new whole.

Good models are assembled under the presiding influence of the future. They come out of imaginative and bold responses to questions of "What if?" But they are not self-indulgent. Their feet are on the ground. They respect costs. They even may regard money as profound. They try to pack in as much change as they can. Above all they have to be tough and resilient, because the system is relentless and crushing.

What thus finally distinguishes optimal and reconfigured educational models from manipulative mechanisms is that they also must be system resistant. There is no way the monolith will willingly change or become enlightened. It finally may collapse under the weight of its failures or, more likely, be crushed by its economic bloat. But bureaucratic systems have a strong survival instinct. They will sacrifice a limb rather than remain trapped. In short, the ultimate strength of an educational model is whether it can protect its inhabitants—teachers, learning teams, and students—from oppression.

CHAPTER 5

The Teacher Culture

Part of the recommendation of the Carnegie Council on Adolescent Development, in its Report of the Task Force on Education of Young Adolescents (1989), focuses on teachers and administrators in a very special way:

> Empower teachers and administration to make decisions about the experiences of middle grade students through creative control by teachers over the instructional program linked to great responsibilities for student performance, governance committees that assist the principal in designing and coordinating school-wide programs, and autonomy and leadership within sub-schools or houses to create environments tailored to enhance the intellectual and emotional life of all youth.

There is a special art to reading the recommendations of national commission reports. It involves not only the familiar practice of reading between the lines, but also perceiving the negatives that lurk behind the recommendations that in fact may prevent them from happening or being sustained later on. Here then is a blow-by-blow translation of the not-so-hidden agenda and assumptions behind this recommendation:

1. Teachers are generally not empowered.
2. Teachers typically do not have control, creative or otherwise, over curriculum.
3. If and when it is granted, teachers as a quid pro quo have to accept responsibility for significantly improving student performance.
4. Committees are not normally forms of governance.

5. Rather, committees of teachers are essentially and mechanically operational and administrative in nature.
6. Teachers are limited to making recommendations, which the principal may or may not accept.
7. Often teachers are not asked to make decisions, only to accept and obey them.
8. Seldom if ever do teachers coordinate schoolwide programs.
9. The domino theory prevails. Often, even the principal has limited autonomy.
10. Local or site-based governance is often constrained by policies of the school board or the central office, but always contingent on and checked by multiple layers of external approval.

No wonder a recommendation was needed! There is so much that is not going on, and so little coherence within what is, that it would be accurate to sum up the situation of many teachers as a series of gaps between ability and opportunity. Then, too, as in the case of the emperor who wears no clothes, no one speaks up and the issue of teacher participation remains unaddressed. And when it is addressed, even national reports use doublespeak. In other words, to understand adequately both the present and future of education it is necessary to understand the culture of teachers.

1. THE DAILY GRIND

The teacher may begin the day before the students arrive in order to do some preparation or use the copying machine before anyone else does or the paper supply gives out or it breaks down. The classroom may have been built decades ago and now the paint is peeling and desks totally inscribed; or it may be more modern and even be equipped with a combo TV/VCR or computer, donated by the PTA. On average teachers meet five to six classes each day for about an hour each. When not teaching they catch up on their many clerical tasks. In England that was estimated to total 16 percent of a typical workweek of 52 hours. The only contacts teachers have with adults are brief and either social or disciplinary. Often they skip lunch and snack at their desks.

Work done on the curriculum and on examining student work is done in isolation. Department meetings usually are preoccupied with the latest cascade of announcements from on high. District administrators usually select the texts each grade level will use. Although each text is accompanied by a detailed workbook of suggestions for implementation, essentially the choice of pedagogy and methodology is made by individual instructors. Teachers do their most important work alone, without validation or insight from peers or superiors.

2. THE LONE RANGER

The structure of the school and the tyranny of time, place, and workload provide little opportunity to reflect individually or interact with other professionals. Teachers are like a plant manager who also works on the assembly line. They have to plan and produce at the same time. To shift the metaphor, they are like the quarterback who throws the ball and then has to run down field to catch it as well. Then, too, no one teaching a particular subject or grade level really knows what the others in that subject or grade level are doing. They are all like parallel lines that never meet.

Teachers, new or old, routinely experience benign abandonment. They are left to their own devices to interpret and select classroom techniques. The only feedback they receive is from the annual evaluation of the principal, which may be so partial or petty as to be either useless or irritating. Occasionally a student or a parent will make their day with praise. Teachers have thin skins and their egos bruise easily. The more dedicated and original among them seem to suffer more.

The value of understanding the routine and general isolation of teachers is that it constitutes the culture of instruction. As such it serves as a benchmark against which proposed changes can be intelligently evaluated. For example, reducing class size or extending the length of the day or of the school year may increase student access to learning, but it does not increase teachers' access to planning or to other teachers. The further problem with such single-focused and quantitative strategies is that they provide only partial solutions. They are exclusive, not inclusive; they do not incorporate all the players. They are worrisome because they deceptively pass off a half as whole. It is like bumper-sticker wisdom: "It is not only the hole we are in but the whole we are not." What is the value of reducing class size if what actually takes place with fewer students is still the same old questionable stuff decided on in the same unconsultative way? We have improved the scabbard but left untouched the unsharpened sword. Worse of all, when reductions in class size do not work or fail to accomplish all that was initially claimed, the public or parents are either confused or throw up their hands in despair. Nothing seems to work. Look at all the money we throw at the problem. It is hopeless.

3. THE TEACHER CULTURE

But teachers themselves are partly the problem. They prefer being lone rangers. They have a fetish about being totally in charge. They relish closing the door of their classroom and, like judges in a courtroom, reigning supreme. But it seems odd that for a profession that is based so totally on communications skills to be reluctant or downright resistant to sharing ideas. In other words, the chosen isolation of teachers cannot be finally understood without understanding their total culture.

The teacher culture paradoxically combines being isolated and yet wanting to share. Meritocracy must never be allowed to prevail. No one teacher can be seen as better as or more expert than another. To do so is to break the unwritten and unspoken rule that no teacher may be considered more talented, worthy, or capable than any other. The teacher culture not only enforces isolation and precludes collaboration, but also enshrines the average and often endorses mediocrity.

Cynicism also often becomes a norm. Those singled out for praise are usually put down as the principal's pet or perceived as self-serving public relations experts heavily engaged in self-advertisement. Those who receive bonuses or incentive pay for increasing test scores are perceived as political animals who, like their students, know how to work the system and to make it pay. Awards—local, regional or national—do not really bring about change among the core of the teacher corps. Like the top salesmen who every year win the trip to Hawaii, everyone already knows in advance who will receive the Golden Apple award or be subsidized to undertake national certification. In fact, they are all visibly engaged in a campaign to win recognition. And it generally works, but it seldom if ever changes the teacher culture or alters the mainstream of collective ordinariness and anonymity.

4. THE DOMINATION OF THE MAINSTREAM

Why and how did that mainstream come about and become so dominant? Competition in other professions seems to work: Why doesn't it work in education? There are two reasons, perhaps. First, schools employ thousands locally and millions nationally. Thus, the bell curve rules. The small percentage of the best is offset by the equal percentage of the worst. The bulk is in the middle. Neither outstanding nor inadequate, these teachers are average. Further, it is the role of unions and of professional associations to protect the average and to argue, not unconvincingly, that it is good enough to be acceptable. That middle group creates the mainstream of the teacher culture. To preserve its centrality, it must remain intact. It must not invite or suffer any comparison. It must wear the hair shirt of isolation and endorse the average as its common identity.

Failing to understand the inertia and quiet opposition of the teacher culture itself leads to bewilderment when obvious or highly touted solutions fail. They fall short of engaging underlying realities. For example, a favorite campaign is to raise starting salaries so that they are more competitive or to designate certain teachers as master teachers who will then earn more. But that does not alter the basic mainstream or affect the distribution of the bell curve. It may increase slightly the number of those who are outstanding, but it does not alter the basic numbers or the inward solidarity of the average teacher culture. It is not unlike the distribution of SAT scores. Although many more are taking the exam, the percentage of top scores has changed very little. If education is really to change, the focus must be on the big middle group.

The second reason for the dominant isolation of the teachers stems from the fusion of American culture with teacher culture. Generally teachers are not expected and hence are not taught to work together. In Japan, where the national culture stresses the group rather than the individual, the school day is made longer for teachers, not students. It is done precisely to facilitate grade-level or subject-matter meetings. Teachers discuss with their colleagues their teaching plans and methodologies. Suggestions are made and often incorporated. Perhaps because it is done privately and in a face-saving manner, teachers can go forth armed with the feedback and insights of others and still be perceived as in charge.

Consultation in Asian cultures tends to be not only a norm but also comprehensive. That is the way Japanese corporations, for example, develop their strategic plans. Unlike the American version, which hurries forward by minimizing input and often falls apart later, Asian corporations take longer in planning but implement faster because everyone already has had the chance to provide input. A favorite Korean proverb is: "The nail that sticks up gets pounded down."

But national cultures are subject to changing dynamics. In the United States competition has forced business to change its culture and paradigm of operation. Workers and customers have been invested with greater importance. To increase productivity, employees used to working individually under the all-knowing gaze of supervisors have become problem solvers and work in self-managing teams. Indeed, much of the gains in productivity, profitability, and even quality in the last two decades have been the result of these new structures and cultures of cooperation.

Teams require the elevation not of the superior individual performer but only of the collective effort. The bell curve still operates, but it floats and is sustained at a higher overall level. Thus, although the ability of members of teams still varies, the mainstream is notched up by virtue of its collective aspiration and upgrading of its goals. The superior teams set the standards. The poor teams shape up or are dismantled and reassembled. But the teacher culture faces a double problem. First, the profession itself generally has not been trained to work as a team. Second, the work environment and administration do not encourage or facilitate collective engagement.

5. INTEGRATION OF ADMINISTRATION AND INSTRUCTION

Outsiders are often puzzled by the contradictory images of teachers: tigers in the classroom and pussycats at meetings; decisive and clear in parent-teacher conferences, tentative or quiet in public. In November 1993, then secretary of education Richard Riley called a forum of teachers together to discuss the Goals 2000 program. The title of the issued report was Honor What We Know, Listen to What We Say. Unlike the recommendation from the Carnegie Report, which had to be tweaked and teased to get at its hidden meaning, here the title of the report says it all:

- Teachers are smart.
- Teachers know what they are talking about.
- Do not ignore or bypass their knowledge.
- Tap and use it.
- Above all, listen to what they have to say.

The report goes on to describe how, in many ways, teachers are not taken seriously. If they were, they would be actively involved in policy making at all levels.

Would all teachers agree? Surely, all would concur in the basic premise that they know what they are doing and that their knowledge is seldom tapped. But many would step back from engaging in political decision making, let alone at all levels. Most would argue that political decision making is not what teachers do; it is what principals do. Further, if that is what some teachers want to do, then they should become administrators. That is how some teachers unknowingly devalue the knowledge of their colleagues and in the process establish the limits of their governance.

In the future, such either/or choices may not operate; teachers may not have to leave the classroom to be leaders. But the mind-set of separation persists in most schools and school districts. Principals still rule, and the title of the report remains unheeded.

6. THE LEADERSHIP OF DOMINANCE

The leadership style of educational administrators can be characterized as "follow me" leadership. Teachers not unhappily follow that kind of leadership because it has the authority to command obedience in the same way they wish their students to obey and follow them. Then, too, principals are often adept at bribery and instilling fear, distributing goodies or dispensing devaluative looks or memos. Teachers submit to the establishment of a hierarchical form of authority and accept the role of subordinates who must be constantly watched over lest they fail or stray. Not unlike the social parable in Ibsen's *A Doll's House*, it is the duty of the father to prepare the subjugation of his daughter to pass on to the new authority of her husband. Given the number of women in teaching and the number of men acting as administrators, gender may play a key role in sustaining the dynamic of father always knowing best. Significantly, as feminism took hold and as more women became principals, teachers became less submissive.

But the net effect was and still is to some extent the same: teachers often are not aggressive because they work in a structure that tells them they know nothing or little. In addition, the lack of support for teachers as professionals is reinforced often through in-service workshops designed by administrators.

Principals affect teacher response. In a number of cases, they reinforce teacher isolation through divide-and-conquer strategies, or the dominance model of influence. To take hold, it requires regular demonstrations of dominance. Of course, motives must never be impugned. For example, a principal, concerned with a school board's recent discussion about students' unhappiness with school, announces that all teachers have to meet with their students individually in their homerooms to discuss their feelings about school. He proudly strides back into his office and sends a note to tell the superintendent about this initiative, copies every member of the school board, and subsequently includes it in his monthly report to parents. Meanwhile, the teachers, whose work conditions have been altered without their consent, are asked to undertake something that is questionable if not downright dumb. They know that it won't answer the concerns raised by the principal in the first place; they shake their heads in familiar bewilderment and chalk up the experience to another demonstration of dominance.

But the fallout is severe. Cynicism drives withdrawal and withdrawal drives cynicism. Even new teachers quickly learn that real participation and competence are not valued or evaluated, that obedience has to be given its superficial due, and that they are playing with a deck stacked against them. Perhaps saddest of all is that teachers' trust and competence are lost. Their performance significantly improves when teachers converse with colleagues more openly, on the one hand, and when they are working with an authentic and nonmanipulative principal, on the other. But the absence of opportunity and the persistence of dominance continue the vicious cycle: sadly, not trusting the administration is directly correlated to not trusting other teachers.

7. THE OBSTACLES RESTATED

Pulling together the discussion of teachers, their culture, and their role in affecting school reform and student performance, the following common obstacles emerge:

- The culture of teachers and their working conditions compel isolation.
- Reducing class size or increasing salaries fails to engage the issue of fostering teacher consultation.
- The knowledge of teachers is routinely undervalued and underutilized.
- The structure and design of education frustrates or precludes intelligent and collaborative planning and learning exchanges between teachers.
- Ultimately that trickles down and affects the exchanges between teachers and students, between teachers and parents, and between students and students.
- Dominating administrators secure token obedience at the expense of quality participation.

8. THE DOUBLE SOLUTION

In class, teachers generally are independent, sometimes excessively so. In meetings, especially those presided over by the principal, teachers generally are dependent, sometimes excessively so. What is generally lacking is a culture of interdependence. That in turn is shaped by two dynamics: relationships and community.

Ideally, schools should be noisy places. Silence between teachers signals acceptance, even affirmation, of their isolation from one another. Respect for one anothers' privacy and domain makes a virtue out of independence and turns it into an end rather than a means of respectful exchange between colleagues and partners. Kids have to be taught not how to take but how to share. Teachers have to learn both.

Teachers have to use each other not because they are weak or dumb but because they know how hard it is to be effective in class and thus need the help that fellow professionals can give. Genuine and authentic interdependence is never judgmental. Rather it is the way a community of best practices is shaped by professionals. It is the way they live and work together. Indeed, teachers need to be empowered to recognize that such a community is not given or prescribed but in fact has to be shaped and created by teachers themselves. Moreover, coincidental with the emergence of a culture of community is a pedagogical model that inclusively and interactively involves all learning partners: teachers, parents, and students. Inevitably, some teachers push that envelope further by seeking direct and comprehensive involvement in schoolwide decision making and policy formulation. Inevitably, an interdependent community seeks interdependent governance.

As teachers develop closer and more interactive relationships with one another, it is perhaps inevitable that they recognize the extent to which administrative decisions and policies constrain and even determine their teaching options and even their independence. Often they are locked out of definitions of what constitutes student success, even though their expertise should clearly be valued. The issue is thus joined. The ability and freedom of teachers to forge a new dynamic of interdependence with one another and their constituencies runs smack into the wall of limited governance and authority. What intensifies the situation is that the role of teachers has gradually increased over time through empowering governance structures, to the point where those greater freedoms cannot be taken back. In fact, the empowerment process and structures contained within it generate an expectation of further or greater spheres of influence. Above all, the pressures of accountability and high-stakes testing have put the spotlight so intensely on teacher performance that teachers are asking for a greater say in how and on what they are to be judged. Thus, a new agenda has emerged: finding a form of community that welcomes professional relationships—in short, shaping a culture of interdependent governance.

9. THE EMERGENCE OF A NEW CULTURE OF COLLABORATIVE PARTICIPATION

It is happening in two ways. The first is gradual and evolutionary. It involves a rapprochement of supervisors and teachers. Although the arrangements may vary, equity is replacing dominance. The other approach is more radical and discontinuous. It involves teachers stepping forth as leaders in their own right and running schools, as if they were principals, but remaining in the classroom as teachers. That is new. To be sure, it is burdened with the task of creating both a new collaborative culture and a democratized governance structure, and ideally fusing the two.

10. PRINCIPAL AND TEACHER PARTNERSHIPS: THE CULTURE OF LEADERSHIP SHARING

Site-based management mandated in the 1970s established a degree of consultation between educational constituencies that could not be reversed. Indeed, an increasing number of principals took the initiative subsequently of forming or expanding governance relationships with teachers. Predictably, these relationships ranged from a still tight administrative control at one extreme to near total equity at the other. Often, such initiatives were criticized by other principals in the same district; and when that enterprising administrator left or was replaced, the structure of consultation often was abandoned. Nevertheless, progress continued. Indeed, progress was given a strong boost by the recent call for principals to play a greater role as instructional leaders. Although that involved change in many areas, clearly a central change was greater cooperation and involvement by teachers; and the movement toward teacher governance was thereby reinforced.

The net result is the increasing recognition, as one advocate put it, that "the days of the principal as the lone instructional leader are over" (Lambert 2002). What has emerged, admittedly more as a promise than a pattern, is the structure of shared leadership. To many principals that is anathema. They would rather quit than share. Others, especially those newly entering administration, have a more open mind and are willing to explore new options. They want to know what they have to give up or share, and what the research shows as to the linkage between governance and teacher performance and its effect on student achievement.

Right now leadership sharing is more the exception than the rule. Although for many schools it is a next step contemplated but not generally taken, its gains are real and substantial. To appreciate how far leadership sharing can bring the culture of teachers, the list of gains below should be set in the context of the recommendation of the Carnegie commission cited at the opening of this chapter.

- Teachers will be increasingly equal partners.
- Others may be consulted, but teachers will remain central and listened to.
- Teachers' definitions of what constitutes student success will be sought and valued as indispensable.
- Leadership will no longer be the monopoly of administrators, schools boards, or state departments of education.
- Principals will increasingly interact with teachers as colleagues, not as supervisors.
- Governance structures—councils, teams, partnerships—will be developed and put in place.
- These working councils, made up of the principal and teachers, will address both instructional and administrative matters.

11. THE CHALLENGE OF TEACHER LEADERSHIP AND COLLABORATIVE GOVERNANCE

But the above straddling for many teachers still fell short of meeting their objections and matching their aspirations. The next step of partnership did not go far enough. It still was too dependent on the largesse of principals. And they in turn were ruled by superintendents and school boards. Curricula often were not teacher selected; and even when they were, texts were selected by the district. Above all, access to decision making was partial and limited. The plan did not really offer democracy. In short, changes in governance had all the characteristics of a political and expedient compromise designed to raise test scores and pacify discontent.

But for some spirited teachers that was not good enough. They valued the special leadership teachers alone could provide. But they did not wish to leave the classroom, since only there do things really happen. They wanted administration to be allied with instruction—with teachers as leaders administering what they teach. In other words, teacher leaders wished to position the classroom and curricula as the central focus of administration and thus have the entire enterprise managed, as it were, from within. They also wanted to explore creating a different structure of school management that would be multiply democratic and that would include and be shaped by all its constituents: teachers, parents, students, and board members. Above all, they wanted to bring together professional conversations and systemic planning, and thereby align classroom objectives with school and community objectives. Thus would emerge a new world in which teachers are leaders and the culture is interdependently collaborative and democratic.

Can it happen? Given a chance, it would work. It would exhibit all the energy and confusion of a start-up company. The obstacles would be enormous. Initially and even subsequently it would be an ad-hoc world. Everything would have to be created daily on the fly. Improvisation and spontaneity would be the order of the day and even the hour. What was put together one day might come apart or have to be revised the next day. Everything would be fluid. Transition would become not only a norm, but also a permanent condition. Just surviving and managing the turbulence would be sufficient. Anal types would never be able to do either. At the end of every week, the structure of putting Humpty Dumpty back together again would be reviewed. Whatever pride was initially expressed would be matched by the conclusion that the goal hadn't been reached yet. At times it would appear that nothing would ever achieve final status, because the scaffolding would be constantly redesigned.

Other difficulties would be both psychological and cultural, self-defining and structural. First, no one is currently being trained in colleges of education as teacher leaders. Educational leadership is reserved for administrators. Second, most teachers reflect the values that the national culture puts on rugged individualism and pulling oneself by one's own bootstraps—hence teacher independence—and the respect Americans generally show to their elders and authority in general—hence dependence. The new culture would require interdependence, which is not a familiar value of the national culture. Third, teaching does not initially attract, or retain for very long, renegades, reformers, or ambitious types.

Besides, ambition has only one way to go: leave the classroom and become an administrator. Fourth, most teachers believe that their plate is already too full, especially for what they are being paid. Why take on more, and more that is unknown, for the same salary? Fifth and finally, bewilderment and skepticism would be problems. Is teacher leadership another flavor of the month—a new flash in the pan—that may not last or offer any security? And what if teachers tried it and found it not their cup of tea—where would they go from there? On the basis of the above it would appear that there would be no takers. But there are; they comprise a small minority, accompanied by a larger group looking teacher leadership over to see if they should take the plunge.

Who are these teacher leaders? One group is involved in some dozen charter schools in Minnesota operating as part of a consortium called Ed/Visions. These teachers range from inexperienced recent graduates, to mature teachers with twenty or more years of experience, to some former principals who wanted to go back in the classroom, to some retired teachers who wanted to get back in harness in a different way. Generally, they have no administrative ambitions and their commitment to teaching is absolute. They usually find it especially attractive to be involved in curricula options such as project or service learning, which require a high degree of student involvement and decision making. Above all, the experienced teachers have concluded that no real or lasting change in education is possible given its generally systemic inflexibility and top-down administrative control. They are tired of not being listened to or, when asked, being ignored. They believe they are as smart as the best administrators and know what it takes to set up and run a school. And they alone know what is required to create and sustain a structure that accommodates and optimizes teacher leadership and a learning community.

12. THE CULTURE OF COLLABORATIVE GOVERNANCE

A learning community led by teacher leaders constantly links what is learned to the way it is learned. Collaboration rules all. Teachers meet and develop shared lesson plans and strategies. Students are asked to meet with one another to the same ends. Parents and board members are folded in at every opportunity. Broader issues of curricula directions, goals, and what determines student success and evaluation are joint governance occasions for all constituencies. The time it may take for comprehensive input is often extended by an agreement to proceed by consensus rather than by majority vote. But all this attending to structure is perceived as part of the teaching load and the learning process, not as extra committee work. The democratization of the process is the structure—it is the school. Collectively, teachers as leaders and learners, with students and parents, would run and manage the entire school. The students would undertake custodial tasks. The parents would function as teacher aides. The teachers would take turns meeting with visitors and prospective parents and students. In that capacity they would not be called the principal but the go-to person of the week.

Perhaps, only with such a collaborative culture of governance is it possible to achieve that rare integration that has proved so elusive to all educational systems: the seamless integration of administration, instruction, and evaluation. In fact, one can go further and claim that given the current incredible demands being put on all teachers and all schools, perhaps the best chance of accomplishing those tasks with integrity and intelligence may lie with structures and cultures that inherently seek the integration of all systems as the ultimate form of collaboration and democratization. What may be education's future is a system that is the least systemic. It will accommodate flow, not impasse; share, not hoard, information; and build relationships and communities, not adversarial oppositions and gaps. And above all, because teachers will dominate, it will always love learning.

CHAPTER 6

The Economics of Education 101

We regularly underestimate the power of money and its offspring, the desperation of deprivation. Although both often function powerfully in tandem, we are routinely lectured that just throwing money at a problem won't solve it. Surprisingly, that was affirmed unexpectedly by school districts with lower per-capita allowances outperforming those with higher allowances (*Education Week* 2002b). And of course no one wants to admit that education is desperate. Surely, there must be some other and better ways to respond to repeated failures. But it is the argument of this analysis that economic forces are driving education into a number of desperate corners. If this is understood and responded to in advance, there are some significant alternative options.

If education is to regain control of its fate and future, minimally it must become increasingly anticipatory and intensely innovative. That process of change will involve three stages: crisis, creativity, and consolidation. Below is a tripartite rendering of a series of crises perceived primarily from an economic perspective, followed by a number of creative solutions, which are then embodied in a series of ongoing future consolidations and restructuring.

Economic threats will come from three major sources: administration, instruction, and bricks and mortar. Costs in special areas such as school discipline (metal detectors and burly guards) have spiked. Technology has pretty much become a standard and predictable budget item. Worrisome is the increasing cost of special education (often twice the normal cost per student) required by state or federal mandates as a result of lobbying and lawsuits. None of these expenses show signs of abating. Still, they have all been manageable—not so what may be coming down the pike.

1. ECONOMICS OF ADMINISTRATION

Crisis

The first economic problem is the salaries of educational administrators. In many districts their current salaries are not much higher than the highest paid teacher. And principals work longer hours and are not separately compensated for summers. Already principals are being lured to poorly performing schools with salaries that are as much as 50 percent above the standard wage. In addition, the call for principals to play a greater role as instructional leaders was accompanied by a companion request to increase the budget and appoint more assistant principals. Moreover, over the last ten years expenditures for administration have generally exceeded those of instruction (*Education Week* 2002a).

The situation is particularly acute with the office of district superintendent. Average tenure has shrunk to between two and a half and three years. A number of school districts have advertised for superintendents as CEOs, a job title traditionally reserved for business. That is paralleled by advertising for and hiring administrators not with standard master's degrees in education but with MBAs or DBAs. Edison already has hired principals with MBAs. CEOs and MBAs who apply for educational positions come with greater salary expectations as well as different managerial mandates, especially those of productivity and cost control, unheard of in most schools. Moreover, because of expected shortages of outstanding educational administrators, the law of supply and demand will dictate the salary increases. In short, costs for administrators may be double or even triple over what current budgets allow.

Creative Solutions

A number of manufacturing plants and businesses have significantly reduced, and in some cases virtually eliminated, supervisors, with no adverse effects on profitability and productivity. Indeed, the general thinning out of middle-level managers has directly contributed to the bottom line. The development of self-organizing and self-managing teams has filled the gap; so much so that in some plants supervising engineers have become marginal.

Many schools already have functioning teams or committees. Elmore (2002) and others rightly characterize that as distributed leadership. At many schools with site-based management, such committees function in an administrative capacity, with their recommendations becoming decisions. But in some schools and districts—some dozen schools in Minnesota, for example, all part of Ed/Visons—the next step has already successfully been taken: the replacement of administrators by teacher leaders.

Typically, teacher leaders are responsible individually and collectively for all administration, instruction, and evaluation functions. Indeed, the integration and interfacing of all three key areas seldom happens in a traditional structure. Administers manage, teachers teach, and various supervisors evaluate. But with each teacher leader heading a learning team consisting of specialists, tutors, techies, and mentors, and responsible for a cohort of about one hundred students, the rare integration of all three areas happens.

If viewed purely from an economics perspective, it is a compelling innovation. The entire cost of administration can be reapplied to teacher leader and team salaries, staff development, database systems of tracking and evaluation, and so forth. Principals can be given the option to become teacher leaders. The increased salary plus less grueling schedule and overtime, including summer, may make it more attractive than their present grind. In short, it is a win-win solution. The structure compels fiscal accountability.

2. ECONOMICS OF INSTRUCTION

Crisis

Routine increases in teachers' salaries are compounded by the graying of faculty. Many school districts have as many as 30 percent of their teachers at the higher pay scales. That will continue and even increase over the first decade of this century as teachers advance to higher pay steps as they approach retirement. Although a million teachers nationally are expected to retire by 2010, the savings of high salaries may be lost in some bonus wars to attract certified teachers in states and districts that have difficulty recruiting such new teachers. In addition, a number of school districts have signed teacher contracts over budget because their feet already are being pressed to the fire to secure passing grades on state exams and to meet the deadlines and criteria of NCLB. In some states if schools fail twice in a row, the students are offered vouchers to attend schools of their choice.

Another drain on the instructional budget will be the projected increase in the number of students. Already portables are being purchased and utilized. Such demographics will drive up not only costs (hiring more teachers), but also impact on class size, maintenance, and new construction. An often overlooked area of increased costs is increased pay for substitutes. In many areas, it is more difficult to secure substitutes than regular teachers. Although the daily pay rate has gone up nationally to an average of $75 for a seven-hour day, many classes remain uncovered. Some districts have even experimented with using students. A few enterprising recruiting companies have now accepted contracts for securing substitutes. The dilemma is that substitute teaching is not teaching. It is maintenance. In short, it is generally a thankless job and there is increasing evidence that a separate national association of substitutes will be formed or that existing unions may absorb them. In either case, the costs of substitute teachers will steadily increase. If that is combined with other instructional costs, the net result may be a doubling of the teacher budget over the next two decades.

Finally, school choice is becoming increasingly an economic issue. Home schooling poses no financial problem because, as when students attend private or parochial schools, there is no direct budget loss. Not so with charter schools, which directly take away the per-capita allowance for each student. It is estimated that there are over two thousand charter schools operating nationally. The number is increasing especially in urban areas, which have felt neglected for years and now have the unique opportunity to run their own show.

Creative Solutions

The teacher shortage problem in England, especially in math and science, is being solved beginning this September with the use of videoconference links. If this is successful, modern languages courses will be next (*Independent* [London] 2002). The international organization Room to Read provides teacherless classrooms in countries all over the world as part of a broad basic information technology kit. It consists solely of four computers, a printer, software, and, most importantly, dial-up service. The program will begin with Nepal and Vietnam (CNet 2002). Cyber schools, partial or total, in the rural United States successfully have offered AP options, retained students, and helped raise passing rates on high-stakes testing.

Technology is an obvious solution to multiple problems: teacher shortages, costs of instruction, diversity and accessibility of curricula, and so on. Downsides are depersonalized instruction, the sometimes low quality of the software used, the loss of teacher jobs, and so on. The fact is, there is an almost Luddite-like resistance to technology in education, which may account for the current dismal level of integration of technology into the curriculum. And that deflection often comes in the face of available and often abundant equipment, software, and even support technicians.

The basic reason technology will become increasingly the preferred choice is that no one wishes to make decisions of desperation. If we have to choose between an unqualified teacher and a qualified teaching machine, we typically choose the unqualified teacher. If we have to choose between canceling summer schools because of budget shortfalls and using a cyberschool, we cancel summer school, often ignoring that schools will have to spend more time and money later when students have to repeat grades. It is like the false economy of dropping drug-prevention programs and later paying the higher social and economic costs of recovery (*Christian Science Monitor* 2002). Besides, cyberschools, totally or in part, already have saved AP programs in rural areas and gone a long way toward stemming brain drain and the further migration to cities. In short, there is a very good chance technology will go far beyond being a Band-Aid solution and emerge as a new and innovative education and economic partner.

The biggest problem will be union opposition and the fear that teachers, in implementing technology, are in the process of putting themselves out of a job. The other reason for resistance is the belief that if education converts wholesale to technology, it will no longer be education but a business, which already is supplying most of the hardware and software. Although many vendors employ teachers and educational instructional designers, they will still be perceived as odious corporations driven by profit. As such, technology vendors will be grouped with the increasing number of for-profit educational management companies, like Edison, and tarred with the same brush.

Consolidation and Structure

So how will technology be implemented in education? Gradually. A corps of teachers will serve not just as midwives, but as the new experts on software and hardware selection. Many will be graduates of online master's programs. Vendors will provide training at no cost. Some teachers will be double employees. They will work for both software companies and the district. They will be new hybrids bridging the two and earning more. Teachers will have to forgo their customary direct method of instruction (which the technology will now provide) and switch to side-by-side facilitating and mentoring. Far from being depersonalized, instruction may become more personal and individualized.

Certainly, this new relationship with technology will be preferred over the trend of increasingly scripted curricula. The Chicago system does not mince words; curricula are referred to as teacher proof. Not unlike the "for dummies" book series, the lesson plans and learning methodology and techniques are totally prescribed. Teachers are not allowed to deviate. The curriculum is broken up into small segments. Each segment in turn is subdivided into an incredible number of baby steps. The program moves along at a snail's pace. It really runs itself. The teacher just nudges it along and starts it up each day. One teacher who had successfully integrated Shakespeare into his reading program was told to cease and desist.

Curriculum developers have produced these cookie-cutter programs to compensate for a significant number of teachers who do not hold a qualifying credential and/or are inexperienced. Schools do not have the resources, time, or inclination to train them. The administrators are under the gun to produce results. The scripted curriculum is so foolproof that even newly certified teachers welcome such support, especially in their first year. Then they are addicted. The downside is that because the curriculum is directed at the lowest common denominator, reasonably bright kids get bored and act up. The same holds true for reasonably bright teachers.

At least with educational technology the machine, not the teacher, is scripted and programmed. The teacher in a tutorial relationship at least can have some independent input as a professional, rather than a robot. Given a choice, most if not all teachers would probably prefer a working partnership between teacher and technology to being a cog in a curriculum machine.

3. THE ECONOMICS OF BRICKS AND MORTAR

Crisis

School buildings and maintenance are depressing subjects. A record number of school districts have had their referenda for new buildings turned down, even though their demographic arguments are convincing. Many citizens, especially increasing numbers of retirees, do not wish to pay extra taxes or bond interest for schools. And many of the proposed new buildings are expensive, way beyond the normal costs of inflation because of the higher costs of building materials and workers. Some include elaborate sports facilities, libraries, computer centers, and so on. Then, too, whenever buildings are turned down, there is a hidden cost. The pressure on existing facilities increases maintenance costs.

The general aging of school plants, like that of teachers and administrators, has substantially increased maintenance costs. This is particular true in urban districts. (A personal note: the elementary school I attended, which I thought was ancient then, is still operating at full capacity today.) Then, too, school buildings receive more wear and tear than comparable public facilities. Kids consume furniture at a rate that would make termites blush. They do the same at home, but their parents don't replace what they destroy or damage because the parents are not compelled to follow state safety codes. Indeed, recently one school district was prohibited from beginning the school year because of some 130 fire infractions. A compromise was worked out, but that district now has to find nearly three million dollars to bring everything up to code.

Finally, the push for longer school days and an extended school year is forcing aging plants to perform at maximum levels, and at the same time removing those buildings from scheduled major renovation or maintenance. And some districts have been shocked by the increased utility costs of longer days and an extended school year. It pays to optimize the plant, but only if the plant is an optimum facility in the first place.

Creative Solution

Following the solution for instruction, schools have to become in part cyberschools. Instead of building ten new schools at a cost of $60 million (not including annual maintenance), only to have half of them empty in ten years as the demographics changes, build five. Convert programs, especially in middle and high schools, to electronic delivery, link home and school so that every student is being homeschooled, set up electronic portfolios, and factor in computer monitoring and evaluative functions to track attendance, work progress, time on task, and daily progress.

Consolidation and Structure

Cyber instruction functions in time, not in space. School is available 24/365. No separate budgets are required to extend the school day or year. Summer school is economically seamless. A total tutorial support program to help students understand test design and to pass high-stakes testing is available for $69 per month per school from Smart Kids. Consider the cost of teacher instruction plus the wear and tear of using expensive talent in the role of drill sergeant. In addition, more real time is thus made available for genuine, not token, service learning and school-to-work programs. If other states follow Florida's lead of integrating K–16, motivated students working at their own pace and under their own initiative can earn college credits before they graduate from high school. Again, if made part of the teacher leadership solution, students would always have a secure anchor and home for face-to-face interactions.

SUMMARY AND CONCLUSION

Given the combined economic pressures of the increasing costs of administration and instruction, the shortage of supervisors and teachers, and the incredible expense of building new and maintaining old school buildings, does it not make sense to pause and to recognize that a historical and financial convergence, the extent and depth of which has never occurred before, is looming right in front of education? As often has been noted, the Chinese sign for crisis is the same as that for opportunity. Do we really need new school buildings if we possess computer delivery systems? The handwriting on the wall is clear for those willing to read it and gutsy enough to call a spade a shovel and not trade off the future for the momentum of the past.

What we have learned from examining companies that last and excel is three principles:

1. Nothing is sacred.
2. Nothing lasts forever.
3. The future favors those who anticipate and innovate.

Education needs to supplement its commitment to the traditional three Rs with the above future-oriented trinity if it is to stay around to successfully deliver the original three Rs.

CHAPTER 7

Money and Teachers

Imagine the following future job description:

Wanted: Ten New Teachers

Utopian School District, located in the unpolluted, rolling hills of upper Aspiration Township, is seeking ten certified teachers for a new high school. Pay range is $75,000 to $95,000 to start. There is an initial $5,000 to $10,000 hiring incentive depending on qualifications. Bonuses are available annually. The ideal candidate should possess the following five attributes:

1. Technologically skilled: integration of human and machine instruction and intelligence.
2. Managerially adept: effective and efficient operation of a learning team serving a cohort of seventy-five to one hundred students.
3. Financially focused: maintenance of budget limits, cost controls, and fund-raising.
4. Accountability oriented: monitoring a comprehensive electronic assessment database.
5. Planning centered: solid scheduler and planner of complex activities and anticipator of future opportunities and problems.

E-mail mission statement and curriculum vitae to collabutopia@ tommorrow.edu. Initial contact will be by e-mail, followed by conference calls. A short list of candidates will be brought to Utopia for final interviews.

This advertisement may appear whimsical, but in truth it is determined by the hard reality that a trinity of motivating factors—money, challenge, and professionalism (probably in that order)—will alone attract quality. (Massachusetts, for example, has been offering a signing bonus of $20,000 to attract one hundred talented teachers to the state.) In many ways American public education has become a subsidized Peace Corps, and talent will not come or stay unless there is pay and pride. We know that talent can turn schools around; short-term urban school projects using Ivy League students have proven that. And we are also aware that education is so teacher dependent, on the one hand, and historically so exploitative, on the other hand, that it does not have the means or mission to lure and to keep educational professionals in a style to which they have never been accustomed. Over 50 percent of education graduates decide not to go into education. Of those who do only 50 percent stay after two years. No other profession drains its own talent pool like education.

What is dramatically different about the ad above is that it is a do-it-yourself solution. If the money can't be found outside perhaps it can be found inside. If the environment is less than professional, teachers put in charge can change that. If students need both comprehensive and individualized instruction, allowing a knowledge team to design and deliver a distributed learning system would be the answer. In short, what is being proposed is turning the problem on its head. If teacher salaries are insufficient to attract and keep talent, and additional funds are not available, the only other option is for money to be generated by the teachers themselves.

To generate income, teachers have to run the schools. Teachers have to shape the learning community in which they and their students work and live. That requires them to be the mangers not only of learning but also of operations. Specifically, they should shoot for the elusive triple crown: integration of administration, instruction, and measurement. Finally, their professionalism has to manifest itself in quality outcomes, parental support, testing accountability, and financial solvency. In short, I am arguing for turning the entire problem of education over to educators and having them put in place an economically driven model of educational excellence. Indeed, it might be the last-ditch effort to turn education around before all the forces that have been nibbling at its sides become the center itself.

The immediate objection to giving teachers a totally free hand is that it is like issuing them a blank check. But the amount already would be written in. Strings would be attached—they always are. Five conditions would be stipulated for generating the economic returns needed:

1. TECHNOLOGICALLY AMPLIFIED INSTRUCTION

Two major trends will converge by 2025. First, the spike in global populations will be accompanied by a spike in computer power. Second, intelligent machines will occupy a position of mastery. In other words, Arthur C. Clark's classic science fiction space odyssey may become science fact. In fact, we already are halfway there. If education is teacher dependent, everything else is computer dependent. When computers go down, everything, including us, stops. President Bush's new education budget proposes a 50 percent cut in support for technology in the schools.

All future teachers have to be trained to be technologically amplified for a number of reasons, ranging from the practical to the visionary:

- All teachers should function in the same way as doctors treating patients. Diagnostics should be followed by appropriate treatments. If preparation is needed for state-mandated tests, there is no point employing and frustrating expensive and creative teachers as drill sergeants. Besides, they probably would not be as good. So the first yield is to save instructional money and time by using effective and efficient computer programs that already are sustaining homeschooling, for which cost is a deciding factor.
- Another value is that software introduces students to important principles of learning and test design. Computer programs do not just teach specifics. They provide the opportunity to learn how to learn, and how to display that knowledge on tests.
- Finally, technology is a rehearsal for an overpowering future that may come—the creation of sentient machines that have the potential to be our masters. Perhaps, current and future students may become technologically sophisticated enough to leverage control so

that we do not lose our freedom. In any case, it is their problem to live with and to solve.

2. LEARNING MANAGERS

If teachers are to be masters of their fate and environment, they have to manage both. That is not a totally radical proposal. It is site-based management pushed to its ultimate point, at which teachers do not just make recommendations but make and implement decisions. But the key is the recognition that school operations have to be stripped of multiple layers of approval, and that bureaucratic bean counting and reporting, which are overwhelming, duplicative, and expensive, must be reduced to the minimum. Here are a few specific examples of managerial reengineering:

- A new hybrid is envisioned: the teacher/leader. Such a fused role replaces all administrators at all levels and reaps the benefits of enormous cost savings. Indeed, because administrative costs have increased over the last five years at a rate five times that of the instructional budget, the savings can be substantial.
- The teacher leader is in charge of a learning team consisting of subject-matter experts, techies, tutors, counselors, teletutors, and so on. Some are unpaid volunteers and retirees, others are parents. The budget for the team is at least 10 percent below the per-capita contribution level for students in the cohort.
- Each cohort consists of seventy-five to one hundred students, grades seven through twelve, but ungraded. Instruction is individualized—that is, decentralized and distributed. A special learning plan and contract are negotiated with and signed off by student and parents. The specifics of each plan and its progress are entered into a database monitored daily to determine progress or lack of it. It also can be accessed using a protected security code by parents.
- Homework is redefined as something a student does not take home but rather does at home. In other words, the various economies of homeschooling are tapped and become part of the

operational range of the program. The technology makes that possible.

3. FINANCIALLY FOCUSED

Education in general is badly run and needlessly expensive. Costs typically exceed the rate of inflation. The tuition of private colleges has been scandalous for years. Now only the very rich or the very poor can attend private colleges. New high schools are built as gigantic palaces that the community pays for but cannot use. They house thousands of students only to break them up into smaller schools within the larger school. Education is often inefficient even on the level of basic supplies. On the average, teachers spend over $700 each year of their personal income to purchase school-related items. In short, there are significant savings possible.

- Each cohort manages its own budget. It determines salaries and raises. Purchasing is centralized to realize economies of scale. Payroll and benefits are also centralized, and may be outsourced. Complex data reporting to the state is outsourced, as well as the general review of income and expenditures. If a unit exceeds its budget, its members do not get paid.
- Cost savings options are identified by teachers and students. They include custodial duties, transportation, lunches, school materials, and so on. In all instances, gains are listed: special software, art equipment, special trips, invited speakers, and so on. Decisions are made collaboratively through consensus by the learning team, students, and parents.
- Surpluses at the end of the year are not vacuumed up but stay with the unit and may be carried over to the next year. Fund-raising is a regular activity of each unit. In almost all cases the units cooperate and undertake common activities. Preferences are given to fund-raising through community service. All students are required to give a minimum of thirty hours per year of community service.
- Grant writers are hired on a percentage basis, like attorneys. If the grant is received, they receive a percentage of the overhead. A

public relations and contact person may also be helpful to work with the grant writer at times, both to secure gifts from donors or businesses and to maintain good relations with vendors of technology and software, who are encouraged to contribute new and experimental hardware and software. The school may wish to consider becoming a beta site.

4. ACCOUNTABILITY ORIENTED

Financial accountability is obviously important because it helps to generate the funds to hire and keep talent and to fund operations. But equally and increasingly important is educational accountability. Actually, the two should be fused but seldom are. In fact, there are schools that seriously lapse in both areas. Budgets are lopsided in order to throw teachers and specialists at schools that have failed state-mandated tests. The fear is that if they fail again, takeover or vouchers will be forthcoming. But often the success is temporary. Accountability has to be total and integrated, not just added on.

- Test prep and test design can be taught by computer. Tutors are assigned only for the weak areas defined by diagnostic tests. In other words, test mania need not become, as it has in many schools, a major budget item.
- Diagnostics also moves across specific subjects, classes, and individual teachers. What emerges are weak links in the chain that serve as feedback to the learning team, allowing them to take corrective action. Occasionally, the weakness may be in the software program. An experimental program in math, for example, produced and tested by Johns Hopkins, may then be put in its place. In other words, accountability need not be perceived purely or primarily as an area of drudgery; it deserves as much creative attention as curriculum.
- The assessment of learning is supplemented with an assessment for learning. The process of evaluation, like the process of test design, is made part of learning accountability. Students become increasingly self-sufficient.

- Students are given more opportunities for leadership. They have a share in and are part of governance. They serve on committees and boards, and student-led parent-teacher conferences become routine. Students take turns at being part of the go-to team when anyone visits the school. Students undertake on a revolving basis custodial and lunch duties, and have a say in how the monies saved are spent. In short, students sustain the economy of their community. They learn that it does not happen automatically.

5. ANTICIPATORY AND PARTICIPATORY PLANNING

Reduced costs require a double shift: from administrators to teachers, and from teachers to students. In the process, students have to become more self-reliant and actively accept more responsibility for their own learning and performance. Remediation is expensive. So is repeating grades or subjects. Using expensive certified teachers for drill work is economically counterproductive. Students need to be given the tools for self-management; teachers need to be free to raise the levels of expectation. But technologically amplified programs that are student individualized are dead in the water without extensive planning and its companion, monitoring. Moreover, the planning must display a comprehensive range from short- to mid- to long-term.

- Data tracking sustained electronically follows the total activities of the entire instructional world and the individual profiles, plans, and progress of each student for a time span of at least ten years.
- Each student maintains an electronic portfolio that is projected forward at least five years after graduation. A disk of that portfolio is given to each student with his or her diploma. The portfolio is future oriented and anticipatory. In fact, students are evaluated on their trend scenarios.
- Career planning and pathing are no more separated from academics than the development of interpersonal relationships. Work in fact becomes a cognate subject of study. Anticipating changing career patterns is regularly linked to research directions and findings. An annual postgraduation survey feeds back patterns currently operative.

- One of the most difficult tasks is to link and align anticipation and participation, and to persuade students that collective forecasting often has great power. Tapping diversity is often regarded as a source of strength and creativity but seldom applied to looking ahead. Each year the senior class generates collaboratively a forecast that represents their graduation gift to the school.

In summary, then, the value of an economically driven model is that it positions reform at the heart of the system and makes all participants individually and collectively accountable to themselves and to all others. Above all, it invests governance with not only political but economic goals. Collaborative leadership is thus always budgetary. That encourages the negotiation of new designs for learning and living together in a common community of learners, scholars, and workers. Financial solvency is not perceived as irrelevant to educators or standing apart as a responsibility or activity of external professionals. It becomes part of day-to-day viability. It is leverage. It is positioning. It puts money where your values are. That is the ultimate version of accountability.

As always, skeptics demand to know whether it can happen. Of course, it can. It already has in many plants in which team leaders are given a credit card with a limit of $10,000 to quickly order parts to maintain production. But in education all things have to go slowly. Gradual acclimation is required. The prospect of operating in and within a budget would paralyze many teachers, just as running a school without a principal would. Adults who have been managing their bills for years suddenly appear inept when they have to face a school budget. But with a gradual introduction of change, and a slow movement from one success to another, teachers can become effective financial managers, especially when they see the relationships between expenditures and quality student outcomes.

What will turn education around are incentives not from without but from within. A bonus earned through cost-effectiveness is both a psychic and a financial reward. Besides, what do we have to lose by trying and trusting? It could not be any worse than what we already have.

CHAPTER 8

Teachers and Technology

Proving or disproving the efficacy of technology vis-à-vis teacher instruction has often ignored student impacts and failed to note surprising findings. And hearing directly from students and placing their comments at the center of the debate is rare. Most of the time the dominating points of view are the concerns and fears of teachers, unions, and administrators on the one hand, and the issues of curriculum equivalency, exposure to pornography, and distraction from high-stakes testing on the other hand. But what is striking about student-focused findings and may disturb educators is that such findings—which are generally missing from the discussion of the pros and cons of technology—tip the scales toward the use of machines.

The reason technology is being discussed in the chapter on teachers is that it is a teacher in its own right. To appreciate the extent to which a teacher can be extended by technology is to consider a win-win game. There are now two teachers, the human one who is face to face with students and the "teacher" inside the machine. Direct instruction is built into the computer program. So is correction, amplification, challenging extensions, links, and so on. Set up as a class, synchronous or asynchronous, it is also interactive. So are teachers' interventions, but now by not having to be the only one offering direct instruction teachers can be free also to facilitate and target discussion. But perhaps the most important reason for educators to embrace technology is so they can be student and reality advocates.

The current and increasing process and practice of dialogue via machine partnerships and interfacing exchanges more accurately reflects current and future work processes than the traditional class model of direct instruction. No matter what the job or profession, work and research are increasingly technology dependent and even driven. In fact, since the 1950s, recognition has been given to the existence and impact of an information economy. So in addition to the prospect of not sufficiently valuing student learning preferences, we now have a reality displacement problem. School reform is primarily focused on improving a process that may more accurately reflect the ways things were than the way things are and increasingly will be. Fixing schools according to the traditional model may only produce a much-improved dinosaur. Increasingly, the reality that all students will have to face is what some students already experience in cyber learning environments. In short, given the dynamics of the workplace and student preferences, if educators really believed in student-centered education it would have to be technology centered.

So how do we get ourselves out of this mess of misplaced foci? We begin by telling the truth, or rather many truths, about technology and teachers. First, a balance sheet on technology itself:

- Technology is no panacea. What may be wrong with schools, technology cannot fix.
- Technology can never be a substitute for inspiring teachers. They alone help students catch fire.
- Technology, however, is formidable. It has three major curriculum strengths: first, it is an excellent drill sergeant and can prepare students for tests; second, it is ubiquitous and can offer direct instruction at any time of the day, in all subject areas at all levels of difficulty (even AP courses), that is adjusted to different learning styles; third, it can offer the jaded or bright a number of imaginative simulations and learning journeys—"hard fun" experiences.
- Technology is not limited to learning but extends seamlessly to monitoring, managing, and measuring learning.
- Technology comes with all the behind-the-scenes interfaces that enable student work to provide important sources of diagnostic interventions and correctives.
- Technology through the Internet is the supreme connector. It can link anyone, anywhere, anytime. Thus, it enables students to visit foreign lands and sites and, more importantly, establish relationships

with students from different countries. It has done more to prepare students for living in a future global world than anything else.

• Finally, technology can present students with the ethical challenges of technology itself, especially medical and bionic developments, and job displacement. What does it mean to live in a primarily technological society?

In addition, we have to stop lying to teachers. We have given them false assurances that machines will never replace them or make then obsolete. It is the same lie told to the hand-spinning textile workers in Luddite in early nineteenth-century England. The truth is that teaching machines can, have, and will replace teachers. They already are replacing essay readers and scorers, and that is a very complex programming process (*Education Week* 2002d). Cyber schools, in toto or in part, are on the increase. For example, Florida's totally virtual high school services the entire state. It is highly likely that the basic reason technology has not been integrated into the curriculum is that teachers are not about to participate in what they intuit to be their own gradual demise. Besides, they listen to their unions, which seek to protect their jobs and are rightly fearful of the motivations of administrators advocating increases in technology as cost cutting.

So what will happen? Three scenarios appear likely. They range from the resistance of indifference, to reluctant accommodation, to indiscriminate acceptance. Although the speed with which each will unfold will vary, all three options will coexist in different proportions, as in fact they do now.

1. THE RESISTANCE OF INDIFFERENCE

Most teachers have no leanings one way or the other. They have so much else on their plate and are so battered by testing mania that the issue of technology does not enjoy a high priority. Besides, they generally feel outclassed by the experts on the one hand and the passionate opposition of their unions on the other. Most are spectators watching a prolonged and often boring tennis match. Although administrators are often absent from the debate, enjoying the rare opportunity to escape the hot seat and believing that whatever finally happens their jobs are secure, many are compelled by scarce resources and the need to produce increased test scores to become technology advocates. But they often are misinformed. That is not surprising: only three states in the country require computer literacy as a prerequisite for an administrators' certificate. And even when administrators are computer literate, many have been out of the classroom so long their understanding of the demands of current curricula precludes intelligent application.

Alan Warhaftig's attack on technology and his strong defense of "education as a human enterprise" appeared recently in the "Commentary" section of *Education Week* (2002c). It is a classic argument, although often smug and elitist, about all those wonderful teachers like himself who stir students to learn in a classroom community. And as already noted and conceded, technology is not inspiring; so no one seeks to eliminate the Warhaftigs, especially those who carry the impressive credential of national certification. Incidentally, technology is not designated as one of the core competencies of that national board; so there is a good chance all the nationally certified Warhaftigs never were presented with the rigors of technology theory and design. But that is not totally surprising. Only 23 percent of recent education graduates believed they were technologically literate. And yet virtually every advertisement and job description for educators lists such literacy as a desirable requirement. Why such duplicity?

The basic argument of Warhaftig and others against technology is that sufficient research has not been done. But when will it be enough? We already have done extensive research on instruction and discovered that generally teachers are technologically illiterate, that uncredentialized and inexperienced teachers compromise student learning, that smaller classes generally produce better results than larger classes, that teaching has the highest attrition rate of all professions, and that most high schools in the next two years (as well as the colleges that already have accepted them) will face the major embarrassment of a significant percentage of seniors failing to pass the graduation exam.

Can technology solve these teacher problems? Not all, but well-tested programs are better than unprepared and underperforming teachers; computers in effect can generally reduce class size to more manageable ratios; machines won't quit if stressed or overwhelmed, or be intimidated by unruly or defiant students; and, finally, computers generally can serve as a better, less expensive, more focused drill sergeant for test prep than regular teachers. In short, the sound and fury has been so overwhelming that teachers have generally been prevented by the research smokescreen from perceiving technology as basically a solid instructional aid that may be able to restore some professional satisfaction and sanity. Of course, we should do more research. Of course, we should test and develop the best possible technology and software that we can. But the Warhaftigs will never be satisfied with computers because they are already so totally satisfied with the Warhaftigs that they will admit no comparison. In the meantime, all the non-Warhaftig teachers—and they are in the majority—are lulled into admiring an ideal that eludes them and shortchanges their students.

2. RELUCTANT ACCOMMODATION

Compromise will be the order of the day. An increasing number of schools will become in part cyber schools. Sometimes that will be done to solve administrative problems of truancy and absenteeism, or to build bridges between school and the home, teachers and parents. Rural schools with declining enrollments have no other choice unless they gut their curriculum. Budget shortfalls will lead schools to seek a technological bailout. Inadequate funds to operate a summer school will result in offering an electronic summer school. The same solution for the same reasons will be used to extend the day and the school year. But whatever the driving forces, what increasingly will emerge is the hybrid school: a combination of real and cyber time and place, real face to face and electronic face to face, two teachers partnering to produce the results listed at the beginning of this discussion.

If learning teams are used, at least one member will be technologically sophisticated. School districts will centralize the purchase of hardware and software, wherever possible forming consortia with other districts to increase price leverage. State departments of education will follow suit. Professional development for teachers will focus on machine learning and diagnostics. Much of it will be done by vendors as a benefit of purchase. The final hybrid will be the interface between regular schooling and homeschooling. Homework will be redefined as home learning, taking place in the home and ideally assisted by parents, and according to a weekly and daily schedule more accommodating to all involved.

3. INDISCRIMINATE ACCEPTANCE

Wholesale and speedy implementation of technology may regularly involve at least two excesses: exaggerated claims of rapid achievement, and increasing dominance of education by the business sector. The two are correlated. The claims will tend to be driven by marketing rather than educational research, just as the gains will be a mixture of better scores and economics. Left on their own, most students would be so involved in playing computer games that access to games will have to be blocked more than to porn sites. More vocational and health-related training programs that do not require a baccalaureate degree will be introduced at the high school and community college levels. Business partnerships and internships will be set up to ease the transition from school to work. These popular programs will be supported especially by parents and students who do not wish to assume college debt. With business presiding overall, education will service the new societal employment needs of an increasingly technological service economy. More students will be trained in the health field and thus reduce the serious shortage of technicians and nurses. The ultimate trade-off will be the replacement of education with training.

There is a strong possibility that such technological exuberance will overshoot the mark, just as the current resistance and indifference pulls it in the contrary direction of inaction. Inevitably the forces of balance will act as correctives and restore equanimity, but not before much damage, dislocation, and misunderstanding have occurred. If looking ahead has any value, then it is to urge a proactive and preventive position that offers more sanity and less strain. In particular, the limited matrix shown in table 8.1 may serve as a recommended course of action for teachers (T) and technology (t) (the one listed first plays the dominant role).

Table 8.1.

Area	Hybrid Roles	Balanced Outcomes
Instruction	t + T	Generic + Customized
Monitoring	t + T	Rubric Multiple Goals
Test Prep	t	Data Tracking Correctives
Essay Review	t + T	Profiling/Patterning of Student Work
Diagnostics	T	Intervention Design
School/Home	T + t + parent	Extension of Learning Calendar/Site
Work/Career	T + t + Service Learning	School-to-Work Alignment

We can persist in pursuing an all-or-nothing direction: only teachers or only technology. But it is perhaps time to recognize that technology is not an enemy but an ally. By doing so, educators will not be at odds with their students but share their mutual future. Learning machines may turn out to be the best new colleagues and partners teachers can have.

Part III

EDUCATIONAL ADMINISTRATORS
AS MAJOR PLAYERS

CHAPTER 9

Leadership Expectations and Job Descriptions

One can learn a great deal about a profession from reading want ads. Position descriptions in advertisements and postings offer a rich mine of information. They can tell us a great deal, for example, about how educational leadership is perceived and promoted. Such descriptions also may acquire anticipatory importance. Changes coming about in the field may surface first, no matter how tentatively, in these postings.

One obvious new development is the encouragement of professionals who do not come from educational backgrounds or experience. A few large school districts already are advertising for CEOs instead of superintendents. After a long and difficult search, the Los Angeles Unified School District finally settled on an ex-governor. New York City and others have split the position into two equal jobs—academic and business. For-profit educational management companies, like Edison, view the MBA as an acceptable substitute for the MS or MA in education when hiring educational administrators.

Another new trend has to do with economics. Administrative salaries, often too close to those of the best-paid teachers, are going up, especially because of the law of supply and demand on the one hand, and the greater salary expectations of MBAs and CEOs on the other hand. The traditional opposition to using business leaders and employing management approaches may lessen, as witnessed recently when Edison and a major urban district signed a contract to work together. Clearly, we are entering uncharted waters with respect to the future of educational administrators. It might therefore be helpful to pause and to examine what districts say they want and expect from their educational leaders. What follows is an examination of a comprehensive sample of advertisements for superintendents from *Education Week* and from association journals.

The basic candidate profile of superintendents that emerges takes the form of five major categories in descending order of importance:

1. Leadership
2. Management skills
3. School performance and reform
4. Curricular and staff development
5. Technological literacy

1. LEADERSHIP

Leadership is invariably presented as a calling, management as a task. The one occupies the high road, the other that of mundane day-to-day operations. In any case, here are the quoted leadership qualities that are sought:

- Exceptional leadership
- Visionary of the future
- Strong and energetic leader
- Proven record of accomplishment
- Passionate educator
- Strong moral character and high level of energy
- Servant leader
- Accessible, visible, honest, and firm

One has the uneasy feeling that some of these qualifications may have been crafted as correctives to what the last incumbent failed to do. But what is curious is that no descriptions include what would be prominent in business job descriptions—decisiveness. The frequent mention of the need for high energy conveys the impression of a nonstop job in which the holder of the office who can outlast his or her crushing schedule will remain a leader—a kind of trial by exhaustion. But what emerges clearly is that the superintendent must pursue the high road, inspire followers, and implement his or her vision. At the same time, he or she must also run a tight ship and possess the management skills enumerated below.

2. MANAGEMENT SKILLS

- Manage a large and complex organization
- Faculty planning, recruitment, and retention
- Financial planning, budget, and oversight
- Strong implementation skills
- Comprehensive fiscal and performance accountability
- Develop new initiatives
- Continuous quality improvement
- Diversity management
- Communication and interpersonal skills

One reason the tenure of superintendents has shrunk to its present average of three years may be the combined expectation of being both an educational leader and a business manager. Although clearly it is not impossible to integrate the two halves, the combination may be unmanageable, or manageable only by minimizing one-half of the dual role, usually the leadership half.

Is this why New York City split the position into two jobs—because it was increasingly too much for one person to manage and to succeed at? Some superintendents are better at one half or the other, or just average at both. Moreover, the ante is being upped on both sides of the street. School reform and performance have been used to hold the feet of leaders to the fire; and costs, salaries, and now performance incentives have strained financial resources. The daily and even hourly crush of operations and oversight, as well as the grueling process of meeting after meeting, creates a no-man's-land that consumes, dilutes, or fragments both high-level leadership and operations management. The net result is low-level leadership and low-level management. The high energy level called for describes a superintendent who is perpetually in motion, working fourteen to sixteen hours a day moving paper off his or her desk, attending endless meetings often dealing with "administrivia," and making sure he or she can offer some inspiring words at the pep rally. At the same time, he or she is supposed to provide educational leadership to accomplish the double agenda below:

3. SCHOOL REFORM AND PERFORMANCE

- Mandated state performance standards
- Testing goals
- Student-focused curricula
- Parental and community involvement
- Continuous reform and quality initiatives
- High morale and performance

4. CURRICULAR REVIEW AND REVISION, AND FACULTY RECRUITMENT AND RETENTION

- Awareness of recent research
- Literacy standards
- Homework judiciously assigned
- Team teaching
- Grade-level planning
- Board involvement as community representative

Typically this laundry list is compiled by the school board. Its function is to hold the superintendent accountable for everything that can go wrong, a state of affairs that burns out so many superintendents and accounts for high turnover.

For the most part, school boards are dreadful bosses. For some members, it is a full-time passion. For others it is a part-time civic commitment. So naturally members thrive on excesses. They either micromanage or become visionaries. Their not-so-hidden agenda is their own school experiences, good and bad. Nostalgia becomes data. They often possess an unfortunate tendency to lecture others about the good old days, the point of which is always to convey an impression of how strong and committed they and/or their parents were.

School boards also are the most politicized aspect of the school system, especially if their meetings are aired regularly on community TV. Board members often appear at such meetings waving newspaper and magazine clippings dealing with various panaceas across the country, asking indignantly: "Why can't we be doing this?" And the poor superintendent, probably going on four hours' sleep, has to once again perform his weary dance: "We can't do everything and do it well."

A new report recently appeared dealing with the issue of the superintendent and the board, produced by the Education Research Service and the New England School Development Council. One of its principal findings bears on this discussion: "School boards should be limited to policy-making and long-term planning, leaving superintendents to manage day-to-day operations." What a wonderful endorsement and affirmation of educational leadership! To avoid micromanagement, the trade-off is to put the key educational expert in shackles and have him trot obediently behind a group of stargazers.

The report totally misses the mark. The superintendent is supposed to be not a business manager but an educational leader. He or she, not the board, is the critical contributor to long-range planning and policy. It is not surprising that, locked out of those opportunities to exercise their expertise, many superintendents become convinced they are nothing more than secretaries to the board, fall guys when matters fall apart, and hacks in the eyes of principals. In short, school districts should not advertise for leaders when what is really wanted is lackeys. But one last item has to be included.

5. TECHNOLOGY

- Computer literacy
- Knowledge of electronic curricula
- Computer-aided instruction

- Distance-education modalities
- Electronic AP courses

Curiously, only two position descriptions asked for technological literacy and familiarity with the above menu. It is a strange sin of omission, given that the economics of schooling may necessarily lead to electronic instruction. If the last shall be the first to enter heaven, then perhaps all the agenda items listed at the end should be moved to the top. In fact, many meetings of administrators leave the future as the last item to be discussed; but because they run out of time (ironically) the future is carried over to the next meeting and then to the next. The assumption is that the future can always wait. Finally, the only ads offering prospective applicants further information refer them to websites or instruct them to make e-mail inquiries.

So what is the upshot? We seem to be engaged in creating or perpetuating the myth of the super-superintendent. Have we doomed our leaders to failure by nailing their operational feet to the ground, asking them to run ahead of the pack and ascend the high road of educational excellence? Or conversely and perversely, have we compromised their managerial competency by also demanding visionary foresight? As if that were not bad enough, when one adds all that is omitted from the ads, the burden is crushing. Leaders above all also are supposed to:

- Hold the enterprise and its people together
- Instill pride and steadiness of purpose
- Reiterate what is central and has stood the test of time
- Value the development of intelligence and imagination
- Resist the fads and fashions of the flashy and the false
- Build character and caring
- Share with the board the journey to the future.
- Prepare principals to be educational enhancers of all the above

School reform may have to start with leadership reform. We need to allow our superintendents to succeed. But that can't happen if, from the start, we overwhelm them—or worse, deceive them. Why should educational leaders constantly be made to go up a down escalator? Are we trying to prove that in education martyrdom is required? Leadership does not have to become less of a calling if the leader is protected, supported, and helped. Must it be a thankless job in which burnout and, ultimately, insensitivity are guaranteed? Perhaps we should be rewriting the position descriptions we post for vacancies. That might be a good place to start.

CHAPTER 10

Survival Skills for New Principals

The job facing new principals is often so intense and unrelenting that nothing perhaps will make it doable. In other words, the problem is not the survival of principals but the viability of the principalship itself. Moreover, each year the work of principals grows in complexity, and demands multiply. The job exhausts experienced principals, and beginning principals feel overwhelmed. First-year principals have been known to stare at their paychecks and exclaim, "Is it really worth it?"

In many districts the pay of principals is only slightly higher than that of the top teachers. And principals work longer hours and year round, have more headaches, and are responsible for a list of duties that expands almost daily. In some districts that have gone to a longer day and/or a longer year, teachers' salaries have been adjusted, but not those of administrators. Clearly, current salary differentials will not be sufficient to attract enough new principals to the job—some five to ten thousand are needed, according to the Department of Labor, by 2005. But the problem goes deeper.

The position of principal is really two jobs: educational leader and business manager. Hopefully, educators are drawn to the job by the difference they believe they can make in the arena of education. But immediately and constantly they encounter the business side of education and all its paperwork. Rooney acknowledges that "the work never gets done. New principals may work late in the evening and on the weekend to finish paperwork" only to find the treadmill start again on Monday morning.

Principals are going up a down escalator. After a while the day-to-day pressure of the job takes its toll. They do not read proposals for school reform or curriculum revision carefully or reflectively. Increasingly, decisions are made not based on excellence but based on expediency. Principals develop a new kind of expertise; they choose what will work with minimum supervision or intervention from their office. They become adept at detecting crushing paperwork or procedures. They hoard their public visibility for the optimum moments or settings. Their priority list is totally pragmatic, and often teachers, students, and parents are not at the top. They generally stop reading. The journals pile up on their desk or night table. In short, they become what Rooney calls them—survivors. When administrators meet, they show one another their respective stigmata.

It's time to decide what a school district wants: an educational leader or a business manager. New York City finally split the job into two positions. The current situation is impossible. It results in leaders who do not lead and managers who do not manage. What kind of profession creates positions with built-in failure and makes surviving exhaustion a sign of leadership?

The job has to change. For starters, increase salaries, hire business managers, provide an executive coach, and rewrite the position description for principals to stress only the educational role. Then share with them all the well-intentioned, intelligent, and insightful observations of Rooney. Those observations might then have a real chance of taking hold.

CHAPTER 11

Principals as Instructional Leaders

The National Association of Elementary School Principals (NAESP) issued in November 2001 a new booklet calling for principals to increase their role as instructional leaders. Entitled "Leading Learning Communities," it is a bold and stirring call for nearly thirty thousand principals to step in and fill the breach of educational leadership and to enhance school achievement. Although research clearly documents the impact principals can have on schools' instructional performance as instructional leaders (Fink and Resnick 2001), achieving the goal is not without its difficulties and even some built-in potential failures. Indeed, there are at least five major obstacles that need to be addressed and overcome if this new initiative is to succeed.

1. RECONFIGURE THE JOB

The first task is to free up the principal to have the time and energy to function as an instructional leader. That is in fact the central recommendation of NAESP. The standard answer is that the principal needs an assistant principal. But that requires an enlightened school board and funds. Some aggressive superintendents, committed to a more assertive role for instructional leadership, may dramatize the need sufficiently to persuade boards to provide support or engage in fund-raising or securing grants. In other words, the enhanced leadership roles of principals have to be supported by all levels of administration, inside and outside of the district. Besides, if the role is important it deserves not a piecemeal but an across-the-board solution.

To be sure, throwing money at the problem may not be the only or even the best solution. Currently, the position of the principal is on overload. The demands have increased exponentially. The principalship has become more political, legalistic, therapeutic, and often confrontational. Current certification training does not include public relations, negotiating skills, security, and zero tolerance. In other words, even if funds were found to hire an assistant principal, the problem of overload would remain; and, with the momentum of add-ons, it would get worse.

More imaginative experimentation has included outsourcing selected administrative functions. This has a cost, but not as high a cost as bringing on another administrator. A few districts have grown their own administrators in anticipation of personnel shortages, recruiting administrative interns to absorb some of the workload in the principal's office. In other schools teachers have been persuaded to assume, as members of committees, some administrative duties. In a few instances, extra pay is provided. Parent partnership schools also have made use of talented parents in an administrative capacity, but there is generally a problem with their long-term continuity and commitment. Although these solutions may fall short of the mark, there is a need to make the job of principal more manageable and less martyred. If his or her position were reconfigured, the principal could indeed become an instructional leader; and, equally important, singular leadership would be replaced by distributed leadership (Elmore 2000).

2. SHOULD ALL PRINCIPALS BE INSTRUCTIONAL LEADERS?

That question is seldom asked, but it is potentially too compromising not to be identified and addressed. Not all principals would be effective as instructional leaders. Most were attracted to the position for many reasons, few if any having anything to do with setting instructional standards. Some would find that primary focus uncomfortable, even uncongenial. This would hold true especially for principals with longevity in the position, who, at the outset of their career and for many years after, were not required to be primarily instructional leaders. That task then did not have the urgency it currently has. And when it occasionally surfaced in the past, it usually required minor tweaking and was left almost totally to the faculty.

A number of principals are superb managers. They move paper, meet all deadlines, and the school runs like a top. They might find the challenge of leadership withering; and if forced to accept it, might conclude that it would be at the expense of the well-oiled machine. However, if the determination is that everyone in the district participates, then some well-chosen consultants functioning as instructional coaches may have to be brought on board to assist the reluctant rulers. In fact, consideration should be given to using such consultants generally for catch-up professional development. But if the enhanced role of instructional leader is to succeed, the honest review of each member of the entire administrative force is required, lest expectations exceed capacity. Not everyone is an instructional leader. Not everyone wants to be one. Above all, not everyone should be forced to assume that role.

3. TIME AWAY FROM THE CLASSROOM

If the principal has not been in the classroom for more than five years, that may pose a problem; more than five, definitely a cause for concern. The issue is one of creditability. Teachers generally are reluctant to listen to moralizing about the way things used to be or hearkening to dated teaching techniques and curriculum goals. Nostalgia is perishable and will not carry far; in fact, it generally is counterproductive. But surely, some will argue, principals are current by virtue of classroom observations and are familiar with different kinds of students as a result of office contact, although admittedly for disciplinary reasons.

The truth is that administrators really are not familiar with contemporary classroom dynamics. Nor are they often knowledgeable about cutting-edge pedagogy, especially best practices, classroom research, collaborative lesson plan development, brain research applications, and so on. Without teaching on a daily basis, having to deliver curriculum to unmotivated students, and building the knowledge base for high-stakes testing, principals as instructional leaders may appear in the unattractive light of failing to practice what they preach. That can be deadly.

The solution, however, already has been anticipated by a few principals, mostly at the middle and high school levels. Many have gone back into the classroom, not on a full-time basis but often enough so that they can understand everything the teachers gripe about. Indeed, the knowledge of those discontents provides important positioning or leveraging points for bringing about instructional refocusing. In short, if the leadership role is to enjoy acceptance on the one hand and precision of application on the other, principals may have to go back into the trenches.

4. SUBJECT-MATTER COMPETENCE

This obstacle has less to do with pedagogy than with subject-matter competence. All principals initially possessed subject-matter competence at least in one area, especially if they taught middle or high school. English teachers generally are comfortable with administrators who have taught and like to talk about literature and grammar. Not so math, science, foreign language, or computer science teachers. Even social science teachers might be uneasy. Indeed, if principals tried to present themselves or claim presumptuously to be well versed in all subjects, the degree of disengagement would be deservedly total. The operating law in education is that the further principals move away from their academic knowledge base and center, the more they distance themselves from those who are supposed to follow their lead.

One way of dramatizing that dilemma is to examine the efforts of the Education Development Center in Newton, Massachusetts. For the last six years, the center has provided professional development for principals. One of the most successful programs involves helping administrators understand basic changes in math education based on the standards of the National Council of Teachers of Mathematics. Typically, a small group of administrators, many confessing math phobia, spend a year observing math lessons and preparing lessons to teach. The gains are impressive, but the implications are disturbing.

What about biology, French, geography, computer science, and so on? Should all principals spend a year, away from the demands of their intense job, to acquire competencies that teachers rightly still may not respect or accept as equal to theirs? A better compromise might be for principals to master leadership content knowledge, which is distinguished from the depth of knowledge required by teachers who actually teach the subjects. Without such knowledge, principals cannot select effective professional development for their schools, evaluate high quality instruction, or understand the struggles teachers are going through as they learn to teach in new ways. In the New York City school system, leadership content knowledge is defined as instructional literacy—a horizontal base of teaching effectiveness coupled with subject-matter essentials.

In other words, all principals need to be equipped with such leadership content knowledge and instructional literacy if they are to be effective instructional leaders. The competence required is not subject specific but generic in nature; and what it lacks in depth it offsets with its horizontal span and linkages between subjects. In effect, the principal is asked to function as an interdisciplinary generalist, and to take the high road of overview—not unlike that of a conductor leading an orchestra. That makes a great deal of sense, especially when weighed against the time-consuming approach of acquiring deeper knowledge of all subjects. Combining the new and the basic may be the essential stuff of professional development for future instructional leaders.

5. LEVERAGE LEADERSHIP POINTS AND LEVELS

This final obstacle is frequently and mistakenly overlooked. On what level and at what points should the leadership be exercised? The general recommendation is across the board, with the principal acting as prime mover and cheerleader. Although that brings much-needed visibility to the cause, perhaps the most important level of implementation is with each individual teacher. And that in turn can best be done in conjunction with evaluation.

Perhaps no other area has been criticized more extensively—especially by teachers—than the annual or semiannual evaluation of teachers by principals. However, with the new commitment to instructional leadership, it may be possible to kill two birds with one stone. Instructional review has to be built into personnel review in a more intense and integrated fashion than ever before. In other words, leadership has to be delivered to the pivotal point of implementation. The first thing that must be changed is the timetable.

Evaluation should not be a single-shot occasion but a series of meetings stretched out over a period of at least six months. The initial meeting is a benchmark meeting. It establishes points for measuring progress and change. The principal explains his or her leadership agenda and its rationale. He or she then asks the teacher to discuss the extent to which those agenda items are currently being addressed in the teacher's practice, how, and with what success. The principal may make some suggestions for further consideration and ask the teacher to think about and develop some responses for the next meeting.

At the second meeting, the relationship is more equal, more an exchange between partners. The principal listens more, asks questions occasionally, and is almost totally nondirective. The agenda is one of change and identifying the avenues for how that change is to be effected. That meeting concludes with the essentials of an unofficial change contract generally understood and in place. The principal then requests a final meeting, in which the teacher, after reflection, presents his or her short- and long-terms plans for accomplishing the changes agreed on. At that meeting the leader listens and learns, expresses admiration in specific terms for the plan, and finally asks if there is anything he or she individually can do to be further supportive and what the school can provide in the form of professional development. When done well the final result of these meetings will be seamless, ownership will be secured, and it will not be possible to determine where the principal begins and the teacher leaves off because both will be instructional leaders.

In summary, then, the worthy goal of increasing the role and visibility of the principal as instructional leader requires identifying and addressing any obstacles to success. The obstacles identified here may not be all that exist or even the most critical ones. And that is equally true of the solutions or approaches suggested. But they may be good starting points for superintendents and NAESP to involve groups of principals in a new dialogue about their future in general and their future as instructional leaders in particular. Toward that end, I would recommend that the exchange be structured along the lines of the evaluation meetings outlined above. That would be a particularly instructive format, especially for establishing the new set of relationships that instructional leadership will require in order to succeed and flourish. According to an ancient Tao proverb, when leaders lead well, the people always think they did it themselves.

CHAPTER 12

Models of Integrative Leadership

The basic issue to be acknowledged is that the current situation of principals is impossible. It results in leaders who do not lead and managers who do not manage. What other profession would allow sources of failure to be built in and make surviving exhaustion a sign of leadership? In short, the issue is not solely the survival of principals but the viability of the principalship itself. Given that more serious and comprehensive statement of the problem, it is necessary to explore the basic current, new, evolving, and futuristic models of educational leadership.

Because distributed leadership has taken so many different forms and is likely to continue to do so, it might be helpful at this point to list what appears to be common to all:

- Leadership is not a monopoly of the top: CEOs, superintendents, or principals.
- Leadership is not limited to any one job description but should be included in all.
- Leadership is thus both individual and collective, operating both in classrooms and in governance structures.
- Participatory leadership minimally grants teachers access to policy formulation, decision making, and definitions of outcomes.
- School leadership thus becomes not singular but multiple, not unilateral but collaborative. Its principal focus is integration.

The new reality that administration will have to operate under is the increasing prevalence of distributed leadership. Schools will have to become increasingly cooperative, collective, and collaborative. Principal-teacher leadership teams absorb and solve many of the problems mentioned earlier. For example, the issue of limited subject-matter competence is answered by the team, miniaturizing all or most of the subject matter areas. Teacher evaluation becomes a daily, normal process not requiring extraordinary and elaborate arrangements or time schedules. Above all, the consultative process assures that once teacher input has become part of a decision, the decision is likely to happen. In part, leadership sharing has come about because the job is too crushing on the one hand and because, in the generally more competitive environment of education, teachers wanted a greater say in how they would be managed and judged on the other hand. Three general paths are available to help salvage the role of the principal:

1. OUTSOURCING

To some extent following the model of teacher-led and teacher-owned schools, principals need to define what their core competencies and responsibilities are and consider outsourcing the rest. That requires that principals be given discretion over their budget and personnel. Rather than going the unacceptable route of asking for more assistants to run the office, principals in effect have to outsource those add-on duties that preclude their being effective instructional leaders. Outsourcing will be discussed more later.

2. SHARING STRUCTURES

Leadership and evaluation sharing opportunities would simultaneously reduce workload and raise the quality and level of decision making and performance improvement. Part of that sharing would involve principals acknowledging the increasing managerial role of teachers mandated by the specific demands of certain curricula and of accountability on the one hand, and the expanded leadership expectations of shared governance on the other hand. In other words, administrators, not teachers, would step in to fill the breach and in the process tap and share their own extensive administrative and leadership experience.

3. INTEGRATION

The key future role is to become an integrative leader who bridges gaps between the traditional basics and new curricula, between teacher workshops and technology, competence and testing. Whether principals find any of these alternatives attractive or choose to remain historically paternal, the future in the short term will be an incredible mixture of all positions—past, present, and a little bit of the emerging future. The traditional role will remain the dominant model. Principals will insist on remaining at the center of authority and monopolizing leadership. A wide range of versions of leadership sharing characterizes the present. Although somewhat unclassifiable, all share a new partnership between a principal and his or her teachers, each half stretching sometimes in opposition away from the other. Administrators and teachers interface. Although largely an outgrowth of earlier stages of teacher empowerment, teacher leadership stands apart as a bold incarnation of the future. Although only a minority development at this point in time, it tasks teachers and administrators with an ultimate version of what additional forms leadership sharing should take.

Which form of leadership will be dominant in the twenty-first century? The last two will take precedence. The first will gradually disappear as those principals retire. But responding proactively to that prospect, current principals should be given professional development workshops in leadership sharing, and all future administrators and teachers should be required to take courses at colleges of education in collaborative leadership governance. The future therefore looks brighter as a result of experimental principals and assertive teachers.

Whatever arrangements prevail or coexist, the overriding administrative and learning problem that still plagues education is the lack of integration. Unfortunately, integration has taken the token form of listing a series of incremental add-ons when it is really a way of rearranging the items on an already crowded plate. But nothing really changes. For integration to be authentic it must be multiple. It has to reduce fragmentation, reconfigure all the essential parts to bear collectively on improving school and student performance, unify the multiple directions that scatter the focus of principals, and reorganize and redistribute their overwhelming workload.

Although integration can be applied in many areas, the discussion here is focused on engaging the essential elements that structure a typical school system:

- Vertical Chain of Command
- Horizontal Connections between Grades and Grade Levels
- Relationships between Administration, Instruction, and Evaluation

Perhaps it would be helpful to step back and to practice viewing the whole of things—perhaps in a new way and with new metaphors. In other words, invoking the perspective of holistics might be helpful. In his essay on "Lessons from the Rain Forest," Taduchi Kiuchi (1998), CEO of Mitsubishi Electric, does exactly that by asking himself, "What is the principal value of the rain forest?" His own initial responses are predictably commercial: wood, botanicals, food, medicines, and so on. But that is not its essence. He finally concludes that the unique contribution of the rain forest resides in its design.

Kiuchi marvels at the incredible diversity of living forms and the capacity for unity. Each species has minimally a double niche: an individual one and a series of relationships to others. Coherence of the whole is always a blend of the singular and the multiple. What maintains order in diversity is the overall commonality of collaborative relationships. Everything has its place, but everything is related to everything else. Everything contributes and in turn is used. The miracle is in the design.

Kiuchi left the rain forest and reorganized Mitsubishi. He united departments that had been separated, established linkages between divisions that had been discrete, and announced that in the future company productivity and creativity would be determined by its commitment to synthesis.

The structures of organizations tend to be too divisive and mechanical. Everything is sorted out into boxes that are comfortable but separative. A more inventive structure is that of a river that starts at the top and flows through and touches every part of the organizational chart, linking its disunited parts with a common purpose. In both instances, the value of overlaying biological or natural metaphors of integrative design onto previously mechanical and divisive structures leads to the transformation of organizations into living systems.

If the metaphors and design principles of synthesis are applied to the three educational areas of the vertical, the horizontal, and the circular, what diagnostic conclusions emerge?

1. *School Leadership:* The hierarchical separation of principals and teachers compromises opportunities for multiple leadership.
2. *School Operations:* All functioning parts are essentially more disconnective than linked, more solitary than related.
3. *School Structure:* Administration, instruction, and evaluation do not function as a unified whole.

Although, happily, there are holistic solutions to each of the problems identified, the temptation is to champion one cause or another and thus ironically, in the name of integration, pursue a piecemeal approach. Coherence requires the involvement of all parts if the serendipity of reinforcement is to produce a new whole. But the vertical dominance of leadership evidently can leave its residual mark on everything underneath. Each division is programmed to gaze upward in obedience or loyalty and await marching orders. In addition, because there are no or only limited bridges between parts, the relationships tend to be competitive rather than cooperative, inward facing rather than outward facing. What conversations take place between teachers at the middle school and those at the high school?

When Motorola wished to cut in half the total number of days required to produce a cell phone, the greatest gains emerged between, rather than within, divisions (Hamel and Pralahad 1994). That was where the slack or waste was. Closer to home, the classic case is the general inability of academic departments to mount successfully an interdisciplinary program. In some cases the only way it has been done is to form a separate college outside of the system with its own professionals. Indeed, that follows the general research findings of Christensen, who found that the only innovative initiatives that survived took place outside of the established system and its deterministic operations.

What then seem to be the major separative flaws of the typical educational system noted by Elmore, Lambert, and others? The list is formidable and cuts across all lines:

- Teachers do not question whether a classroom problem is individual or schoolwide.
- The school separates knowledge into discrete parts that in turn are often the basis for resource allocation. Fragmentation follows budgetary incentives.
- The separation of grades coupled with singular teacher focus on his or her class precludes the integration of cumulative learning.
- Professional development is always focused on how to improve student learning, hardly ever on how to improve teacher learning.
- Elmore (2002) claims that most school reforms are largely symbolic and public relations rituals. The teachers do not really know why they are doing them; the structure of the organization that helped to create the problem in the first place remains intact; and there is no significant change in the way resources are allocated.
- Leadership and learning generally are not linked. According to Lambert (2002), "Being responsible for the learning of colleagues is at the center of the definition of leadership."
- Reflection on teaching practice is hardly ever extended to reflection on organizational design. As a result, microchange fails to affect the macrostructure.
- Above all, knowledge and practice have to be "stretched across roles rather than being inherent in one role or other" (Elmore 2000).

How then can integration be applied to this level of separatism and effect transformation? And what roles should principals play in effecting such changes? Integrating leadership is the first step. Administrators and teachers standing side by side and collectively facing the same problems together may bring about solutions that fuse both roles and administer learning. Then too there is the increasing recognition by a new wave of principals that they cannot accept the status quo but have to take on the challenge of structure. In a sense they have no other choice, since their position alone offers such leverage, and their experiential knowledge of organizational structures is singularly expert. Moreover, educational researchers like Lambert and Elmore have provided both the diagnostics and the correctives. It is no longer enough to review the nature of the work; how the structure organizes and even determines that work must also be considered. That double perspective, that blending of form and function, is what integration seeks to accomplish.

In many ways changing the structure is more a challenge and opportunity for principals than for teachers. After all they are the administrative professionals. But it does require that they become advocates for integration and the integrative process. They never should have been asked to be instructional leaders in the first place. Teachers should be the instructional leaders. Rather, principals should take on the whole ball of wax—they should shape and articulate a new holistic set of partnerships between parts that traditionally have remained apart or unconnected to the whole. If the ultimate goal is to integrate administration, instruction, and evaluation, and to bring harmony to otherwise discordant and counterproductive relationships, then principals minimally have two ways to go.

The first approach is from the outside in. The three areas must be redefined in terms of one another. Classroom management is also the way one teaches and evaluates. Administration does not exist solely outside the classroom; it has to focus on learning environments. If the classroom does not remain the central pivot, nothing will really change. Administration also must keep evaluation focused on curriculum and learning. Otherwise the school will always be at the beck and call of outside forces of accountability, and the focus will be on isolated rather than cumulative results. In many ways the goal of integration is the constant search for commonality.

The second approach is from the inside out. It engages the basics of governance. The structure of the school has to be reconceived as a collaborative tied together in a governance network. Each collaborative stage at every point can step back, see its horizontal extent to the left and to the right, and envision itself as part of a total circular whole, not a series of hierarchical parts sorted out by division of labor. The design should be always visible, busy, and even noisy. Each part should know that it has the power and jurisdiction to affect the whole; and that in turn it will be shaped by the negotiated unity of its discrete partners.

Above all, each collaborative has to be defined as a miniature of the whole. The one-on-one curriculum, for example, cannot drop the problem of administration or evaluation on any other group. The proposed curriculum must be total and seamless. It must be accompanied by its appropriate form of management and evaluation to be considered for adoption. Anything less will result in its being turned back as incomplete. And clearly it cannot be sent to the principal to be fixed, since he or she is now as much a part of synthesis as the staff is.

Will educators naturally take to such collaborative governance? No more than newly formed teams would. Teams are not born but made. Ask any coach. Governance training for principals and teachers may not please many who like to preserve the gap of adversarial relationships, but it is the key form of professional development to anchor leadership sharing and organizational redesign. Given time and a commitment to holistics, it will take hold. And in the process principals will be given a bracing future and mission: to pursue, align, and integrate the parts of a new whole.

CHAPTER 13

The Principal as Plato

In general, the bridges between instruction, administration, and evaluation are occasional, unilateral, or unused. Teachers teach, administrators administer. Each views his or her task as indispensable in its own right, as well as to the other. But the linkages between teachers and administrators are often not articulated. They travel in parallel lines that never seem to meet. Even if there is some alignment on the outcomes of evaluation, their perspectives are totally different. The teacher sees a student with a name, a personality, a family, a story, whereas the principal examines columns of performance data. Such separative and myopic foci preclude much. There is little or no coherent environment or culture all share. Although the rallying cry is for a collective effort to increase student performance and accountability, it usually falls on the individual ears of teachers, not on those of the group. When the results are disappointing and uneven, the determination to push harder still acts on the assumption that a unifying culture exists. And when an attempt at improvement does not work, again, each side may blame the other. The search for scapegoats precludes introspection.

The culture of each school is not a given. It is not predetermined or cast in stone. Teams are not born; they are made. The task of principals, often unacknowledged or unacted on, is to shape an interactive, coherent, and collaborative environment. A school should be a busy, friendly, caring, and stimulating place to work. It should produce interesting tales, not a litany of complaints later at dinner. It also should be on balance a source of satisfaction, with the good stuff outweighing the bad. Above all, it should not be dreaded as a place to go to every morning.

How is that to be accomplished? The first answer of workers is frequently "Get rid of the bosses!" That underscores—negatively, to be sure—the centrality of leaders and their effect on employee attitudes and motivation. When pressed further as to what makes bad bosses bad, workers tend to respond, "They don't listen. They are know-it-alls." So, it turns out, leaders should not be bosses. Ordering people around and not listening to them is not what leaders do.

Communication and culture always have to be paired. Each is a creative and reinforcing means to the other. A group that does not talk and listen seriously, frequently, and equally is disconnected and fragmented. The infallible sign of a coherent culture is that it is held together by communication. The glue is conversation. The principal, in short, is responsible for the conversations that take place or do not in his or her school.

The first step toward improving the culture of schools is for principals to rid themselves of all claims to ownership. The school, teachers, and students do not belong to anyone, because they are held in common. Top-down possessiveness jeopardizes genuine exchange between equals and partners. The next step is to accept the task of building culture by stirring conversations. But a goal for the talks is needed. A significant one would be to integrate instruction, administration, and evaluation—to create coherence by talking coherence. Introduced and nurtured by the principal, such conversations require no outside or additional materials, workshops, or costs. But to take hold and to bridge all involved, the strategic exchange has to involve three directions:

1. *Horizontal:* Distributed leadership connects instructional practice with teacher and student common learning, on the one hand, and bridges instruction, administration, and evaluation through a common empowering process, on the other. The key focus question is: How can we be more effective, collectively?

2. *Vertical:* Instructional goals are aligned with schoolwide and districtwide objectives so that top down and bottom up are not opposed to but in synch with each other. Differences and even disagreements are not ruled out but are contained within the mission of alignment so that neither mutiny nor apathy reigns. The key focus question is: How can we work together to achieve common goals and in the process align the micro and the macro?

3. *Circular:* Structured mutuality requires a match between how the organization works or does not, and how it provides, stirs, and enhances learning (including the self-learning of administrators, teachers, and staff). The critical focus is on environment and how it supports or deflects from achieving shared horizontal and vertical purpose (Elmore 2002). Such so-called externals are thus made part of the design and action. The key focus questions are: How and why is our work as educators organized and structured the way it is? How does it relate to student learning, and how is it supportive of collective effort?

To set all this in motion requires a dialectic common to all three agenda areas. As noted, an emerging and significant area of research is that of structured interviewing, strategic questioning, and scenario building nicely summed up and applied by Ratcliffe (2002). It is both qualitative and quantitative, and often incremental. It has been applied to many and different complex problems and yielded impressive scenarios of cities and industries. All applications, however, are governed by the same model, as developed in the seminal work of van der Heijden (1996).

THE MODEL

Strategic conversation defines organizational design and flow as consisting of three components:

1. All organizations are communities. They are sustained by interactions and exchanges. The principal mode of interaction is conversation. When the conversations are genuinely strategic, a community of common purpose can emerge.
2. Strategic conversations are multivalued and functional. They are learning loops, perceptions, concepts, and actions. They are invariably dynamic and as such interactive and always interconnected. They structure the interpersonal relationship of working together.
3. Focused and purposeful strategic actions growing out of conversations become the basis for developing a coherent action plan. Whether remedial or futuristic or both, the plan is designed

to intervene in the evolution of the organization. One of the permanent goals of all such plans is to optimize strategic conversations by having them extend leadership sharing to all levels.

The model is attractive because it is simple, generic, and above all participatory. It avoids the mechanical architecture of organizational charts or the engineering clutter of functionalism. Its scale is familiar and available. Thus, a school is a community in which conversations take place. If it is a genuine community, the conversations strategically are sustaining and evolving. If it is an aspiring and goal-focused community, its environment always features intervention and accommodates planning. If it is a future-oriented community, its curricula are always longitudinal and anticipatory. If it is democratically driven, then both teachers and students experience leadership and evaluation sharing.

Although applications of the model in the literature are frequently ambitious, and the methodologies elaborate (Ringland 1998), a simpler, scaled-down version may be extracted that can serve as a basis for introducing and stirring strategic educational dialogue. With some adjustments, such structured exchanges can become part of a principal's tool kit. Although various approaches and entrée points are available, one process that enjoys the benefits of extensive practice (Silverman 1997), and is particularly amenable to the role of the principal as Plato, involves five stages.

1. Meetings

The principal announces that every meeting of teachers/staff from now on will include a professional development piece. It will emulate the best of workshop environments in that participatory exchange will be the dominant mode. The focus of such platonic dialogue is reflection. The aim is to encourage a self-conscious awareness of work environments and an understanding of how they support or don't support teaching and learning.

The principal might begin by saying: "I would like to make part of our regular meetings a more reflective series of conversations in which we collectively think and share our views about our work environment and the way it operates and is organized. In fact, I thought we might start with meetings in general—committee meetings, lesson plan meetings, rubric meetings, and so on—and list what is good and not so good about them. This is a genuine, no-holds-barred exchange. There are no sacred cows. All I ask is that the context of effective teaching and student performance guide all exchanges. Let us divide up into three groups of about five each. You know the drill: select a spokesperson to record and present general observations and any recommendations for change. I think we have enough time to put them all in priority order."

2. Feedback

The principal compiles, prints up, and distributes a composite list of observations and recommendations from the first discussion. In addition to praising the interesting results and noting some exchanges that were less than productive, he also may wish to offer some general remarks about the nature of strategic conversations along the lines of the following to-do and not-to-do list (Ratcliffe 2002):

- Stay focused.
- Keep it simple.
- Remain interactive.
- Pass on ownership.
- Communicate.
- Employ consensus.
- Eschew despair and cynicism.
- Enjoy each other.

Following that, the principal puts together a distributed leadership implementation team to process recommendations for change. He may request that the group decide not by majority rule but by consensus.

3. The Mission

Building on the base of initial feedback about meetings, the principal adds other microareas so as to build confidence and to help internalize the process of self-reflection. These microareas may involve current modes of evaluation, mentoring new teachers, resource allocation, state-mandated testing, parental involvement, and so on. Once a significant base of success has been achieved, the principal needs to up the ante by introducing the most comprehensive context within which future exchanges will take place. That inevitably involves the mission and vision of the school district.

Even if an official mission statement exists, it can still be reviewed, and supplements can always be added, especially to express the individuality of each school within a district. Indeed, to the standard list of teacher effectiveness, student performance, evaluation accountability, parental involvement, and community relations can be added strategic self-reflection and scrutiny. Above all, the review of mission led by the principal should employ as a guiding overlay the three structural dimensions of the horizontal, the vertical, and the circular, as noted above.

4. The Retreat

Once a critical mass of strategic questioning and recommendations has been centered on the mission, and once the mission itself has become an affirmed strategic document, then there is a need to put it all together. That cannot be accomplished at a single meeting, but minimally requires a day or, better still, a two-day retreat. Two such retreats spaced at least a few months apart would be ideal.

The goal of the retreat is to put together the micro and the macro, and position the findings of the various distributed teams within the context of the mission, now reviewed and perhaps supplemented. As discussion moves toward action, strategic questioning converts to scenario planning. The outcome of the retreat is the creation of a series of alternative scenarios for how and why the school should organize or reorganize itself, what new questions need to be asked, and what new forms or processes need to be put in place.

5. Reality Check

The scenarios are sequenced into stages according to a timetable. Following the retreat, the recommended changes are not implemented wholesale but phased in experimentally. All understand that this is on a trial basis. As changes are gradually introduced, tried, and evaluated, the distributed leadership teams shadow and monitor implementation teams. The findings are reported regularly to the principal, who is responsible for keeping a cumulative running record. He or she issues a weekly scorecard and progress report.

The principal also may opt to share results on a timely basis with a representative parents group, community leaders, union reps, superintendent, school board members, and so on. But if the process is to be shared with external groups the principal has to prepare a detailed description of the process from beginning to end. Once sufficient time has been allowed for implementation to do its work of reality checking, then the second retreat is scheduled to adjust and finalize the agreed-on future school.

Will it work? Positive results abide in the literature of strategic conversations (Ratcliffe 2002). Besides, in a sense it cannot fail. The only issue is how inclusive, how spirited and stirring the dialogue will be. Even a minimal effort will encourage teachers and staff to be increasingly self-conscious about the work they do and the environment in which they do it. The research conclusively proves that when professionals own their environments and can prioritize their work so that it is aligned with organizational goals, the gains in productivity and morale are significant. Equally important are the role changes that strategic questioning and scenario planning can bring about.

The Principal

Principals are restored to their comprehensive role of leadership. They do not have to choose between being an instructional leader, a professional development advocate, an accountability champion, and so on. All can be folded in as the principal once more becomes the 360-degree leader of the micro-macro whole. He or she may or may not wish to evoke the model of the philosopher king, but he or she can legitimately appear as the advocate for platonic dialogue. To achieve the integration of administration, instruction, and evaluation is no small feat. Besides, strategic conversations can carry the same productive focus for individual teacher evaluations.

Teachers

Invited to reflect on and scrutinize not only how they teach but also how environments both small and large, intimate and external, shape and perhaps blunt their well-intentioned efforts, teachers are encouraged to apply learning to structure and structure to learning—and in the process to discover the interfaces that work and those that do not. Encouraged subsequently through distributed leadership to spread those insights over various instructional and evaluative areas across the board as well as up and down, teachers further discover the extent to which horizontal and vertical flows intersect, and what linkages and bridges may be needed to produce the circular formation of common purpose.

Students

Whether invited to be part of the reflective process or not, students are the ultimate beneficiaries. Learning becomes more thoughtful and involving. Teachers appear to be all of a piece. Why, what, and how they teach now is matched by environments that are a better reflection of policy, place, and process. Conversations between teachers of the same subject and/or grade level result in more supportive, interventionist, and gradual rubric development. The expectations of success become a self-fulfilling prophecy.

Mission

Here the benefits accrue to all constituencies. The review of the mission, its general approval, and the creation of supplements provide a center of affirmation for the entire educational community. The improved mission steadies the focus, keeps developments on track, and above all speaks the common voice of shared purpose. In fact, it would not be an exaggeration to claim that the most important task of the principal is precisely this search for commonality. His infallible guide is Plato, who models the power of strategic conversations to generate shared purpose and coherent cultures.

CHAPTER 14

The Principal as CLO (Chief Learning Officer)

Three factors are currently converging to compel a reexamination of the principalship and an exploration of administrative alternatives. The first is demographically driven. According to recent estimates by the Department of Labor, 40 percent of the current 93,200 principals will be retiring. It is further estimated that vacancies will range from 10 percent to 20 percent—between ten and twenty thousand openings—nationwide by 2005.

Second, the job is apparently not as attractive as it used to be. Many administrative openings remain unfilled and the jobs go begging. Los Angeles finally had to settle for a former state governor to run its system. Professor Thomas Sobol of Columbia's Teachers College summed it up: "It does not pay as well as it used to and you get dumped on all the time. Who needs it?" Evidently it also has become a tougher, more stressful, and less satisfying job. As Franklin Dean Grant, executive director of human resources of Georgia's DeKalb County School District, noted, "The training programs as they were designed in earlier years are grossly inadequate. Principals need a course in public relations, a course in school law. They need a thorough understanding of budgeting and finance and accounting."

Third, administrative training is being revised. A dozen states currently are offering alternative certification routes for principals. Even more striking, a number of districts, especially those facing immediate shortages, have undertaken special initiatives. Jefferson County in Louisville, Kentucky, has formed a consortium with local colleges to train administrators. Austin, Dallas, Rochester, and San Antonio have taken a different but not unfamiliar tack: grow your own. In short, exploring alternative roles for principals has led to exploring alternative ways to train them.

To partially summarize, then: there is a demonstrative need for producing more principals; the position is not as attractive as it used to be; teachers or other educators who want to go on beyond the classroom and help deliver programs have no alternative other than becoming a principal; there seems to be a need to review the way principals are trained; and, finally, as a result of all of the above, the position itself perhaps should be reconfigured.

A good way to start may be to step back and consider a different vision of educational management to guide how learning is to be delivered in the twenty-first century. Specifically, there is a need to examine and perhaps reengineer the position of the principalship as well as to find more attractive alternatives to persuade others to become leaders.

In business, when new areas of responsibility and growth open up or current arrangements are insufficient, a new office or new hire is prescribed. The recent creation of CLOs (chief learning officers) to handle e-business and the informational dimension provides an excellent, forward-looking example. The proposal, then, is that the job description of "principal" be rewritten as that of "CLO."

This is not semantics. Although current and new principals obviously could apply for the position, this new alternative would not be limited to current educators but open also to those who currently manage learning and training in business and at corporate universities. That is not so odd. After all, the titles of some superintendents have been changed to "CEO," and a number of senior-level positions in the central office now accept the MBA instead of the MS or MA in education. The three key goals of current learning managers would basically remain the same, with a few changes:

- Integrate learning and management to be seamless.
- Have learning and the evaluation of learning become so intertwined that the one cannot go on without the other.
- Blend learning and e-learning in a fusion of school and home.

Learning leaders would manage through the creation of a learning leadership team. Its collective task would be to design, administer, monitor, and evaluate a multiage and multigrade individualized learning program. The team would consist of a learning leader, teachers, tutors, computer technicians, curriculum instructional designers, parents, and a roster of community support professionals and organizations. Each team would totally manage an individual elementary or middle school. A large unified high school would be subdivided into smaller academies or schools within a school. It would be multigrade, multiage, and, in many urban school districts, multicultural and multilingual. Each team would develop and negotiate its own curriculum to meet state or county mandates and require all its students to pass state proficiency tests. The instruction would be basically a blend of face to face and electronic. It would thus be available in school and at home and combine the best of both worlds—classroom schooling and homeschooling, teachers and parents.

To provide existing and new principals with a fighting chance to become a learning manager, what different kinds of training would be needed? Perhaps the best way to start is to examine what is already going on, in the Rochester program for example. The district is growing its own administrators—some ninety candidates over three years. The first thing to note is scheduling and incentives. Because all the candidates are currently teachers, courses are offered on weekends and during one summer. Later, when internships have to be undertaken, the district frees up time for participants. Sixty percent of tuition is covered by the district, but the graduate has to agree to serve at least five years. The instructors are current superintendents of Rochester schools. The instruction uses a case studies approach. One size fits all does not apply: the differences between urban, suburban, and rural schools are stressed in the case studies. Could it serve as a model for retraining principals? The answer is yes and no. The way it has been started and designed addresses the basics, but it falls short of engaging the future and serving as a genuine alternative.

The Rochester program would benefit from a number of additions that would bring it into the twenty-first century:

- First, the program should recognize that team leaders need to be given a comprehensive battery of skills: conflict resolution, negotiating skills, agreement by consensus, coaching, group dynamics, managing and valuing diversity, the MIT Dialogus project (dialogue and the art of thinking together), innovation strategies, and so on.

- The second area for improvement is instructional design. Future learning managers should know not only what makes for effective training, but also how follow-up monitoring insures implementation of training and provides feedback for training improvement.
- The third area is educational and informational technology, in particular the evaluative research that benchmarks effectiveness and identifies best practices; the compilation of a multiage, multigrade, multicultural individualized electronic curriculum; and a monitoring and evaluation system for tracking the performance and hopefully the improvement of each student.
- The fourth area is knowledge of testing, test design, and test taking; exploring alternative ways of determining knowledge and measuring skills; developing conceptual building programs through inquiry and questioning methodology. (When something goes wrong, the Japanese use *kaisen*—asking the question "Why?" five times to get to the root cause.)
- The fifth area is knowledge of student, parental, and community involvement as part of learning and life skills growth, with service learning not treated as an add-on but built into the curriculum.
- The final area is following basic budget and accounting principles to manage cost control and to insure that any money saved is not vacuumed up at the end of the year but rolls over and is used by the unit that earned it.

If current educators could be sufficiently trained or retrained to meet the new and future challenges of learning managers and then also be joined by those from the world of business and instructional design as colleagues, what a new alliance and synergy would be formed! And what a new energy and intelligence would be driving education!

CHAPTER 15

The Principal as Broker

No one looks forward to performance evaluation. Many are petrified. Few are calm. Postmortems invariably involve matters unsaid, points unmade, communications stillborn. Must it be that way? Solutions have been proposed. Much of the literature exploring and endorsing coaching has as its explicit or indirect aim softening or diffusing the pressure of the annual review. But the role of coach is not easily acquired by many supervisors; and even when it is, it is often not sustained. Many managers revert to a directive style in which, in no uncertain terms, and often using finger or hand gestures, they inform the poor soul what he or she will do, starting next week or at least before the end of the month, when a report will be sent in.

Generically, evaluation is plagued by three major problems. First, it is one sided. The evaluator holds all the power. If the role of coach is chosen and sustained, the power is muted. But it never disappears. At best, it is held in reserve or put off to the side. It is less confrontational, more deflective. But as long as there is someone on top or in charge, there has to be someone on the bottom who takes orders. In short, evaluation is essentially adversarial, not cooperative. Second, there is an incredible range of supervisors. There are some who cannot wait to straighten someone out and others who cannot be critical at all. In a number of organizations there are employees who have not been seriously evaluated for years because their supervisors just could not bring themselves to say anything negative. They solved the problem by not holding the evaluations in the first place or scheduling perfunctory or token sessions. But when those employees are promoted or moved to another division they frequently encounter a very different, more assertive supervisor, and they are in shock. In other words, personnel evaluation in many organizations inhabits the extremes of being paramount or ignored. Finally, there is the issue of change and timetable. Work assignments routinely are altered. We even signal that process by calling certain objectives stretch goals. And yet, because annual evaluation may be all that is done, it frequently is based on goals that are no longer current or operative. Ironically, evaluation thus always lags behind performance when it should be on top of it, and is perennially involved in catch-up when it should be future oriented.

Curiously, professional development is generally plagued by the same types of problems. It tends to be determined from the top. If it is focused on the rank and file, supervisors generally are exempt from attending sessions, and thus intelligent follow-up is jeopardized. It is almost always generic training that limits individual and precise job applications and invites general slippage of alignment with company objectives. Above all, it is irregular and at the mercy of budget cutting. When things are tight, the first thing to go is training. Sadly, that may be precisely the time when more, not less, professional development is needed. Above all, what is lamentable about the loss is that when evaluation works and when training is focused and challenging, the impacts on productivity, profitability, and quality are significant. The recurrent dilemma is how not to throw out the baby with the bath water. Is there a process whereby the problems associated with performance evaluation and training can be minimized, and what they appear to hold in common be tapped by joining them together at the hip? In short, what would an integrated evaluation and professional development process look like? How would it work? What would be its gains?

I was fortunate to be involved with two very different clients (one in manufacturing, the other in a service industry) in helping to introduce, design, and implement just such a converged process of employee evaluation and professional development. Like all professionals in the tough field of increasing performance, productivity, and general morale, I feel that any promising way of achieving such an integrated goal needs to be shared—the journey involved as well as the results.

The proposed fusion of performance evaluation and training rests on five key principles:

1. Relationships between supervisors and employees should be collaborative, not adversarial.
2. Performance evaluation is to be recast as performance improvement and tied to professional development.
3. All performance objectives are to be projected horizontally over time to accommodate changes and vertically to reflect alignment with company goals.
4. Follow-ups are to be multiple, averaging a minimum of five meetings over the year.
5. Both a short-term and a mid-term professional development plan are to be produced and signed off on by supervisor and employee. That plan embodies evaluation sharing and in effect constitutes a seamless version of evaluation set in the context of continuous improvement.

The dynamics of the process generally follow three basic stages: preparation, planning, and progress.

PREPARATION

1. At the initial meeting the supervisor does most of the talking. He or she shares the five basic principles above and walks through the three-stage process of preparation, planning, and progress.
2. He or she then gives an assignment that is due at the next meeting, in two weeks. Each employee is asked to compile in draft and electronic form a document that consists of four components: job description (job parts), job dynamics (relationship to others and other divisions), job process (job flow and sequence), and job measures (review criteria and timetable).
3. At the second meeting the roles are exchanged. The employee talks and the supervisor listens. Both accept the principle that no one knows the job better than the one who does it.

4. The supervisor, in addition perhaps to raising some questions of clarification, gradually broadens the base of discussion by linking preparation to planning. For example, he or she raises for later discussion issues of alternative and more effective ways of doing things and establishing work priorities to reflect business objectives.

PLANNING

1. Planning invites speculation by the employee on what he or she knows best, his or her job. The following questions are asked: If you had the option, what would you do differently? How would you reorganize the work or its schedule? In short, what would you change? While you are at it, think about the future of your job and whether that is likely to change. If so, how? And what training would you need to do that new job? In short, what do you see as your own future as an employee? Let us discuss that at our next session.
2. The exchange now centers on how the job process might change and have a greater impact on company goals. Gradually, the focus on the present has been extended to include the future.
3. Once negotiated and agreed on, the new and projected versions of the job are placed alongside the initial version and assigned a timetable for implementation.
4. The supervisor then gives the employee a new assignment: What kind of training would be needed to maximize suggested changes, achieve greater productivity and quality, and factor in future directions?

PROGRESS

1. It is here that all the components come together. The supervisor reviews all the stages. He brings forward the original job description and its alignment with company objectives. He identifies each job change over time and how that will affect alignment. He brings in the future dimensions and sets those in a time line to indicate how they will extend and even stretch performance. Finally, he reviews and adds to the cumulative profile the em-

ployee's suggestions of what kinds of professional development and training would be needed to get from here to there. Throughout the summary, the employee is invited to step in and offer any corrections or amplifications.

2. And then comes the closure of ownership. The supervisor asks: If all that we have discussed and now laid out is acceptable to you, largely because it is mostly your own design, can we also finally agree that this integrated and projected job profile will be the basis of your performance evaluation from this point on?

3. The employee agrees with one stipulation: that the training required to enable and support change be given in full and not shortchanged.

4. That stipulation is written into the final version and both sign off.

There is one last step. All negotiated work documents are aggregated upward and examined by human resources for areas of commonality. Minimally, in my experience, two common denominators emerged. First, the companywide goal to maximize each job and to implement both job performance and personnel evaluation over time was affirmed as an across-the-board process for all. Given the extent and quality of employee input on the one hand and the increasingly collaborative role of the supervisor on the other hand, the expectation was the optimization of the process. The second common denominator was the commitment to training. That was likely to be more honored now than in the past because this time it was employee and future driven, it was tied inextricably to the outcomes of the evaluation process, and it aligned worker change and growth with company present and future goals.

In summary, then, if training is to be retained, and if personnel and job evaluation is to grow out of a more collaborative give and take between manager and employee, and if stretch goals are to be aligned with company objectives, then performance improvement specialists need to adopt the strategy of integration and champion the process of seamless convergence. All the raw materials are there and await the hands of the knowledgeable practitioner who unites past, present, and future and brings to disparate parts the art of holistics.

The Principal as Outsourcer:
Economically Driven School Reform

Outsourcing is a standardized way of doing business. Its current use has been accelerated by five forces:

1. Lower costs than in-house work
2. Equal or better quality
3. General internal unavailability of work skills
4. Review and redefinition of core mission
5. Speedy electronic communication and transmission

Today, outsourcing is a staple of such diverse organizations as Kraft Foods, Motorola, UNISYS, Kellogg, Six Continents Hotels, and CNA Insurance. The Detroit public school system recently adopted outsourcing.

SCHOOL OUTSOURCING

Clearly, other schools and school districts might benefit from the Detroit experience. On an experimental basis, Detroit assembled a list of what were designated as potential "externals": bussing; food services; and the maintenance of fields, parking lots, lights, and sidewalks. They also outsourced "internals": medical and nursing services, security, and payroll. Purchasing was on the list but turned out to be more efficient managed locally and centrally. Also under consideration was subcontracting to private teacher recruitment firms to fill vacancies, especially from international sources. The unions were not happy because union membership was not made part of hiring; and those from English-speaking or commonwealth countries like India were not culturally sensitive to the importance of collective bargaining. The district in turn was concerned that unless the new hires remained for at least three years it would not be able to recoup the original heavy costs of recruitment. So although much of that is still up in the air, an uneasy compromise between district and union may still be worked out, with hiring restricted to American teachers who become members of the union in their second year.

The specifics of the Detroit example might serve as a model for other budget-tight school districts. But the examples should not obscure the larger issue of what is driving the change. In particular, the participation by a major school district focuses on a number of issues currently impacting on and inviting the initiative of educational administration. Although some of the trends are not altogether new, they may be newly perceived and appreciated in the context of outsourcing.

1. THE BUSINESS-EDUCATION GULF

The first issue is narrowing or bridging the gap between education and business. The typical go-it-alone attitude of education is gradually changing. Superintendents, in particular some who are now called CEOs, are viewing what the business of business has to offer the business of education. Hopefully this is a sign of a general trend, with the two fields perceiving each other more as allies than enemies.

2. END OF THE MONOPOLY

No longer the official public monopoly, education has found its mainstream position eroded by the some two million homeschoolers on the one hand, and the over two thousand charter schools on the other hand. The latter ads insult to injury by draining off per-capita dollars. In some small or rural school districts, the loss of funding has left behind schools whose enrollments are so reduced that it is not financially viable to run the school or to offer a full curriculum.

What is perceived as a common threat has unexpectedly brought educational administration and unions together in opposition to the charter school movement and its empowering legislation. In some cases, unions are creating their own charter schools as ways of preserving their membership, leverage, and school budgets. This redefinition and expansion of school choice now also includes the entrepreneurial introduction of private school management companies.

3. PRIVATE MANAGEMENT COMPANIES AS OUTSOURCING

Although Edison may turn out to be essentially a mismanagement company that does not know how to run its own house, it is not the only one around; and even if it fails it probably will be replaced by others that have learned from past mistakes. In effect all private management companies are a type of outsourcing. To be sure, the outsourcing takes the form of insourcing, but in essence it is no different from contracting with another company to run employee benefits or payroll.

Typically, the district offers Edison a contract to run a school—in Philadelphia recently it was thirty schools. Regular administration is replaced by or rehired as Edison employees. New curricula may be introduced, professional development workshops scheduled, data tracking and monitoring installed, and so on. All private educational management companies claim to be "branded" and that their special style is what will make the difference. But such changes are really not that different from what some schools have tried and are doing. What sets Edison and others like it apart is the new perception of education as an economic investment.

Because the annual expenditures of education match those of the defense budget, business has been drawn to education. Indeed, all major universities created in the last twenty-five years, which now have combined enrollments of nearly one million students, have been and still are proprietary institutions. Created by or currently owned by venture capitalist groups, they often increase their economic value through mergers or acquisitions to enhance, extend, and even accredit business operations. Sylvan Learning recently purchased the regionally accredited Walden University for $80 million. In short, educational administrators now have to confront a double economic reality: the familiar tight budgets and increasing costs, and now the challenge of direct economic and entrepreneurial competition. The embarrassing accusation that surfaces is: If private management companies can turn a profit from the same resources and activities, why cannot regular public administration do the same; or at least not increase costs?

4. IMPACTS OF ACCOUNTABILITY

Schools are drowning in calls for accountability and improved student performance. Such calls come from various reports of national commissions, from professional associations of administrators supporting the role of principals as instructional leaders, from state legislatures and departments of education, and now, with No Child Left Behind, from the federal government.

Educators have responded by kicking and screaming, as well as by buckling down to solve the problem. The first response appears in apparently endless and often angry editorials, articles, and topics of plenary speakers. But the characteristic problem-solving approach bears on another dimension of outsourcing.

What makes outsourcing attractive is that it provides immediate, proven, and available expertise to turn things around. Such competence is usually not available at all or only in a limited way in house. In either case it would require time and support to happen, and both are in short supply in house. That does not mean that districts are not motivated to fix the problem. In some states, students at schools receiving failing grades on state tests two consecutive times are eligible for vouchers. Some school districts have been taken over and made wards of the state department of education. The most recent embarrassment is the number of high school seniors failing mandated high school exit exams.

Outsourcing has come to the rescue with an impressive cornucopia of solutions for education under the gun of accountability. Thus, not only have new curricula been rushed into the breach, but test-ready curricula—with federal- and state-mandated goals built in. Then, too, the hardware and software for tracking student performance, as well as analyzing teacher effectiveness, generally exceed the ability of most if not all school district in-house computer operations and personnel. Besides, the data results offered by outsourcing are already formatted to satisfy state and federal reporting criteria and displays.

One of the most significant additional values of outsourcing is catching up with incremental needs or discontinuous developments. The gap is often too great, the issue too immediate, and the pressure too great and unavoidable for catching up to happen in house. Besides, why would an administrator risk turning his entire operation upside down and inside out trying to reach a level of competence that finally may elude him and his staff, at a time when his task is to preserve stability and morale so the school can survive and implement the outside solutions? Indeed, if he is both smart and caring, he outsources.

5. MISSION REVIEW

The key question that organizations periodically and wisely ask as part of mission review is: What are we about? What is our core business? What is our central focus and competence? The answer is then used as an overlay to survey all operations to determine what belongs and what does not. For example, many major state universities maintain an extensive fleet of state vehicles and employ a number of their own mechanics to service their fleet more economically. But is that an essential part of the educational mission? The answer has led to outsourcing to car rental agencies; the contracts negotiated even provided a return to the universities.

Another example is online curriculum development. Many individual schools and states have developed virtual high school courseware. Recently, a consortium of midwestern states sought to consolidate such courses into a comprehensive network that could be tapped by all schools in the consortium. The project was viewed as education's proud answer to the electronic curricula being offered by business, and was supported by the rallying cry that local educators are as good as the outside competition. But the consortium floundered. The diverse curricula were not formatted to be interchangeable; they ran on different operating systems; the performance goals varied too much; quality control was uneven; and some had not even been tested thoroughly using controls. The cost of reconciling many of the above problems was so enormous that the consortium folded. It could not compete, nor should it have tried in the first place, with the purchase of a uniform, tested, and expert set of curricula produced by educational technologists whose only mission was to create quality software learning programs. The strategy is clear: outsource to those whose mission is to serve yours. That way integrity can be maintained and expertise can be value added. Match competence with competence, focus with focus.

6. A FUTURISTIC POSTSCRIPT

Leaving behind for the moment present pressures and realties, and looking ahead to what may occur in the next five to ten years, what is the role of outsourcing in the future? Two patterns emerge, one predictable, the other not.

Outsourcing will continue. More school districts will emulate that of Detroit. Gradually, a school district will become a hub serviced by outside centers or networks of centers providing products and services in support of an educational mission. Preferred vendors may develop materials according to client specs. Some may even be directed to link or interface their services or products with those of other suppliers.

The selection and quality maintenance of such partners will be the responsibility of educational administrators who increasingly will be evaluated on their ability to manage outsourcing. Matching the increasingly integrated instructional, administrative, and evaluative needs of the school with the competence, costs, and just-in-time delivery schedules of outsourced suppliers will establish and define future roles and tasks of administrators.

A more radical option is for schools to serve as internal clearinghouses of educational alternatives, including the possibility of outsourcing students to other schools. This requires, admittedly, such an extraordinary act of educational leadership that it may be a high road too difficult for current administrators to contemplate, let alone accept. Here is what would be involved.

The school district would accept the comprehensive responsibility for providing a total counseling and planning service, pre-K–16. Instead of reacting negatively and often subversively to competition, each school district would provide parental guidance and student testing so as to help families make informed choices from among all the options of school choice. The central office of the district would be staffed by a core of administrative professionals whose task would be to facilitate the management of educational choice as part of the new mission of the district.

The proposal is that the comprehensive control, direction, and planning of educational and school choice be accepted as the total facilitating responsibility of the central administration of an entire school district. Instead of viewing different schools as competing options and rating them as inferior or superior, the district would perceive all as legitimate and equal alternatives whose value would be determined by a matching process available to all parents and students.

What needs to be addressed and why? Educational choice has become too complex and confusing to many parents even within a single school district. Moreover, there are too many eager advocates pushing one choice over others. Parents not only need guidance; they need impartial and objective guidance. They also need to have their sights adjusted so that school choice is perceived as school choices—as a series of branch points along an extended line running from the selection of a preschool to the choice of a college. Parents also need objective guidance from educators, not financial advisers, about college savings plans, especially when grandparents already have indicated that they plan to open one when a child is born or enters kindergarten. In addition, parents need to better understand the developmental stages of their offspring and how at different points their educational choices and strategies may have to change. Above all, parents need to recognize that because the future their offspring face may be quite different from the present, the availability of careers may have to retroactively determine schooling. In short, education is increasingly a complex labyrinth requiring a road map for families to navigate their way from the present to the future.

The process would be holistic and longitudinal. Serving as brokers, central office staff would help parents and students select what at any given time may be appropriate and beneficial. Thus, it is conceivable that a student would be advised to be homeschooled for the first three years, then switched to a traditional school, then enrolled in a magnet school, then switch to a completely or partially virtual cyber arrangement. If supervised internships are required or recommended, that too may be factored in and aligned with the student's program. If the range is K–16, high school courses would be matched with college courses as acceptable equivalents on a college campus or through a college online program. In other words, all options would be brought under one wing. School choice would be coupled intelligently and proactively with student development. Progress would become a more directed, varied, continuous, and ultimately seamless professional process.

In this configuration, public education would assume or regain its leadership role and once more become the mainstream by becoming, paradoxically, the center of outsourcing. Combining differentiated needs with quality controls, every central office would thus become the advocate not so much of different versions of education but of the developmental needs of students. Because students are different and have different needs at different times, one size fits all or one choice for all time makes no sense. To allow the current external and internal competition to drain energy and resources also makes no sense.

The current crisis in education is in many ways the crisis of a vacuum. Competing solutions, each one passing a half off as a whole, empty the center of common ground and focus, and deprive students of a menu of programs best suited for them in a continuous and developmental spectrum of options. Rubric testing and tracking can be factored in, as well as the diagnostics of cognitive research. The net result is that the most complete composite profile of student performance, strengths, and areas of improvement would be centrally maintained and tapped for school choice.

What would it take for such a blending and advocacy of alternatives to occur? Would it take another generation of administrators more comfortable with outsourcing, or more holistic leaders who have the vision to look ahead to make such a clearinghouse happen? Would it take a foundation grant to a state department of education to set up such experimental centers in selected school districts, especially those in which there is considerable hostility or suspicion? My favorite suggestion is to have the clearinghouse serve as a profit center, and provide such a guidance and planning service for all parents for a fee, whether they plan to send their kids to a private, parochial, or public school, or even to homeschool. It also might be attractive to parents as an outsourcing alternative to some of the major private tutoring and test services, like Sylvan and Princeton Review. For those parents who could not afford to pay for guidance and planning services, it would seem that a better use of vouchers would be helping students and parents to be proactive.

As to present prospects, it is difficult to take the high road when mired down in contention and when squeezed by competition. But as districts and administrators gradually implement outsourcing in all or many of the forms outlined above, they may also come to recognize that outsourcing can be more than a process to solve problems. It can become the educational mission of an entire school district.

In that capacity, it would be basically inclusive, not exclusive. It would honor the offerings of all others and their educational missions. They would be recognized and accepted as kindred, though different, souls engaged in the same enterprise. With school choice increasingly in the driver's seat, administrators who opt for the big picture and for bringing school choice under one integrated umbrella may become, in effect, the outsourcing experts and champions of all students of all ages and stages. Thus, the immediate value of outsourcing may gradually be extended to the longer term as current administrators back their way into the future. Perhaps that step-by-step process is the only, or even the best, way for such a new vision to take hold.

Part IV

PARENTS AS MAJOR PLAYERS

CHAPTER 17

Parents and Educational Change

There are ten basic sources of student success. The first five are totally parental:

1. Show up
2. On time
3. Washed
4. Fed
5. Dressed decently

The first item appears obvious. Why list it at all, let alone at the top? According to the Department of Justice, 81 percent of all those in jail began as truants. The figure jumps to 95 percent for juvenile offenders.

The next set of five factors are shared by parents and students but still strongly influenced by parents:

1. Tools: pencils, pens, and paper
2. School books
3. Homework done
4. Curiosity
5. Reasonably happy

The involvement and intervention of parents or the lack thereof is as important, and in some cases more important, than that of teachers. In fact, knowledgeable and experienced teachers acknowledge that without parental support, teaching children is like going up a down escalator. It may or may not take a village to raise a child, but strong and committed parents make strong and committed schools.

SOME EXAMPLES OF PARENTAL ADVOCACY

In a later section on school choice, the discussion begins with a description of over seven hundred parents standing in line early in the morning to request school choice. Although applying the first day or early on does not mean they stand any better chance of securing their first choice, they defy logic and stand there. One remarks that she would hate for her daughter to think that her mother did not do everything she could to get her first choice. All those parents on line are a teacher's dream. Here are some other examples.

A father works in an assembly plant. Two of his older teenage sons are thinking of applying for a job there during the summer. The father learns of it and calls them in and reads them the riot act: "If I ever catch either one of you in that plant I will break both your arms and legs." The boys protest: "What's the big deal? It's only a summer job." The father responds, "I did not put up with that kind of job all these years so that you would choose it. If you did, you would be both failures in my eyes. Worse, so would I."

A registered nurse is talking to her daughter about college and future careers: "Don't sell yourself short. My mother brainwashed me into not going on to medical school. 'Be a nurse instead. Besides, most men don't want wives who are too smart or earn more than they do,' she said. Well unfortunately I listened. Now I spend a lot of time bailing out and making dumb doctors look good. You go for the gold. Don't settle."

The PTO of a middle-class neighborhood wanted to do more for the middle school than just run bake sales and sponsor coffee klatches. They noticed how well equipped the computer labs were at the high school and in private schools. They embarked on an ambitious fundraising campaign called "Operation Upgrade." They applied for help to the Beaumont Foundation and to the Gates Foundation. They asked Dell to designate the school a beta site. Within one year the school opened its lab. The first day was payback. It was devoted to computer literacy instruction for parents. That was to be continued at home and/or in school by their kids.

Probably all parents consider their kids special or different. Many also hold strong moral and religious beliefs about what schools should teach and not teach. For a variety of reasons, nearly one million households have elected homeschooling, which may be the ultimate form of parental involvement. These parents receive no subsidy from the school district. In fact, they have to buy their own textbooks and all the supplementary enrichment materials they need. Homeschoolers regularly have won national merit scholarships and subject-matter awards and secured admission to colleges and universities of their choice. When they elect to enter regular public school, they generally perform above average and are remarkably self-organizing and self-supervising. Finally, homeschooling usually brings the participating family closer together.

Steven Spielberg's mother was interviewed and asked to explain what child-rearing approach she had taken. Her son was constantly restless, would stand on coffee tables, and would always pretend he was taking pictures. She indicated that she did not follow the guidance of Spock or anyone else. What then? She answered quietly: "I never said no."

I will finish the examples with a personal anecdote. My mother always claimed that she went to college with her son. Well, in a way she did. I commuted to college. When I came home my mother was waiting for me in the kitchen with a sandwich, usually one of my favorites. With a cup of coffee in her hand, she began the kitchen seminar with the standard invitation: "Well what did we learn today?" I started to recite what had taken place. She knew all my subjects, so I did not dare to leave any out. She asked questions all the time. Sometime I felt like I was being grilled on the witness stand. Her questions became tougher and tougher; some even were slippery and tricky. In any case I could not answer them all. Some I wrote down, vowing secretly to raise them in class. I remember raising one of my mom's questions in a literature class. The professor responded: "I have been teaching this class for over twenty-five years now and no one ever raised that question. Let me think it over." I never told my mom what had happened; I would have never heard the end of it. But I did intensify my efforts to share and listen to what she had to say. I realized that whatever I was doing to help her go to college she was equally helping me. And she was a third-grade dropout!

How important is parental involvement? According to the research, there are five factors that determine school success: time on task, high expectations, parental involvement, safety, and school leadership. Parental involvement is the only factor outside the school and yet enjoys a higher ranking than safety and leadership. And when time commitment and high expectations are also made part of home environment, as invariably they are, then parental involvement moves up to join the first two factors.

EFFECTIVE PARENTS

Effective parental involvement in turn rests on three activities: communication, participation, and governance.

Communication

For parents to be involved they must know what is going on. That requires frequent communications between teacher and parents, and between the school and the community. The two time-honored communications are receiving and signing report cards and the follow-up of parent-teacher conferences. That barely scratches the surface. In fact, the recognition of the significant contribution of parental involvement to student performance has led teachers and schools to develop more invasive and intervening communications tactics. These include:

- Home telephone calls in the evenings, especially for two-income families
- Home visits
- Student-led parent-teacher conferences
- Electronic sharing of attendance, tardies, homework assignments, and so on
- 360-degree evaluation sessions: participants such as clergy, case workers, and neighbors identified by parents

Participation

Parents often are invited directly to participate in school as teacher's aides, tutors, and guest lecturers. Many teachers welcome the added expertise and often further benefit from the good will and links to the larger community. Often such involvement results in financial contributions and donations of equipment.

Governance

This involves political access by constituencies to public institutions supported by their taxes. They are entitled to some voice in key school decisions. Such public participation was given a significant boost in the 1960s and 1970s with the passage of Title I and the federal requirement of parent advisory councils, or PACs. Although later legislation removed the requirement, PACs had and still have a residual effect on schools.

How many parents value such governance? Parents are generally not interested in micromanaging, but they want to know about programs and practices that bear directly on their children. Finally, to what extent can home environment make a big difference? And what are the best kinds of environments and parenting styles?

HOME ENVIRONMENTS

Conventional wisdom is that what basically determines successful school performance is socio-economic status (SES). In fact, the documentation is so strong that SES has been used as the basic predictor of success. But later research examined the SES more closely and found that it consisted of four factors: income, parental education, parental occupation, and home atmosphere. Remarkably, home atmosphere turned out to have the strongest relationship with student achievement. For the first time researchers had unearthed a basis for understanding how students with a low SES but a positive home atmosphere could do so well in school. In short, nurture triumphed over nature, for a change. Equally as important, the research opened the door to exploring what shapes a good environment and what parenting styles work best.

PARENTING STYLES

Three key elements determine an effective home atmosphere: communication, supervision, and aspiration. Supportive parents always find the time to discuss school and what is being studied and learned. In the process, alert parents learn to detect problems when their kids avoid the subject or quickly dismiss it. There may be something deeper going on. And so they gently probe and prod. In other words, effective communication often involves hard work and ingenuity. It is never automatic or easy, which is why many parents give up.

Supervision involves remaining always a mom or dad and not being tempted to become a friend or pal. It involves constant monitoring: when they leave for and when they return from school; where they are going with whom and when they must be back; how much time they spend on their homework; how much time they are on the phone or watching television or playing video games. Not surprisingly, studies have found a negative correlation between watching television for many hours and school achievement.

Finally, parents support learning when they show signs of continuing learning themselves—when they read, for example, rather than watching television, attend lectures or cultural events, or watch educational programs on TV. They also are effective when they communicate academic aspirations of finishing high school, going to college, attending graduate or professional school. If they can back that up by establishing a college investment fund (or a child's grandparents are able to establish one), so much the better.

Because school choice often has provided the consideration of educational options way before those of college, families have the opportunity to discuss with their kids what to choose and why. That may involve visits to prospective sites, just the way a parent or parents may escort their offspring on college visits later. In fact, parent involvement in those visits has become such a standard practice that admissions offices have arranged special sessions only for parents. Finally, a parent can also communicate career aspirations, such as found in some of the anecdotes noted above. Here, though, there are often surprises: for every kid who wants to follow in the career footsteps of a parent there is one who is determined not to. Moreover, parents are given the classic warning not to try to accomplish through their children their own unfulfilled career dreams; although, having said that, one cannot deny the extent to which the powerful motivation of lost opportunity drives parental support.

Last of all, there is the question of how all this is done by parents. Which is the most effective parental style of three types: authoritarian, permissive, or persuasive? What the research shows is that the first two show little relationship to student achievement, but the last one evidences a strong positive relationship. It makes sense. Children, like adults themselves, generally do not like to be bullied or given no opportunities to be part of decision making. In fact, that is why teachers have been advised and trained (parents, too) not to back kids into a corner but give them options.

The problem with the permissive style is that kids want and need structure; boundaries need to be drawn within which they can function securely and happily. Such boundaries are like the rules of the game; one cannot play tennis with the net down. Persuasion works best because it brings together communication and supervision in a nonpunitive and patient way, and routinely empowers kids with choices. It tries wherever possible not to use tangible rewards as incentives. That may communicate a value system that is questionable, and the bribe will need to be constantly increased. The best reward is celebrating as a family and cementing parent-child relationships; it is legitimate to do that at an ice cream parlor, by ordering pizza at home, or by renting a video and making popcorn. The centrality of the family is the core relationship, especially for single parents. That offers the key to everything: emotional health, role modeling, aspiration, and student achievement.

THE FUTURE OF PARENTAL INVOLVEMENT

Accountability and high-stakes testing will undoubtedly raise the standards of performance. This is not by any means a solely American crusade. It is going on intensely in England, and in fact in all of Europe. It has always been a preoccupation of the Japanese; the Chinese are accelerating the pace and level of education. Singapore just announced an ambitious, well-financed, ten-year plan to achieve international preeminence in ten key academic areas. Invitations to professionals, to academic institutions, to research organizations, and to think tanks were extended. The attractive financial offers were accompanied by equally attractive arrangements of relocation, including excellent English-speaking schools for the offspring of teachers from English-speaking countries. The academic areas selected function as a self-fulfilling prophecy of Singapore's future.

The value of anticipating the future is that it compels stepping back, employing the widest possible perspective, and surveying the emerging scene within the most comprehensive parameters. A number of major trends emerge:

- Education has become a global and competitive priority. No country that wants to maintain its current preeminence or seeks to attain such a position can do so without a first-rate educational system. It has even been speculated that China's educational goals have been spelled out privately in terms of Olympic gold medals, world-class performing artists, and Nobel Prize winners. In short, China is behaving like an assertive parent with low SES but determined to create the right atmosphere for achievement.
- Competition has shifted from physical to intellectual resources, from financial to human capital, from brawn to brain. In effect we are going through a second industrial revolution, except this revolution stands not on an industrial but on a knowledge base. It signals the emergence of the knowledge worker functioning in a knowledge culture.
- Learning has replaced schooling. This is not mere semantics. Learning is no longer limited to schools or to a single time or place. Rather, it is continuous and lifelong.
- Traditional delivery face-to-face systems have been expanded to distance electronic learning.
- Knowledge partnerships will develop between machine and human intelligence.

To a large extent much of this has been going on for many decades. It has ranged from TV instruction offered to peasant women in remote Mexican villages to become nurses; to many universities providing education at all degree levels electronically worldwide; to students in small rural areas in the United States supplementing limited curricula offerings by tapping into online courses. But what has all this to do with parental involvement?

Many parents, in the performance of their work, have experienced miniature and professional versions of these global trends. Many professions require annual updating, often in the form of academic credits or certified education units (CEUs). American business spends over $1 billion each year training and upgrading employee skills and knowledge. Ford and Motorola and others run their own corporate universities; even McDonald's has McDonald's U. Workers are finding that they have to undergo several career changes—three to five, on average—in a lifetime; and each change has its own set of learning standards. Many organizations now designate work objectives as stretch goals to signify the constant flux of the job and the need to be adaptable. In short, parents have been compelled and persuaded to change again and again, and they thus bring a new perspective and urgency to raising kids, in the following specific ways:

- The national priority on testing and raising performance standards has increased the level of competition.
- Test taking has become as important as learning skills.
- The test-prep expertise of Princeton Review, Kaplan, and Sylvan now has been applied to K–12 education.
- Parental involvement, communication, and supervision will probably shift similarly to mastering and studying for tests.
- Parents likely will not hearken to teachers who bewail what is lost by all this testing and will pay more attention to professionals and tutors who better prepare students to survive the testing barrage, even if it involves teaching to the tests.

Given these trends, what will parental involvement look like and what forms will it take in the future? At least five major changes will occur:

1. The Environment

Learning and schooling will require more complex monitoring and intervention. To accommodate such complexity, parents may set up a special school and learning table at home. Above it hangs a general month-to-month calendar and a daily one. That visually helps the student to organize and manage multiple educational tasks and activities. The table will be positioned close to the door and used as a daily pick-up and drop-off spot before and after school. In some cases the learning table will be expanded to a learning area or room, especially a dining room if it is used infrequently and only for special occasions.

2. Diagnostically Focused Tutorials

Areas that require improvement as revealed by tests and teachers' comments will be addressed quickly and competently by supportive parents. These will range from specific subjects, to general study skills, even to life skills. By their very nature, some areas are not amenable to class solution but require a one-on-one approach. The importance of the tutorial approach has been recognized in the No Child Left Behind legislation, which provides funds for tutorial services. Parents increasingly may be called on to be tutors themselves, especially if they do not have the means to pay for professional tutors. Small tutorial groups may be formed around play dates to pool the expertise of different parents for tutoring purposes. In short, supportive parents will apply the title of the new legislation to their children to make sure that in this more competitive world their kids are not left behind. That will require that parents increasingly become colearners with their children.

3. Learning Partnerships

The school and the home, the teacher and the parent, will become learning partners. The school must significantly increase the level and extent of communications with parents. It also must provide more free time for teachers to plan and sustain parent-teacher meetings and interactions and thus put parental involvement on an equal level with prep time. It also would be helpful for parents and teachers separately and together to be offered training on what makes for optimum parent-teacher learning partnerships.

4. Electronic Exchange

The increasing requirements of schools electronically to monitor and track student performance by individual, grade level, teacher, and school will provide databases of great interest to parents as well. Already a few schools routinely e-mail parents and provide them with information on attendance, tardies, and homework assignments. In the future such feedback will become a norm rather than an exception. Although some, especially students, may object to this as an invasion of privacy, most parents will find that it reinforces their monitoring and supervising role. In any case, with e-mail the partnership is two-way. Parents may send back documents and seek review of what they are planning to do at home.

5. Homeschooling

The final future integration will be a seamless relationship between the school and the home, between school schooling and homeschooling. The successful model of separate homeschooling will become the model for blended schooling. All the support systems and vendor suppliers that homeschooling painstakingly has built up over the years will be available to the new hybrids.

To summarize: What likely lies ahead? Schoolwork and homework will become not alternatives but two versions of the same thing. Teachers will be supplemented and extended by parent teachers and tutors, in single and cluster arrangements. Learning will not stop at the end of the school day but continue at home. In the process, teachers and parents will have to change their priorities and time allocations. School will have to move closer to the home and the home closer to the school. Teachers once again may become more like parents, as parents become more like teachers.

The only thing missing that would complete the picture and support the process is financial support. If ways could be found to certify parents as tutors so that they could be paid, or if further tax credits could be granted for homeschooling in general, but especially along the partnership lines described here, then we might see the full emergence of the professional parent, a role that parents increasingly are already being asked to play. Teachers who have worked with such enterprising parents know that if there is any way those financial supports can be made available, parents—especially those with low incomes—will find a way to make their commitment happen. For parents the future is not a series of abstract trends; it stands before them in the personal, direct, and familial form of their offspring.

Expanding and involving parents in learning, their own as well as their kids, is not just helpful. It is indispensable. There is no more effective way the ambitious goals and higher standards of NCLB can be reached. But teachers have to change their view of parents. They have to see them as learning partners, not solely as bossy or intrusive advocates for their kids or busy organization ladies running bake sales. Teachers are not trained in college to partner with parents and to use them, as they use their colleagues, to plan, structure, and accomplish learning. Such training must be provided and the means (traditional and/or electronic) of communication established. Above all, teachers must expand their lesson plans to include not only what they plan to do, but also in detail what their students' parents will be asked to do.

Finally, parents have to bring the school into their homes. They have to recognize that raising kids requires not only good psychology, but good learning and success models. More than ever before, parents have become indispensable to student success. Self-esteem has to be integrated with good study skills. All the books and articles parents consume about nurturing have to be supplemented with knowledge not only of all the changes and choices going on in education currently, but also those that will happen in the future. Parents have to become smart and savvy managers not only of home and family operations, but also of the dynamics of student success.

In many ways these new challenges have come at the best and worst of times. The best is represented by the higher levels of education of parents now than ever before, and even after graduation the surge of adult learners (mostly parents) attending school at night or electronically. Two-income families also make both parents more aware of the dramatic shifts in the economy and in work demands. The lesson they have learned is that if one does not change, one does not keep up or last. Finally, the current generation of parents is technologically more literate and educationally and socially more aggressive. They are the "Yes, but" generation of parents, especially when the education of their kids is involved.

The downside to juggling jobs and/or attending school at night is that it may leave little time or energy for parental supervision and participation. Some parents work evening or weekend shifts and are often not home when their kids are, or are asleep when their kids arrive home from school. The demands of work also have increased: more time, more stress, more goals to reach, sooner. Last and perhaps worst of all, the basic family structure is often shaky. There are more single mothers than ever before, more latchkey kids, more grandparents raising grandchildren. In some cases the family is so dysfunctional that kids are made wards of the state. A more enlightened and less punitive solution has been to create boarding schools for such kids. The increase in their school performance has been dramatic. Finally, even teachers dedicated to increasing parental involvement can find it exhausting and frustrating trying to reach parents, let alone meet for a conference.

For better or worse parents have never been so important and even indispensable for the success of their kids. It is that simple and clear. But one could claim that there is a parent shortage that is more extensive and urgent than that of teachers or administrators. Parents not only make the difference; they are the difference. Good schools enroll not just kids, but families. We need a parents' curriculum of student success.

CHAPTER 18

Teacher–Parent Partnerships

In the previous section, the greater involvement of parents in student success was a rallying cry. But that will not happen without a parents' curriculum. What follows is one possible version of such training.

Schools and teachers now more than ever before are encountering pressures related to greater accountability, mandated high-stakes testing, and the demand for higher levels of across-the-board student achievement in No Child Left Behind legislation. The scale, pace, and timetable of adjustment are dizzying, debilitating, and often demoralizing. The relief of smaller class sizes appears to have been stalled, budgets are tight and even shrinking, and many school districts, because of demographic projections, face overcrowded schools unless new construction is started yesterday.

But there is one bright spot and source of help on the horizon. It has always been there and often has made the difference. It is parental involvement, now perhaps more important and pivotal than ever before. In fact, the claim is that parents' involvement not only will make a difference in the lives and homes of their families, but also may help teachers and schools raise student performance to meet and even exceed the standards set. Parents may be enough to offset the odds and provide a more even playing ground for teachers and students.

But to do all that everything has to change. And the change cannot involve familiar tokenism or cheerleading. It must be more aggressive, intelligent, collaborative. It must reflect a schoolwide commitment. Above all, it must be research based.

What follows is only an outline of a teacher–parent partnership students' success program.

THE TEACHER–PARENT PARTNERSHIP STUDENTS' SUCCESS PROGRAM

The program is based on the following factors, which research has found to increase students' success:

- Parental knowledge of the key student success factors
- Contributions of parental support to student performance
- Reinforcing impact of teacher–parent partnerships
- Joint training of teachers and parents
- Two-way communication roles of teachers and parents
- Teacher-diagnosed and parent-implemented follow-up tutorials
- Multiple intelligences opportunities
- Test-prep and test-taking skills for home practice
- Optimum home supportive learning environment
- Effective parenting styles

THE TOPICS AND STAGES

The professional development of the program will explore the above and subsume them under five major topics:

1. Student success factors
2. Parental involvement partnerships: initiatives and activities
3. Designing an optimum home environment and its links to school
4. Suggesting parenting styles in synch with student needs
5. Developing a comprehensive inventory of parental intervention options

OUTCOMES FOR TEACHERS

By the end of the sessions, teachers will be more knowledgeable about teacher–parent partnerships—information that will be backed by current research findings—and what constitutes an effective and individualized parental involvement program. They also will know what gains they can legitimately expect from such an investment of time and effort. Teachers will be able to focus individually on desired changes in terms of student performance, attitude, and behavior.

Above all, teachers must constantly remind parents that their focus is educational, not psychological or sociological; and, further, that the partnerships are designed to facilitate student success in school. The achievement of closer marital and family ties, although very much a welcome and even integral factor in better parent-student relations, is the domain of the home and not the school. Stating this serves to keep matters separate and to forestall the natural tendency for parents to engage teachers in their private affairs, although obviously a win-win situation helps all involved.

Finally, after the program has taken hold and results begin to appear, teachers may increasingly be able to count on parental follow-through and plan their lessons and goals with parent collaborators in mind. They also may welcome being detoured less by behavior problems and freer to devote themselves to achieving higher levels of subject-matter achievement.

OUTCOMES FOR PARENTS

Parents will have a clearer and deeper understanding of the demands and range of curriculum, the expectations of general and individual student performance, and the ways evaluations are conducted. They will have a better understanding also of the teachers' point of view, how they perceive their role, and in particular how they view the parents' child and his or her strengths and areas needing improvement. Parents will learn about the use of learning rubrics and about diagnostic and improvement-planning tools. But the exchange will not be one sided. Parents know their kids very well, including what they are good at, what they are not so good at, and the optimum circumstances that support their efforts and learning. This would be a crucial time and place to discuss and apply Gardner's multiple intelligences.

In the process of the exchange with teachers, parents may develop a better sense of what is happening or being planned not only at the individual school, but also in the district. Such discussions would provide a series of heads-ups for parents to entertain different school or program choices. Because kids generally do not think ahead, parents have to assume a proactive stance of advocacy. In short, the goal of the teacher–parent partnership students' success program is for parents to develop the school smarts they need to undertake a minimum of two activities: developing an overall plan for student progress, K–16; and finding ways at home to support school goals and the individual performance of their kids. The key to teacher cooperative partnering is the recognition that the parental agenda and the teacher agenda are aligned and ideally one and the same. Such shared purpose offers a united front to students that is persuasive and hard to oppose, and a model of school-home relationships that is inevitably reinforcing. When the student at home complains, "You are just like my teacher!" smile and persist. You are getting through; you are succeeding.

Part V

STUDENTS AS MAJOR PLAYERS

CHAPTER 19

Parents and School Reform

Three powerful forces are converging to invest parental roles with greater importance, value, and urgency. First, this generation of parents is far more politically savvy, better educated, and more aggressive than their own parents ever were. Bake sales have been replaced by the incorporation of nonprofit school foundations. The national PTA is a major source of published research. Recently, a survey of Ohio parents indicated that 65 percent were generally satisfied with the public schools. But that approval rate jumped to 85 percent if schools welcomed parental input. In other words, this current generation of parents could be called the "Yes, but" group. "Yes, we will support education, but . . ." In short, parental support is now conditional. Parents have their own change agenda.

Second, teachers generally acknowledge how critical the home is to student performance, although the evidence cited is more on the downside associated with dysfunctional families. A few are aware of the research on student success factors. There are five: time on task, supervision, parental involvement, motivation, and learning leadership. Since the first and the last two are also involved in good home learning environments, parental involvement tops the list. In addition, many educators are coming to the conclusion that without strong parental support, they may not be able to reach the targeted goals of NCLB, let alone sustain them.

Third, many school districts have established electronic communications links between school and home. Parents now know what, in the past, only teachers knew. Big Brother tells all. Recently, Broward County in Florida installed the Virtual Counselor, which in addition to the standard flow of shared information provides total access by parents to their child's entire school record, going back as far as kindergarten. The next step, already technologically feasible, is two-way communication, an electronically facilitated teacher-parent conference.

All seems in place for major transformation of school-home relationships. But, alas, it has not generally happened. Parental involvement in schools ranges from bake sales, to token seats on school-community committees, to experimenting with new formats for teacher-parent conferences, to teacher-parent performance partnerships. Although the last is the most productive of student achievement, it is more the exception than the rule, probably characteristic of less than 10 percent of the total.

Why such a limited number? The trends favor it happening. The goal of improved student achievement is backed by the research. So what is holding the groups apart? Minimally, three factors: maintenance of the teachers' instructional preserve; parental perception that their participation is either unwelcome or undervalued; and a lack of leadership to bridge the gap between the two.

One can develop a five-step model. It would include: identifying the source of and defining the leadership role, eliciting teacher and parent objections, shaping a new basis for working together, negotiating and structuring future relationships, and, finally, articulating both the principles and parameters of that partnership now focused on student achievement and school reform. The dynamics of the model appear below.

Leadership is the linchpin. Without such intervention either nothing happens or nothing lasts. The school principal is the key. He or she alone enjoys 360-degree support. The teachers believe the principal is protective of their turf; the parents value the access associated with his or her office; and both are convinced that he or she is fair and would not favor one side or the other.

Although the stage is set, leaders looking for a quick fix sometimes make the mistake of bringing the representatives of both groups together prematurely. They are not ready to meet, let alone move forward. They first need to vent and consolidate their objections before they can identity a common cause. So the principal sets up the two groups that initially, at least, do not meet.

What are the concerns of each? Teachers object to the following: parents advocate only for their own kids, prefer certain teachers, dump their family problems on the school, fail to show up for conferences, ask for inappropriate information, tell teachers how to teach and even how to run the school, and so on. In turn, parents find that teachers routinely devalue their knowledge of their kids' learning, expect parents obediently to do their bidding, arrange conferences when parents work or have little ones at home they cannot leave, provide only one-way communication, and so on.

Playing the potentially dangerous role of the messenger, the principal conveys the objections and issues of each group to the other. Typically, both groups go quiet and reflective. Both are chastened by the sharing. They confess that this is the first time such cross-perceptions have been provided. There is no attempt to be defensive or act innocent. Seizing the moment, the principal steers the group to the next stage. Without throwing out the baby with the bath water, is it possible both to restrain mutual excesses and develop positive new common ground for the future? Both groups agree to do so, but again separately.

What does each come up with? The teachers agree to the following olive branch: receptiveness to parents' input about the way their kids learn; more two-way exchanges; more flexibility in scheduling teacher-parent conferences, including more frequent contacts by phone; and so on. Parents in turn concede exercising greater restraint, more openness to problems affecting all kids, fewer bossy efforts to run the class or the school, more openness to negotiating the directions of school reform, and so on.

The time is now ripe for bringing representatives of both groups together. The concessions that each group extends to the other are essentially operational rules, not substantive relationships. The building of a foundation for a new relationship has yet to be done. Above all, the principal has to make sure that the focus is student achievement. What emerges from the interaction is an impressive list of common goals and common roles.

Common goals are: to facilitate two-way communications, to align schoolwork and homework, to establish a seamless learning continuum between school and home, and to share strategies for improving student performance. Common goals are to be structured by the principle of reciprocity: teachers and parents should be learning partners, colearners and coteachers; collaborators on behalf of marshalling public support; and not just fund-raisers but resource developers. Both groups agree that given that new congruence of goals and roles, the mission of the school should be expanded to read that it enrolls families, not just kids.

Although the final details of this new teacher-parent collaboration may take many different forms and vary from district to district, three conclusions are clear: it is needed, it has to be negotiated, and only leadership on behalf of negotiated reciprocity will make it possible and meaningful. As they develop, such teacher-parent partnerships unexpectedly become not solely the object, but also the agent, of school reform. Each group gains an ally, and the bridge between school and home sustains the traffic of student achievement.

CHAPTER 20

The Student-Centered Curriculum

According to ads, proclamations, and mission statements, we now have in abundance student-centered school districts, administrators, teachers, curricula, missions, and visions. One district boasted that even its pupils are student centered (or really self-centered?). What educators are trying to communicate is a break from the past, when education was largely or exclusively focused on subject matter. Still, three questions persist:

1. If student centeredness is intended to function as the focus of schools, how are all the other school goals affected?
2. If student-centered schools are new, what existed before? In other words, does the concept of "student centered" have a history (prior or current versions)?
3. Will schools remain student centered or become something else?

The matrix below seeks to accomplish two ends: to respond quickly to the three questions, but to do so in the form of a continuum that includes possible later versions of what it will mean for education to be student centered.

DEGREE AND SPAN OF STUDENT CENTEREDNESS

The matrix shown in table 20.1 nicely captures the following individual and collective emerging patterns:

- Student centeredness, although relatively recent, has emerged quickly to become the universal focus of all education.
- It signals a clear-cut, major shift from teaching subject matter to teaching students.
- Teacher or subject centeredness and student centeredness are mutually exclusive.
- Student centeredness has compelled changes in the relationships of teachers with other teachers, teachers with their students, and students with other students.
- No longer are teachers exclusively in charge of learning; neither are schools.
- Principals no longer have a monopoly on instructional leadership.
- Leadership has become distributed, even being made available to students.
- Curriculum has become a servant, not a master.
- Curriculum alliances to work, character education, values, student relevance, and so on have become an adjunct norm and further expression of education being student centered.
- Technology increasingly is being driven in part by its being already a comfort zone for student-centered activities.
- Single measures have given way to multiple measures. Differentiated education and student centeredness become, increasingly, versions of each other.
- Parents/families/homes increasingly are becoming an alternative educational resource and setting to accommodate student-centered learning.

Table 20.1.

Past Practices	Present Versions	Future Roles
Occasional	Dominant	Total
Subject-matter dominated	Learning styles	Individualized
Teachers indispensable	Partners	Facilitators
Principals essential	Team leaders	Interfacers
Curriculum prescribed	Eclectic	Freewheeling
Technology occasional	Essential	Tutor/teacher
Teacher/teacher	Student/teacher	Student/student
Test evaluations	Portfolio	Self-evaluation
Parental support	Parental participation	Home/family schooling

Spelling out the implications of student centeredness for the future is valuable not only because it anticipates what student centeredness may become and the roles its supporters may play, but because it accommodates countervailing trends and opposition to student-centered education and its alliances. Three such positions are discernible.

First, many constituencies may resist the future implications of student centeredness. Education will be accused of pandering to an already overindulged and self-focused generation of professional consumers. Poor performance on high-risk testing may result in a throwback to subject-matter drills. In addition, many teachers may find it hard or impossible to surrender their traditional role of serving as indispensable providers of instruction, especially because of the emphasis of NCLB on subject-matter proficiency. Principals seeking to recover their role as instructional leaders will be reluctant to embrace a shift of control from educators to students. Nor will administrators find attractive serving as plant managers of educational factories of computers and self-absorbed techies.

A number of traditional parents and citizens also may conclude that student centeredness is not what their tax money should be used for. They may call for a return to traditional forms of no-nonsense education, in which teachers are teachers and kids are kids; and the latter do what the teachers and parents tell them to do. As a result, there may be a significant increase in private and parochial school enrollments and more traditional education. Dress codes (and body ornamentation restrictions) will be developed and enforced. Some schools already require uniforms. The future, in short, may be found in the past.

Second, in contrast, many will find the future projections of student centeredness attractive because it will accommodate their own agendas. Riding on its coattails, advocates of school reform will go further and push for student-led education. Educational technologists will have a field day. Technology will see itself playing an increasingly facilitating role. The cognate commitment to individualizing instruction will tap the almost limitless capacity of computer programs to spin infinite variations on a theme or assignment. Time and space will be reconfigured. School may be available 24 hours a day, 7 days a week, 365 days a year. Computer-equipped homes will give new weight and definition to homeschooling in its own right or as part of regular schooling.

Because student centeredness essentially is a feature of certain curricula, curricula advocates may dominate. Curricula will include differentiated education, project or inquiry learning, service learning, character education, and so on. All combine experiential with academic learning on the one hand, and focus on student leadership development on the other hand. Teachers who have been persuaded that it is more effective to be a guide on the side than a star on the stage will happily be learning leaders guiding students in a project-inquiry-oriented curriculum. Others will provide support to student research projects. In the process, teachers and staff will have the task of facilitating and monitoring the psychological growth and character building of students. The developmental line will run from dependence to independence to interdependence. That will parallel and even dovetail with the medieval developmental model of intellectual competence from apprentice to journeyman to associate to master.

Finally, the emphasis on assisting the emergence of a caring and committed community of students will inevitably build on student centeredness and add an action or experiential component. A commitment to service and to giving back to the community will become part of the value system. Community service or, better still, service learning—which serves as both an experiential extension of the curriculum and as the building blocks of leadership development—will be, for many, a norm. As the above takes hold, schools themselves will become increasingly differentiated as students are encouraged to extend student-centered education to student-managed and ultimately student-led education.

Third, and finally, there is the totally different tack of challenging whether student-centered education is really adult-centered education. Saul Cooperman notes: "Student centered is more a statement of what teachers and administrators wish the high school landscape to be than what is truly is. Reality involves an adult centered curriculum, with both the organization of the faculty and the subject-matter hierarchy modeled to suit the convenience of adults, not necessarily the learning needs of students" (*Education Week* 2003c). Separatist subject-matter departments, like fiefdoms, rule separately with virtually no bridges between them. Students seek connections that would make their studies relevant and whole. Teachers stand in their subject matter all day and see nothing else but that subject matter. In contrast, students are on the receiving end of all subjects. They experience multiplicity without unity—singular and isolated strands of information without coherence. If the curriculum were really student centered the faculty would have to talk to one another about student-centered curricula.

Which trend will dominate? If history is any guide, all three, or an amalgam, will. All the versions of the continuum will coexist, although those who occupy the bully pulpits will argue that such range muddies the waters and will cry out for a single version. Whether we come down, finally, on the side of being subject-matter focused (the past), student centered (the present), student led (the future), or a combination of all three, schooling has become increasingly a matter of choice—in this case, of internal choices as well.

It never used to be that way. But, perhaps without realizing it, educational advocates of customer services and imitators of companies that are customer driven have opened a Pandora's box. In the process, they also unknowingly may have empowered students to be change agents themselves. But at this point one has to pause to take into account a powerful and all-pervasive force that may alter significantly the outcomes of student-centered education.

What cannot be discounted from all discussion is a powerful youth culture that is for the most part anti-intellectual, antischool, and hedonistic, and that has been developed by advertisers into the most acquisitive consumer generation of all time. Indeed, some have cited its capacity for distraction, deflection, and substitution as contributing to the loss of momentum between high scores in math and science in the fourth grade and a serious drop in test levels by the eighth and even more so by the twelfth grades.

YOUTH CULTURE

In many ways, current youth culture is full of itself. It is a pleasure culture, which is counter to an achievement culture. According to the youth culture, smart is dumb, immediate trumps delayed gratification, the group or gang is the real family, and it is always us against them. It has become increasingly a visible culture signaling its separateness, common identity, and indirect defiance by its obviously different dress, body piercings, and even walk and hand gestures. The goal of merchandisers has been in effect to produce a brand-driven youth segment to justify heavy investments in advertising. Recently, two firms, Youth Marketing International and American Greeting, have teamed up to market Clifford and Care Bears to preschool-aged children (*New York Times* 2003). Moreover, such marketing is already standard fare in middle and high schools. Younger kids have enough financial resources to be programmed as outstanding consumers. Unlike studies linking TV and film violence to criminality, there is no comparable research linking consumerism and poor school performance. All this creative talent and commercial investment busily selling and even pandering to a youth culture is, after all, merely entrepreneurship in the best tradition of capitalistic growth.

The youth culture is no abstract sociological concept. Walk through the halls of a high school during the change of classes to experience the wave of mass conformity. That same experience of uniformity is now increasingly available in middle schools. The hardest task for teachers often is to break the mass mold so that individuals are free to emerge, and to encourage responses that are not herdlike. For many teachers, eliciting some independent thinking is a rare achievement in its own right.

Some educators and parents have not been blind to the negatives of this culture. Some schools, both public and private, have restored a dress code or required students to wear a specific uniform. A number of parochial and religious schools have projected themselves as increasingly nonsectarian in order to attract parents and students who are not of their faith but who want a safe haven from the trappings of the youth culture. The substantial and sudden appearance of civic and character education, the attention to managing bullies, and the more aggressive counseling attitude toward truancy are all in large part responses to the counterculture. The decision to break up huge high schools into smaller academies of about a hundred students each is partly motivated by the desire to break up the mass effect of the culture and to make it more manageable. Because of the youth culture's frequent alliances with drugs and alcohol, the general attitude of education is that whether or not individuals are using, the culture itself is addictive and has to be viewed as such. The war on drugs, not incorrectly, has become a war on the youth culture.

Finally, and perhaps unexpectedly, a new social and political attitude seems to be surfacing. Statistically based and guided, it is the increasing recognition that the projected social, welfare, and medical costs of caring for, warehousing in prisons, and curing the excesses of the youth culture are too high. Therefore, a preventive medicine approach is surfacing: to spend more now and make a greater effort before it is too late to rescue the current and future generations from being burdens of the state, or from being unemployed or underemployed by a new global economy that already has shown itself to be a severe downsizer of American workers.

The legislation of No Child Left Behind thus can be perceived as almost a last-ditch effort—not unlike a rescue mission to a area devastated by drought or disease—to salvage students, especially in urban and rural areas, from the kind of educational neglect that has produced the statistics of failure that triggered the legislation in the first place. All such efforts seek a new kind of inclusive, collective, and proactive effort that revives the role of the school in loco parentis. There is also a kind of last-ditch evangelism to provide a firm hand that will not allow our legacy, the current and future generations of young people, to grow up without the knowledge, skills, and caring they will need to be productive citizens and workers.

The fear is that the youth culture is changing student centeredness to self-centeredness. Its excesses embody the worst, not the best, of the historical shift in focus from teaching subject matter to teaching students. In the process, it has downgraded America's ranking internationally, resulted in the embarrassment of seniors failing graduation exams, and elicited the protests of employers, who often find their new employees cannot read, write, or calculate. The current backlash of testing and testing was thus inevitable. It is also unsettling to realize that although education expenditures have increased fourfold over the last three decades, no comparable increase in performance or test scores has occurred. The total budget for education nationally matches that of the Defense Department. International rankings indicate that we are currently a ninth-rate power.

Finally, there is the fact that we are not educating students for an enormously changing and fast-paced work world. The estimate is that the twenty-first century will witness not one hundred, but over twenty thousand, progressions from what was; and that one of the major dilemmas, ironically more so of developed countries, will be whether there will be enough middle-class jobs around for all those high school and college graduates. Two-income families and/or parents working overtime at two different jobs sustain the bulk of middle-class families now. But the somewhat self-indulgent and expansive youth culture is encountering the tough and competitive work culture. Excess triggers counterexcess. Testing will be endless, social promotion will be eliminated, the senior dropout rate may increase, and underemployment may negatively characterize future graduates, as well as affect the spending power of the current generation.

The current correctives may appear harsh and total, but that may be because they are long overdue. They also in many ways may be essentially the educational versions of the hidden hand of the employment market. Above all, such correctives are a wake-up call to return to serious business. We have moved rapidly through future stretch and strain and now inhabit future shock. Increasingly, looking ahead has to become not the exception but the norm. Whereas all that is happening and changing in education may not consciously focus on the excesses, motivations, and behaviors of the youth culture, the youth culture may be precisely where it has the greatest impact and scores its greatest gains. Tough times, now and later, may require tough measures and tough love—the stern command and the embrace.

Part VI

INTRODUCTION TO THE MAJOR DRIVERS OF CHANGE

CHAPTER 21

The Impact of the Global Economy on Education and Work

Ted Hershberg (2003) has defined the three essentials of public education in the last century as follows:

> To provide universal basic literacy; to socialize a diverse population to the demands of a factory system; and, through IQ-type tests and the bell-shaped curve, to identify and sort out the top fifth of students who would go on to college. The rest easily found jobs in a manufacturing economy that required little in the way of high skills or advanced education, but paid middle-class sustaining wages. By succeeding so well at these tasks, our schools were a key element in America's emergence as an industrial superpower.

Although one might quarrel with his versions of the major past goals of public education, Hershberg's subsequent conclusion is correct: namely, that what worked before is not what is needed now, and therefore "it is time to transform our system of public education."

What then should be the essentials of a transformed educational system? Here is Hershberg's list for the future: students should be able to use technology, solve problems, and learn on their own all their lives. Then he shifts ground: all should be educated equally, not just the top one-fifth; and the education of all should be notched up to higher levels of knowledge and performance. The increasing demands of the global economy require that all students "become effective citizens or productive workers in the new economy."

Why is the global economy singled out as so pivotal? What will be its impact on students? Unfortunately, Hershberg and other educators generally stop too soon and expect that catch-all phrase to be sufficiently persuasive. But if it is to be such a critical determiner of educational goals, then what sets off the global economy from previous economic systems needs to be examined.

Kids entering nursery school and kindergarten now at age five will graduate from high school between 2015 and 2020. Kids just born will be the class of 2025. Indeed, if education is to minister to the future of its students it must be shaped and driven by the kind of future they are likely to face. The role of educational futurists is to anticipate the territory ahead and then prepare the new maps to get there. Because forecasting is not an exact science and because trends and data may be fallible, the map offers not one but a number of routes to chose from. But the critical positioning remains firm: the goals of education must be the goals of the future its students will likely encounter; and the role of education is to prepare them for living, learning, and working in that future. To demonstrate the process of futuristic probing and application, the global economy provides a nice case in point.

THE GLOBAL ECONOMY

Goods and services made in less developed countries at lower wages have put better paid American workers in jeopardy. In fact, many companies have exported jobs to enjoy just such a competitive advantage. In addition, many software companies use programmers in India to develop software at lower costs. Dell currently is redirecting its customer tech service calls there as well. Downsizing is a regular by-product of global competition. In this connection Hershberg notes further that in the last twenty-five years virtually all the income gains have gone to the top fifth of the population. But what he does not mention is that for the remaining bulk of the bell curve, middle- and lower-class earning levels either have eroded or, when they have remained constant or increased slightly, it has been accomplished only through two-income families, having no kids or fewer or later kids, working longer hours as overtime, and occasionally starting businesses, mostly in the service sector.

In the early and middle nineteenth century, social critics lamented the nearly total degree to which public education was the midwife of the factory system. Charles Dickens in particular portrayed the extent to which the Gradgrind teacher of the school prepared children for the Gradgrind supervisor of the factory. In a telling caricature of the day, the exit door of the school became the entry door of the factory. In other words, economics in general and the job market in particular propelled social and educational policy, whether or not it was officially articulated as such. If economics and the job market are to reemerge as the driving force of the global economy, why not admit it and spell it out without beating around the bush?

BUSINESS TRENDS

The truth is the transformation that Hershberg is calling for in public education has been occurring first, faster, and more directly in the workplace. The standard recitation of the differences of salaries between high school and college graduates may be leading young people down the garden path. It assumes that the jobs for college graduates will be waiting for them. In truth, in many cases college graduates already have bumped high school graduates out of the marketplace and are working at jobs that really do not require college-level preparation. Is anyone really persuaded that a college degree is needed to run a local McDonald's or car rental agency?

If one studies what has happened to the curricula of two-year community colleges in the last two decades, what one finds is that they have become basically terminal career and vocational, rather than transfer, schools. They more resemble those private, small, specialized, proprietary schools that boast that their high-tech graduates can learn more in just four weeks than college students do in four years. In fact, those schools and many community colleges are doing a land office business recycling the unemployed, the underemployed, downsized college graduates, and former military personnel whose technology training was too specialized or high tech to meet the more ordinary demands of business technology.

Then, too, downsizing also has included not just rank and file but middle-level managers; part of Hershberg's one-fifth. Accustomed to effectively managing cost reductions and savings, middle-level managers suddenly found themselves the object of such cost reductions.

They were replaced not with better-educated or more technologically sophisticated managers but rather with rank-and-file workers in teams (often with only a high school education). One cannot responsibly discuss the future of education, therefore, without being aware of the metamorphosis of management. In other words, educators who, like Hershberg, urge the transformation of education have to become far more expert on all the other transformations occurring now and increasingly in the future if what they are calling for is to be persuasively realistic and relevant on the one hand and dynamically informed and shaped the other hand.

If one were to singularly shape education to the current and future job market, what would be some of the critical operating patterns? They generally would not be uplifting. Here are a few:

- General scarcity of good and challenging jobs in the future.
- Those jobs that are good and challenging will likely not last a lifetime.
- At least three and as many as five career and job changes may be required.
- Being downsized may become increasingly a nonaccusatory or nonjudgmental norm of work life.
- Company and job loyalty, previously assumed, will increasingly be rare.

Given these trends, certain other dislocating or ironic factors emerge. Hershberg's one-fifth may shrink to one-sixth or one-seventh. The gap between the top and the middle may widen considerably. More and more of the middle class will become working stiffs. The selection of a significant other will increasingly take the form of an economic partnership. Current professionals at the top may assure the future of their children in effect by buying it—sending offspring to private schools and thus paying college tuitions from kindergarten onward, and then enrolling them in Ivy League universities at which current tuition and board equals the annual salary of middle-level managers with MBAs. Increasingly the economic elite will emerge as a financial and intellectual dynasty. They will enjoy a lifelong economic advantage that cannot be matched by those attending public schools and graduating from state universities. Except for the occasional exception to the rule, the lower and middle classes will always be playing catch-up. In short, the economics of the future is shaping an aristocratic meritocracy.

The call to make quality education more available to all so that no child is left behind focuses essentially on urban and rural schools with high percentages of poor and minority students—about 40 percent of the school population. The economics of the future suggests that the goal of preparedness has to be provided to this 40 percent as well if they are not to join the ranks of the unemployed or the underemployed. Examining the data of displaced workers from 1984 to 2002, Farber (2003) concludes that job loss exceeded job creation, and, further, that the jobs lost were generally of a much higher earnings level than the ones created.

Education is no guarantee of a job or job choice if the jobs are not there in the first place. The only thing higher education may be able to provide is job flexibility. California is currently solving its teacher shortage problem even in the competitive areas of math and science through economics, not commitment. Many of the downsized employees from Silicon Valley firms, as well as those weary of roller coaster rides of insecurity, have reluctantly joined the ranks of alternatively certified teachers. But if the economy improves, they may be the first to jump ship.

The global economy, when properly understood, may better serve developing nations than developed countries; just as NAFTA may benefit workers of Mexico and Canada more than American workers. Of course, such preferential or free trade arrangements often result in lower prices for goods and services. But unless Americans are working, they may be unable to afford even those lower prices. In short, the global economy and the American dream increasingly are on a diverging course. Expecting education to close the gap as it has in the past shows a disturbing ignorance of the extent and possible permanence of the gulf between the two.

WORK, NOT EDUCATION

Given the prospect of such grim realities, would it not have made more sense for Hershberg and others to recommend that teenagers work part-time or volunteer as interns? Perhaps they also ignored what past and current research shows of the impact of work on school performance and learning. Lawrence Steinberg, in his *When Teenagers Work: The Social and Psychological Costs of Teenage Employment* laments, as his title suggests, the excessive number of hours teenagers work, the menial jobs that are available to them, and what they mostly do with their earnings (fix up souped-up cars). He notes that the only reason American teenage students generally can work more hours than their counterparts in other counties is that schools are not demanding. Although wrapping hamburgers neither is nor prepares students for meaningful work, if the alternatives are cruising the malls or getting high, wrapping hamburgers is preferred. As to the effect work has on grades, Steinberg counters that sadly schools let students generally slide by, promote them socially, and thus pose no barrier to their working as many hours as they wish.

But a completely different perspective emerges from a recent study by Jeyland T. Mortimer, *Working and Growing Up in America* (2003). Mortimer traces the lives, work patterns, and school performance of some thousand randomly selected students over a seven-year period. Her longitudinal study shows, first, that teenagers who work twenty hours per week throughout the year enjoy academic success, especially in college and especially among students who showed low educational promise when they entered high school. Second, those who work in that pattern do better academically than those who don't work at all or those who work more hours. Third, teenagers who work during high school have an advantage over those who don't in finding career-related jobs later. Fourth, even menial jobs teach students how important it is to show up, to be on time, to work with others, to take orders, to exercise initiative, and to mange money (especially the little they make given the number of hours they work). Fifth, and perhaps most important of all, students discover that not all kinds of job are equally satisfying. Sticking with the first one is not a good strategy; trial and error may help to identify both talent and its match with a work environment, and thus better prepare teenagers for the multiple careers and job changes that await them.

Recently, business-school partnerships took a new turn and perhaps provided a new trend in Texas. Outback Steakhouse, an Aussie-themed restaurant chain, built an actual restaurant into Westside High School in Houston. The curriculum is Entrepreneurship 101. Although the course is focused on the restaurant business, the skills are designed to be transferable. The goal is to work from the ground up to, three years later, entering management. Significantly, vocational students so engaged have a higher graduation rate and score higher on standardized tests than their college-bound classmates. And the chances are also that such training will be recession proof and flexibly survive the pressures of the global economy.

NEW EDUCATIONAL GOALS FOR THE FUTURE

Convergence rules the future. The key task is synthesis and integration. What has been divided and set apart has to be brought back together again or reconfigured in a new framework. All future goals of education therefore require holistic contexts, integrative skills, and reframing structures; the following, in effect, constitute the curricula of, by, and for the future:

1. The Politics of Economics and the Economics of Politics
2. Dual Citizenship: National and International Communities
3. Systemic Thinking and Holistic Contexts
4. Independent and Interdependent Learning Technology
5. Anticipatory and Participatory Fusion.

1. Political Economy: Regional, National, and Global Work
Economics and Political Citizenry

If public schools are to be transformed, especially to reflect the new global economy and its demands, a minimal requirement will be the fusion of economics and politics and their application in two tracks: one is academic, the other experiential.

Political economy was an integrated discipline in the nineteenth century. But then the pressure of specialization split the fusion into political science and economics. The former goes under the name of "civics" in school, the latter, "careers." It is an unfortunate split at all levels. It leads to decisions that may be politically astute but ignorant of markets, or to economic policies that are politically inept. The two together approximate reality and should never have been separated in the first place. In the school of the future they have to be reunited.

If economics is not a high school subject, it should be made one. If it already is, but is divorced from civics, then the two have to be combined. If the reunited political economy is offered only in the junior or senior year, it should be moved up to the freshman year. And it should be required of all students; a high GPA should not be the grounds for exclusion. The course should be an in-depth examination of the economics and politics of work. The context should be regional, national, and international in order to demonstrate the extent to which the global political economy affects all markets and politics. Sample multinational industries, their operations, political allies, and their workforce could be used as case studies. The international scene and setting should always be given a national focus. Career trends and patterns should be tapped. Students could individually shadow those holding various jobs.

The course on political economics has an experiential match. Each student is required to complete thirty to forty hours of community service. Character and citizen education would converge in meeting the hourly requirement of supervised, evaluated, and monitored community service volunteerism. This too could be given an academic dimension, as students learn about the role of social services and the ethics of volunteering. Above all, service learning that integrates community service with academics should be built into the curricula options of all schools at all levels. Paying students for their service learning hours so that they can choose that over wrapping hamburgers, pumping gas, or packing groceries at the local supermarket would serve as an incentive system for putting academic learning at the service of the community. In the process, students also would learn the basic values of both work and service to the community, and the emergence of leadership and collaborative learning would be promoted. Above all, such a program would also help to insure not only that no child is left behind but also that no social need is left unaddressed.

2. Dual Citizenship

The global economy is made possible in large part by the increasing globalization of the world. That globalization often has resulted in double loyalties. Thus, the traditional education focus on raising the level of student awareness, knowledge, and practice of being a fully participating citizen has to be given a futuristic supplement of preparing students to be world citizens. Only education is uniquely qualified to address the issue of dual citizenship, and of integrating national sovereignty and pride with global interdependence. Only by dual citizens can the international problems of ecology, health, human rights, and living and work conditions be comprehensively addressed and solved. As dual citizenship takes hold students will carry two passports.

The topic of world citizenship is ready made for class discussion and analysis. It would immediately lead to a compilation of principal international agencies, their missions, and the obstacles they face. Issues such as ecology and health, which cross all borders, could be identified and studied. The question of different languages might motivate more students to become more bilingual or even multilingual. An oath or pledge of allegiance could become the object of writing or multimedia exercises. An appropriate symbol or logo could be designed. Clearly, it is an ideal occasion for discussion and development. At the same time, it provides students with a broader, deeper, more diverse framework for what indeed is the future condition of the planet.

Even if all students were better educated, their qualifications might be in excess of what the economy is able and prepared to offer them. It might turn out to be the cruelest disappointment of all—finally arriving at the end of the rainbow to find an empty pot. It might be like all the kids dreaming of becoming Michael Jordan or Britney Spears or Dr. Salk when in fact less than 1 percent ever achieves that status. Besides, focusing on one's own success is one sided and self-centered. It is preoccupied with individual, not collective, goals, with being an economic, and not also a political, animal. For students to achieve more they have to be more. In other words, if all those who had been left behind in urban and rural environments caught up to where everyone else was, and then all of them equally aspired to and achieved higher levels of performance, would the equity and accountability of access match or find fulfillment in the equity and accountability of opportunity? As long as the bell curve continues to exist, as long as socio-economic factors are predictors of success, and as long as the one-fifth has the means and credentials to insure their continuity and dominance, the only thing accomplished would be higher levels of job disappointment and social dislocation. Only citizens' ethics on behalf of all can counter the aggrandizement of the haves. Only the fusion of economics and politics can support the paradox of dualistic allegiance to the individual and society, the national and the international. The vision of dual citizenship is to banish war as solution.

One of the functions of the future and especially of future curricula is to set up the conditions and parameters of learning. Specifically, plans for the future of education need to address the future of everything else that is changing. It would be a cruel hoax indeed to discover in the future that students are worse off and that raising the level of education removed them from more ordinary but more satisfying opportunities of employment and fulfillment. And would students who endured such economic mismatching be inclined to be good citizens?

3. Systemic and Holistic Knowledge and the Research Frontiers

The sciences are routinely separated and taught as discrete subjects, even though biology is largely chemical and electrical, and even though knowledge is cumulative and regularly subject to cross-fertilization. Psychology currently floats in its own world, even though most applications now are pharmacological. Already noted is the questionable and counterproductive separation of politics and economics, of voting and working, of the civics of public policy and the economics of the workplace. Brain and genetic research are redefining not only human identity but also human expression and language. The cracking of the human genome and its code places the debate between nature and nurture on a much higher plane, which in turn has major economic and political consequences. In short, students have to be introduced to contextual learning, to systemic and interrelated knowledge, to holistic systems as shaping the future and therefore their lives and careers.

But surely many will object to the overwhelming scope of such conceptualization. They will argue that the basics must be taught and mastered as a prelude to such an integrated worldview. But there are two problems with such a gradualized and step-by-step approach. First, given the way education crawls and stalls, the baby steps will be extended so far that the systemic will never be reached at all. Or the entire process will be designated as too complex for all to master and therefore postponed until college. Second, inertia will prevail in both obvious and evasive ways. Singular subject matter will still be taught separately, but in a token holistic context. In other words, subject-matter competence will remain as intact as the subjects' instructors. Or the gap will require such extensive retroactive unlearning, correction, and reprogramming of mindsets that again the contextual framework may never be reached, let alone addressed, and even when it is reached it will be so diluted or diffused that it will be limp and exhausted.

The solution itself must therefore be systemic. Parts are used but they are miniwholes. Each one should be shaped by the degree to which it mirrors and illuminates what is generically its larger version. It can start even at the elementary level by exploring how we think in terms of words and how sound and nonverbal learning shape our identity. In short, the entire curriculum needs to be recast. We need not throw out the baby with the bath water. Much can be salvaged and recycled. But it must be placed within new, more holistic frameworks and its rich linkages identified and tied to what it is allied to and enhanced by. Specialists do not have to abandon their specialization but they do have to become generalists—not unlike the dual citizen. The old question that was asked of those who faced a daunting task was, "How do you eat an elephant?" The answer is: "One bite at a time." We should make sure each bite is generic and typical so that it is always a miniature of the whole, and so that the micro and the macro become versions, not alternatives, of each other.

4. Independent and Interdependent Learning: Face to Face and Technology

The focus of good parenting should be on helping offspring become independent. Those who are tied too closely to apron strings grow up suffering from completion deficiency. Similarly, raising an only child as opposed to siblings often results in an adult who does not know how to share, compete, or cooperate because he or she has not had to. Education, acting in loco parentis, has the same goals: helping, guiding, and structuring students so that they become both independent and interdependent learners.

Technology now plays a new and critical role in the first task and can also be supportive of the second. Virtual (electronic) education is now so totally in place that starting at age five a student need never physically attend a school. The some one million families that have opted for homeschooling are now able to enroll their kids in cyber charter schools and derive most of their learning online. Because such charter schools are also public schools and thus are under the same mandate of high-stakes testing, the effectiveness of technologically amplified homeschooling can now be easily compared to traditional schooling. And because the evaluation tests only knowledge and not mode of instruction, the comparison is apples and apples.

Online learning is not limited to one-on-one but also often occurs in online classrooms. Students still are independent learners but they are aware, through e-mail interaction and common questions and answers posted on electronic blackboards, of the other members of the class. Research has shown that such online interactive courses often achieve higher levels of interdependent learning as well. In particular, students are impressed by the diversity of others' thinking and problem-solving skills. They also generally concede that the questions finally asked by all the members of the group exhaust all the conceivable questions that could have been asked. But still there is something missing.

Important though it is for students to be exposed to and master the technology of independent learning, and to derive some of the benefits of its interdependent dimensions, it does not approximate the totality of collaborative learning, which increasingly will be a dominant mode of the future. Such learning is not so much acquired as negotiated. It often involves understanding and bringing to the surface buried values and assumptions, which, like the unconscious, determine conscious actions and positions. In many schools in the United States, such diversity is masked by geographical or class homogeneity. But in a typical large company as many as five generations can coexist, with racial and ethnic differences added to the mix. But classes are typically all the same generation. They are like many Silicon Valley start-ups: agile but fragile. They can move fast because they are all of the same mind and age, but there is no internal tension of difference to challenge where they are going and to prevent them from going off the deep end.

Totally interdependent learning requires face-to-face interaction. It requires functioning in a team or group environment. It compels an understanding of the special paradox of group dynamics: the learner is dependent in his interdependency; the group can do and provide more than the individual can on his or her own; and the most difficult agreement to accomplish is consensual rather than by majority vote. In addition, learners come to better understand that in a team environment they cannot only be takers, they also must be givers. Learning satisfaction, like job satisfaction, in the future will require each student to provide satisfaction to others. Finally, cooperative learning introduces students not only to leadership in general but to a different kind of leadership. Team leadership is different. It is based, according to Robert K. Greenleaf (1984), on primus inter pares—on being at best the first among equals. Nor is the position of being first a permanent arrangement. It rotates to the person in the group with the expertise to best deal with a new challenge.

So a major goal of future education is to kill two birds with one stone: to introduce students to the technology of independent learning and to the sociology of interdependent learning. Combining and fusing the two may make us better able to produce lifelong learners and may better prepare students for working later in teams. Learning and knowing others will become not alternatives but versions of each other. Above all, learning relationships will provide the glue of communication and community, which share the same root of bringing knowledge and people together.

5. Anticipatory and Participatory Fusion: Proactive Involvement

All students have to a large extent to become futurists, even if only defensively. So much is changing so rapidly—with new research frontiers and findings altering the map of the landscape almost daily—that the only real way of remaining current is to constantly look ahead. What this means in terms of education is the study of the future and its methodologies.

That in turn inhabits two ends of the spectrum: the history of the future in the past, and the history of the future in the future. Students will also become adept at understanding, gathering, and constructing opinion polls, surveys, trend searches, and so on. They will examine in detail the demographics and shape scenarios that reflect cultural trends. They will learn about the value of expert group judgments as structured by the Delphi methodology. They will mine science fiction for its technological foresight and create scenarios of their own future societies. Naturally, those scenarios will have been prepared for and tapped in many ways by the other areas of study noted above. But the critical orientation is that each student functioning as a futurist will become a norm. The only variation will be the degree: whether what they have chosen to be and how they have chosen to live will lead them to be future oriented, directed, or driven—or all three.

SUMMARY

Futurists, perhaps more so than any other professionals, have to worry about how their notions will be perceived and received by different audiences. To many parents, for example, the above may appear intriguing but far-fetched. They would worry that the basics may be neglected, putting their offspring at a disadvantage. But those parents in the current workforce would find the analysis sadly confirmatory and agree that they were not prepared as well as they could have been for the changes they have had to face. In short, parents would have sufficiently mixed views and feelings to both endorse and put the brakes on the five future probes.

Most educators would recoil at the prospect of having to reformulate their areas of expertise and resituate them into new frameworks. Invited to meet and collectively create miniwholes, teachers would raise an incredible number of paralyzing problems and questions; they would identify reasons why it could not be done and state that even if it could be done, it would be beyond the grasp of most students. In short, the future would be acknowledged, just the way Hershberg did with the global economy, but it would remain an unexamined reality that bore little relationship to education, to its future, and above all to the future of its students.

Students probably would be receptive, find science fiction literature and films engaging, and enjoy creating scenarios of future earth societies. They might particularly respond to the blending of the academic and the experiential, and to returning to Dewey's advocacy of learning by doing. Study would not only alternate with work, but be informed by it. Students would constantly be building up an experiential base of expertise. They also might embrace the four-stage progression of achieving subject-matter competence—apprentice, journeyman, associate, and master—rather than grade levels. To be sure, their appreciation of the changes would not always be cumulative. It would require constantly regrouping miniwholes into larger miniwholes, and so on; but the process would be aided and supported by collaborative and interdependent team learning. But then students are often the last ones to be consulted; and admittedly, in this case, even if they were offered a choice, most already have been programmed with a mindset inimical to what is being proposed. The only difference is that the real future, especially that of the global economy, will reprogram them, often unpleasantly.

So if hardly anyone would support these new educational goals, what is the point of introducing them? The point is to challenge inertia, to put matters on pause, to raise prospects, to stir things up, to lead some to rethink the situation, and above all to indicate to those who already are thinking ahead that they are not alone and that there are ways of applying the future in specific and challenging terms to education. At best, futurists should focus on being a minority movement, a persuasive gadfly, on finding leverage. As one futurist noted recently, the sign of his making a successful presentation on the future is that he is never invited back.

But martyrdom is to be avoided at all costs—ditto excessive seriousness and earnestness. The problem with the lone wolf crying out in the wilderness is that he is so full both of himself and his howl that he never shuts up. If he did, he would hear all the other lone wolves crying out in the wilderness, and he could then join them in a collective howl. And he would be reassured that what disturbs him similarly disturbs others, and he and they would find comfort in not being alone and finding companionship with others in a common future. Futurists, in short, should build communities. If it takes a village to raise a child, then perhaps it also requires educational futurists as a group to demonstrate that being student centered and future centered are one and the same.

CHAPTER 22

Competition and School Choice

Few organizations would ever admit it, but they all wish they could be monopolies. Some, of course, are. The most obvious examples are public energy and water utilities. Less obvious are government operations such as the IRS and Social Security. Throughout the United States, public schools are often the largest business in town and the major employer. That distinction sometimes extends to being the only or dominant choice in town.

For many generations, attending the public school historically was a given. Other options were driven by belief or value systems, especially religious. Full-time parochial schools were an alternative especially for Catholics, although other denominations also have created such schools. Historically, if there was a religious or cultural preference of those attending public schools, it appeared in supplemental education, especially Sunday schools. Various ethnic nationalities also sought to preserve their cultural identity through such after-school activities as Chinese school, Irish societies, Swedish folk dancing, and so on. Because private or independent schools were not generally perceived by the middle class as options, public school was in effect a monopoly. But things changed, especially with two innovations, homeschools and charter schools.

Ironically, homeschooling was hastened inadvertently by the public schools themselves. Determined to be as professional as possible in their advocacy of student well-being, schools added sexual education to the traditional knowledge base. Initially, the conduit was the standard course on hygiene, which essentially stressed disease prevention and control through healthy habits of hygiene, diet, and inoculations. Primarily taught by physical education coaches, the course met only once a week and often was not taken seriously by most students. Sex was either never examined in detail or limited to the observation: "Sex is a problem. When you are married it is not." That statement alone testifies to a lack of credibility.

But educational professionals, especially those with a crusading mission, typically were not content to stop there. With characteristic zeal and aggrandizement, sexuality became an increasingly acceptable staple of education. Visual aids of internal organs began to appear. Issues of sexual control and safety led further to discussions of contraceptives. Later on abortions entered the discussion. And so on and so on, as education gradually crossed the line and made part of a public curriculum what many families regarded as a private, moral, and even religious preserve.

Discussions by concerned parents with school administrators failed to alter or arrest this socially driven mission of the schools to prevent unwanted teenage pregnancies and later the spread of AIDS. But to many parents, the schools were perceived increasingly to be morally callous, indifferent, and godless; they were usurping family and home authority. Enrollments at parochial schools increased. Some denominations, especially Christian fundamentalists, created their own schools. But what was genuinely new and challenging was the decision to remove kids entirely from public schools and teach them at home, especially when there were no acceptable alternatives. The monopoly was challenged. A number of alternatives began to emerge.

HOMESCHOOLING

The estimate is that now over two million kids are homeschooled. That choice has become a new direction, articulated by a vocal and often assertive constituency. Initially, at least, it was essentially a moral issue and choice. But increasingly it has become an intellectual and competency issue. As in all things, the proof is in the pudding. In 1998, 20,760 homeschooled students in 11,930 families were tested and surveyed. Depending on their grade levels they were given either the Iowa Tests of Basic Skills (ITBS) or the Tests of Achievement and Proficiency (TAP). Here are the results of the tests and the surveys:

- The test scores were exceptionally high: median scores were in 70th to 80th percentile.
- Twenty-five percent of homeschool students performed in grades above their age level and above their public and private school peers.
- Parents of home schoolers have more formal education than parents in the general population.
- Median income is higher in families that homeschool.
- Almost all parents who homeschool are married couples.

In addition, although some parents could afford to send their offspring to private school, they did not choose to do so. In other cases there was no good private school where they lived. Parents of homeschool students tend to be very enterprising and resourceful. They are well aware, for example, of the social limitations of homeschooling. They devise ways to mitigate the problem with other homeschool families, as well as in conjunction with some school activities and clubs. Although there are only about two million homeschool students in a total pubic school population of sixty million, their impact as a learning model has been out of all proportion to their numbers.

Here, then, are some of homeschooling's salient differences as a model:

- Time and space are not fixed. Schedules vary from a few hours to an entire day; from five to seven days a week; from thirty to fifty-two weeks of the year.
- Learning is portable. It travels with the student and his or her family. Family vacations are no longer tied to the school calendar in terms of time or duration. Such flexibility is not available even in a private school.
- It is ungraded, competency based, and self-paced, the components of differentiated education.
- It spans K–12. Homeschooling has been around long enough for its students to attend college; and university faculty generally find them well-prepared, motivated, and intellectually intense.

- Parents generally have benefited psychologically and intellectually from the experience almost as much as their offspring.
- In families with two or more kids, homeschooling is very much like the one-room schoolhouse, in which different-aged kids learned with and helped each other.

Aside from the general lamentation that home schooling has skimmed off some of the cream from the public schools, it generally has not been perceived as a direct threat. Its numbers are small and it leaves intact school per-capita allocations. It also fails to affect private or independent schools. And yet because of its multiple distinctions, those familiar with the nature of its operations and achievements are determined to keep homeschooling alive as a model central to the future of schooling and learning. Indeed, there are signs, often tentative and sporadic, of three possible further variations or developments of home schooling, reconfigured or redefined, that may shift its position from the periphery closer to the center.

The first would involve economic incentives. If vouchers are not declared unconstitutional and enjoy wider distribution, and if they could be used to underwrite home schooling, or if per-capita school allocations could be made available to homeschooling, that would legitimize and, further, stimulate a significant increase in, homeschooling. Once a family makes a decision to undertake homeschooling it usually includes all their offspring. With economic incentives a reasonable projection is that homeschooling enrollments might increase from two to five million by the end of the decade. One thing is clear: the infallible sign of such an increase occurring would be the demand that homeschooling be intensely regulated, monitored, and even credentialed. The lobbying for that already has surfaced as part of the call for greater supervision of both home and charter schools. The inevitable argument that also will emerge is that if home schools are increasingly to be regulated, then financial support also should be given. Or a test case might surface in which parents given vouchers award them to themselves. In other words, the special and often extraordinary model of homeschooling could become a much stronger option in the future with financial incentives and with increasing political or legal advocacy.

Another way homeschooling might gain wider acceptance is if it were defined not solely as an educational model but also as an agent of familial coherence and social welfare. In that capacity it would be perceived as offering multiple social benefits. It would be a way of preserving the family, encouraging more parental involvement and supervision, reducing absenteeism and unruly behaviors, and even raising the general level of educational competence of parents. A combined educational and social contract could be signed by each household. In return for per-capita grants, which in some cases might be the equivalent of a part-time job salary, parents would have to abide by state regulations and be willing to be trained in knowledge acquisition and subject-matter competency. Cost-benefit analysis might demonstrate that the expense of providing supervision and training would be more than offset not only by student educational, career, and behavioral gains, but also by the societal gains of achieving greater family stability.

But the third option, with a little coaching and pushing, would probably turn out to be the most viable. Rather than operating on the assumption that homeschooling is a separate and special activity totally apart from regular public schooling, perhaps it should be perceived as part of a continuum and as an ideal extension of schooling. Specifically, homework should be reconceived and reconfigured as an opportunity not only for individual drill, but also as a homeschooling activity. Assignments routinely could be designed to be family involving, vacations would be structured to include written and pictorial journals, community service options would be not be limited to individuals but become familial, and so on.

Currently many teachers do not give homework at all. If they do it is either minimal or crushing. But in either case, it generally is not designed as an opportunity for parental involvement and feedback. To capture and integrate some of the best features of homeschooling, public education has to merge public schooling with homeschooling, homework with familial work. The overriding concept then would be that the school enrolls not kids, but families. A continuum is established: learning does not stop at the end of the school day; it continues at home. One of the reasons many advocate cyber schools in toto or partially is that technology makes the integration of school and home easier. In fact, in a number of homes, students have provided their parents with computer literacy.

Forecasters have endowed homeschooling with future importance out of all proportion to its numbers for many reasons. First, it passes the test for being durable and adaptable. It has lasted, increased its numbers slightly each year, and attracted various constituencies. Second, its educational attainments are splendid and wholesome. Third, long-term projections seem to be sustaining the gains. The initial generation of homeschoolers are entering college and doing well. A longitudinal study would confirm or alter that pattern. Extended far enough it also would yield data on careers and on decisions later to teach their own children via homeschooling. Fourth, everyone wins; kids, parents, nuclear families, communities. Fifth and finally, it is a triumph not so much of meritocracy or demographics as of design. And, as noted, often viable models carry the future forward.

CHARTER SCHOOLS

When educators and parents discuss the variables for school change and improvement, the list routinely includes class size, class day, and even year-round schooling. Teacher quality is an obvious priority, but one that may be beyond their control. What individual parents always seem to prefer are teachers for their kids who are not too young and inexperienced but not too old, tired, and far removed from the days of their training. They want in short youth and maturity, perhaps the same expectations they have of doctors—which is the reason so many doctors grow mustaches when they are young and starting out. But seldom if ever do parents discuss school size.

That tends to be a given. Parents are programmed to expect and accept that smaller elementary schools will give way to larger middle schools and ultimately to even larger and sometimes huge unified high schools, as if maturity required adaptability to size. They also have been persuaded that larger offers more. That applies to the range of subjects, facilities, labs, studios, theaters, playing fields, and teams that the modern high schools and even larger state universities have to offer. The typical assumption is that size offers economies of scale. But whereas that is sometimes true, education is so labor intensive that as much as 80 percent of its budget is already determined by salaries and benefits. It is thus not an easy matter for parents—much easier for students—to accept school size, especially for offspring in their teens, as a key variable of change.

Almost all charter schools are small. They average about 100 to 150 students. That size is both imposed and chosen. It is frequently compelled by space availability and construction costs. Many charter schools operate in abandoned or unused supermarkets, factories, warehouses—in short, limited but open space. Students generally find the openness unconfining and even expanding in nature; they welcome the high ceilings and even factorylike environment. When new buildings are constructed for charter schools, they are kept small to control costs.

But necessity also meets and embraces ideology. What is central to the nature of charter schools is that they are in fact created apart from regular schools. The contrast is always consciously maintained. They are not part of the existing system. They are creations of preference, favored in a way not unlike preferred futures. They are established with a mission of difference. They are not continuous with what went before and do not carry its past baggage. They have a point of view, a rationale for being. They may invoke earlier traditions and require students to wear uniforms or follow a dress code. Or they may be far out in the future and in effect virtual or cyber schools. But whatever position they occupy in a historical and educational time spectrum, they are born of choice. And they in turn are chosen by parents and students—otherwise they would not exist at all. What is thus established from the outset is that all those who are there are there because they want to be.

Although other factors enter into the choice, school size is increasingly being recognized as a critical determining factor. In fact, a number of large high schools have subdivided themselves into smaller schools or academies as an antidote to impersonality. A recent seven-year study that appeared in the fall issue of the *American Educational Research Journal* documents the success of reorganizing a failing three-thousand-student comprehensive high school into a network of five smaller schools. The newer, smaller schools, as a group, produced better attendance, lower rates of violent incidents, superior reading and writing scores, and higher graduation and college-going rates than what they replaced (www.aera.net). No Child Left Behind needs to be expanded to no child left unknown, unengaged, and unimproved.

The hope also is that smaller schools offer the best of both worlds: variety and familiarity. Anyone who has been caught in the jammed and noisy hallways of a large high school when classes are being changed will find neither. In contrast, in the charter school every student can know every other student regardless of grade level (they are often mixed together), and the traditional hierarchy of grade levels does not prevail. Every teacher knows every student to such an extent that evaluations of student performance, in addition to being one on one, can also be schoolwide. That is possible only in a small school in which every teacher has informed input. In short, size offers community. Meetings can be like town meetings, providing everyone with a voice and vote. A small school can create an environment that is not only student led, but also teacher led. And that brings us to the degree to which ideology and size affect governance.

Size above all permits school communities to be self-learning, self-managing, self-organizing, and self-governing. School governance is a variation of individual governance; the way one learns is of a piece with the way the school works. As a result, charter schools employ a highly selective recruiting and selection process to attract and to hire teachers and support staff who are willing to be part of such a learning and governing structure. And because in most cases there is no tenure, only annual renewal, charter schools are also rigorous in letting teachers go who are not able to thrive in the worlds of learning and governing. In fact, one of the general functions charter schools provide to the education profession as a whole is a safety net to retain teachers who ordinarily might quit the system altogether. Indeed, many give up tenure to join charter schools.

Are charter schools the ideal? Do they always work? Are there no problems? Of course not, but generally the problems and failures are of their own making. They are correctable because they are human fallibilities, not those of an impersonal and inaccessible system. Although they are a minority movement—there are only about two thousand charter schools currently operating in the United States—what is generally not known, let alone publicized, is that charter schools are and have been a major global movement for many years.

The term that international educators and especially staff of the United Nations use is not "charter" but "micro" schools. In some areas of the world they are called "alternative" schools, while in others they are variously designated as "cottage," "community," "village," "grass-roots," "one-room," or "two-room" schools. The common characteristics of micro schools are as follows:

- Smaller in size than traditional schools
- Employ a small number of teachers
- Accommodate a range of grades; not restricted to one grade level
- Generally amplified by technology
- Operate around the clock
- Accommodate older learners or those with jobs
- Ownership may be either private for gain or non-profit
- Regarded as legal schools whose degrees are accepted by all

In many countries with limited tax and governmental structures entrepreneurs are encouraged to fill the education gap by creating private management companies to offer educational services. The global perspective reminds us of the extent to which the charter movement is in fact part of much larger small business entrepreneurial efforts, albeit using pubic funds. That last point is a major source of contention.

Charter schools are public schools. They operate as such by using the same per-capita allocations that regular public schools do. Actually, they are handicapped in at least one major way. They are not given a physical plant. The acquisition and maintenance of a school building is an additional cost that regular schools do not have to absorb, which accounts for the creativity of those who start the schools. Charter schools must enroll enough students to sustain costs and salaries. If they don't, or go into the red, they fold—unlike public schools, which are not subject to the same pressures and are subsidized and allowed to continue operating. The contrast between the two modes of operating schools puzzles business professionals. They in fact find that charter schools have more in common with competitive business environments than public schools.

But the key claim is that charter schools offer an educational alternative. For many students size is enough of a difference; for parents individualized and nurturing attention is enough. But for teachers contemplating giving up tenure or for new graduates worrying about how teaching in a charter school will look on their resumes and affect future employment, they want more. What is thus established immediately is that many teachers who join or switch to charter schools may not be run-of-the-mill types. They want challenge. They may be oddballs who want to remain that way and who are convinced that finding the right environment for their difference will add to their effectiveness and benefit students. Then, too, charter schools similarly attract students who are often independent and march to their own drummer. Such students sometimes hold strong views on the way a school should be run. So do the teachers, but they do not want to be administrators. They want to remain in the classroom but have a strong say in what shapes that classroom and above all to define what determines student success. Finally, especially the experienced teachers who are also subject-matter specialists are not convinced that the way learning is now generally compartmentalized is the way to go. They are thus open to curricular innovation, even though they may have to learn more, partner and often be on the same level with their students, and generally work harder. The double emphasis on curricula and governance, and especially their integration, requires more acknowledgement and appreciation if the promise offered by charter schools is to be understood and perhaps emulated.

CHARTER SCHOOLS IN OPERATION

In Minnesota there are some dozen charter schools distributed throughout the state that operate under the wing of an umbrella organization called Ed/Visions. They include elementary, middle, and high schools. They operate individually and for the most part autonomously. They do not all have the same curricula, although their governance structures are basically alike. They are generally too far apart to be feeder schools for one another. Each one has to make its way in its own community. But they have been in existence long enough, surviving various changes and crises, to be examined, warts and all, with some detail.

The curriculum most favored is project or inquiry learning. There are no separate subject-matter departments to inhibit or limit interdisciplinary range. All specialists have to be also generalists. The governance structure most favored is collaborative. There is no principal and no administrators. Administrative services such as payroll and benefits are outsourced. Others are insourced; contracts to take care of state- and federal-mandated reporting are issued to independent contractors (no benefits are paid). Some operational tasks are taken over by students and teachers, such as custodial duties, computer repair and upgrading, and low-level maintenance and repairs. Teachers take turns serving as administrative "go-to" persons. Cost control is an absolute. Teacher salaries are reduced to offset overspending.

What is project learning and how does it work? And why was it selected as the curriculum of these charter schools? The focus is on a project chosen by the student. Thus, from the outset the basic motivation derives from student self-selection. But topic selection is neither unilateral nor spontaneous. Selection is a patient and complex process of frequent iteration and negotiation. It has to take time because it must have depth and extent. It must be able to sustain extensive and deep study on the one hand, and cut across and tap various disciplines on the other hand. In the process it must also satisfy state course requirements. It can range from the history of local governments in the county or the influence of the silk route on European culture. It can start out on a personal subject of interest, such hockey or the Boy Scouts. But then it is required to develop and be nested within larger frameworks, such as the history and culture of sports in general or the concept of youth organizations. It may be career oriented as well. A student may select landscape design because he or she is thinking of working in that field. In addition to learning about the design of landscapes throughout history and in different parts of the world, he or she also learns the biology of fauna and flora. But in all cases the project drives the learning. It dictates what directions need to be taken and what knowledge must be tracked down. It is relentless, its appetite and demands endless. In the process, the project articulates its own standards of evaluation. At the end of the school year the student is often exhausted but proud.

The roles of the teacher are multiple, and sometimes teaching is the least of them. He or she may not be completely knowledgeable, let alone an expert, on the topic selected. It is unnecessary for the teacher to have such knowledge, though, because the emphasis is on a generic journey.

The first stage of the mentoring role is providing assistance with topic selection. The teacher-mentor may have to play devil's advocate. Nothing frivolous or indulgent gets through the academic and project hurdles. The mentor may ask that the topic proposed be revisited and even revised a number of times. Students learn quickly the different facets or dimensions of a diamond in the rough. Once the topic has survived sufficiently the ordeal by fire, the mentor requests three written submissions: an outline of the major subdivisions of the topic, a list of resources needed, and a timetable for the compilation of the resources.

As the project gets underway, the mentor-teacher also becomes a broker. Acting as the basic bridge between the project and the academic disciplines and knowledge bases it requires, the broker helps to negotiate general liaisons and individual sessions with members of the faculty who have the subject-matter expertise needed. But frequently the expertise or the depth required is not available in-house. The broker and the student then must extend their search outside the school: to the local university, members of different professions, and above all expert websites and professionals all over the country and even the world who can be contacted by e-mail.

Typically, such experts are generous with their time and knowledge to students interested in their field and work. A more mundane but no less important form that brokering takes is to insure that the basic minimum subject-area requirements for graduation are met and mastered. That may involve the student enrolling in the appropriate classes in English or math or social studies, or taking those courses online.

The final task of the teacher is to facilitate evaluation and presentation. In addition to internal review by the entire faculty involved, the topic selected and the depth of its examination may require external peer review as well. Tapping a small budget for honoraria, the teacher-broker identifies and secures expert evaluation. Finally, after all revisions and corrections have been made the teacher brings together faculty knowledgeable about presentations — speech, the arts, communications, technology, and so on. They explore and recommend some of the best ways the project can be presented at the end-of-the-year symposium, as well as to others outside of the school. Such presentations do more to build community support on the one hand and recruit new students on the other than any elaborate and expensive public relations campaign. Moreover, truth in advertising prevails.

Governance is equally involving. Teachers and students collectively run the school. There is no principal. There are no other administrators. A teacher with accounting ability keeps the books. If none exists or is available, a part-time bookkeeper, frequently retired, is hired. But he or she is not independent. He or she reports to and services a financial committee of faculty and students. That committee, in addition to having overall primary, but not exclusive, responsibility for allocations, is responsible, like every committee, for communicating on the school e-mail network both its deliberations and its proposed actions. The latter must allow at least a week for feedback. Any faculty member may stop the process from going forward by invoking the "square one" rule. That means that an item is to be taken back to its origins and revisited before being presented again.

The governance process is sustained by continuous and clear communications—no gobbledygook language to obscure financial explanations or insider techno-babble for computer acquisitions. To insure participation and involvement, governance is built into teacher evaluation as part of general competency.

The committees run the school. Their recommendations, once they survive feedback, are decisive—unlike those of most school committees. Moreover, transparency rules. Everything is out in the open. There are no secret deals, no limited access. Even personnel discussions and decisions on retention or termination, and salary increases or reductions, are displayed and known. Teachers are reviewed by teachers, not by administrators who often have and reward their pets. Performance is always judged as both individual and collective. To what extent has a teacher contributed to the development and growth of students and project learning, and to sustaining the governance structure that determines and enriches the collaborative community of the school?

The multiple instructional roles are aligned with the multiple governance roles. How everyone learns and how everyone lives together is of a piece. Agreement is not by majority vote but by consensus. Faculty leadership follows the formula of the Roman legion: primus inter pares—first among equals. The same holds true for heads of committees. Moreover, being first is temporary and rotational. If the situation requires another kind of expertise, then the position of being first rotates to someone who is equally qualified.

What are the downsides? The amount and extent of academic work and governance work are enormous. The typical day for faculty starts earlier and lasts longer than it does for students. Sometimes weekends are also involved. As one ex-principal, who went back to teaching in one of the Ed/Visions charter schools, noted: "I used to worry about getting them there. Now the problem is getting them to leave." Project learning frequently strains teachers beyond their subject-matter comfort zones. Many yearn to teach a single and simple class in their discipline. In addition, the job is intensely multitasked. Just keeping track of all the projects and the various stages of incompletion compels teachers to be learning and project managers. Because there are no principals, teachers must take turns serving as the "go-to" person—the one the secretary calls on to speak to visiting officials, unhappy parents, prospective students and their parents, and so on. Some faculty nostalgically yearn for the old arrangement of the central office that took care of "administrivia." Sharing or supervising maintenance and custodial chores is often not high on their list of priorities, although all voted to do it and voted also on what to do with money saved. Consensus is often taxing and often admittedly takes the form of agreement by exhaustion. Some faculty and students are weary of "Yes, but" types and those who always trot out their predictable hobbyhorses. But, as with democracy itself, any other way would be less desirable.

Such negatives do not affect new teachers, because they really do not know what they are getting themselves into. But it sometimes wearies more experienced types. Some may go back to more traditional schools where they can simply teach their subject-matter courses, where they do not have to shoulder the burden of collaborative governance, and where they can come to and leave work just before and just after the students do. It is understandable. Educators, like everyone else, do not want to be martyrs. But such legitimate discontent should not be the final word or obscure the extent to which some charter schools have broken from past practice and established viable alternative models for the future. Here are some of the more radical features of the Ed/Visions charter schools:

Administration: Teachers have demonstrated that they do not have to leave the classroom to be administrators.

Leadership: Teachers are the instructional leaders.

Learning Management: Acting as mentors, brokers, coaches, and facilitators of learning, and as project management, teachers have demonstrated their ability to be operationally multitasked.

Intervention Advocates: Alternatively acting as cheerleader and taskmaster, the teacher has to be a creative and entrepreneurial advocate of interventions that advance student-chosen projects.

Governance: Accepting collaboration and consensuality as the norms of governance, teachers have demonstrated how much the operational and decision-making environment contributes to and determines effective schools and learning; and finally that teachers alone are the best ones to integrate the classroom and the school, instruction and administration.

These are no small advances. Essentially they support a new definition of the teacher as a leader and of the master teacher as a manager of learning. Both instances signal a complete break from past models, which required teachers to leave the classroom in order to become administrators. Equally as important, charter schools revisit and even confront the issues raised by Richard Elmore about educators being self-examining and self-determining about the environments in which they operate and learn.

The charter school answer is simple and direct: bring the external in line and in harmony with the internal; align form and function; make structure and performance cater to and become versions of each other. Collaborative governance and collaborative learning are of a piece. Ideally, one cannot tell where the one begins and the other leaves off. Size permits community but governance creates it. It also goes further and contributes to the community of best practices. Not all charter schools are adventurous or experimental. Nor are they the only schools involved in project or inquiry learning. But if we did not have competition and did not create alternative outlets like incubator labs and industries on university and business campuses, we would never have any actual working models of a significantly different way to structure learning. To be sure, we could always theorize and speculate, but the supreme advantage of having an actual model in hand is that it not only provides a specific and tangible curriculum for altering the preparation of future teachers in colleges of education, but also demonstrates that the future is available and imitable. Curiously, then, competition and choice may be giving education a new lease on life.

CHAPTER 23

Accountable Accountability: Curing the Cure

"Holding public education accountable" has increasingly become the language of its critics and the legislation of politicians. Indeed, No Child Left Behind is essentially an accountability document that not only spells out the kind and levels of student and teacher performance, but also the consequences of failing to achieve stated goals according to a tight timetable. Many objections have been raised to this comprehensive and, to some, relentless commitment to accountability. What are the principle arguments advanced?

- Too much, too soon, too top down
- Testing as the sole basis of evaluation
- States having to align their tests and levels with national standards and timetables
- Too centralized; in effect Big Brother national control
- Increasing student performance to unprecedentedly high levels
- Abolishing social promotion
- Passing tests as a condition of high school graduation

The arguments often become a them-versus-us contest, with local and state rights advocates taking on the feds. Or the debate generates the rhetoric of martyrdom or a litany of whose oxes are being gored. Then, too, educators are protesting that the external pressures for accountability are backing them into a no-win corner: they are being judged by ways and means often essentially foreign to the educational process itself. The intensity and partisanship notwithstanding, three factors restore balance:

1. If education itself had been sufficiently and regularly accountable, there would be no need to insist on accountability now. In short, education brought it on itself.

2. If education had raised its standards of student performance and equalized its accessibility to all students, especially in urban and rural areas, no massive national intervention would have been required. In short, education has been found wanting in both areas.

3. Finally, only a national approach could mediate between the variable tax bases of urban, suburban, and rural areas, on the one hand, and state standards, on the other, to bring about equality of opportunity and of delivery. And only a federal commitment could reflect the need for valuing the future of student human capital as a national resource. In this instance, education is guilty of convenient tunnel vision and myopia concerning social responsibility and accountability.

Given the advantages of hindsight and the failings of education, accountability was therefore inevitable. What to many is surprising is that it came from a Republican administration that generally has favored less centralized control. The administration's further endorsement of vouchers, even for use in parochial schools, has led to the charge that the current secretary of education is out to break up the current configuration of public education, to bust unions, and to encourage and stimulate a more competitive environment in which education will be more accountable. Although there may be some truth to some of these accusations, the problem generally with intrusive legislation, especially on the federal level, is that it always involves playing politics. But those who accuse the government of such tactics play politics themselves, as occurred recently when the Ohio Federation of Teachers took charter schools to court to have them declared illegal. Incidentally, the federation lost the case. Given their own failings and partisanship, what should educators do other than scream and cry foul?

Three options are available. The first and most obvious may be the least pleasant: compliance. Align classroom and school goals with national goals as defined in NCLB, and accept its accompanying tests of accountability. Allow for some catch-up time, anticipate some bail-outs or closures of failing schools, and hopefully see results produced under external pressures to perform.

The second option is flexibility. Educators are not bereft of options. If single-focused tests are distortive, there is nothing to preclude supplements. If acceptable and respectable assessments should employ multiple measures, should display moving pictures and not one-shot stills, and should be organic and integral to the learning process, then correctives are available. Supplemental assessments can restore multiplicity; on-going data tracking can redeem single-shot judgments. Even high school graduation assessment can and has been shared and worked out with colleges that already accepted the graduates. But the third option, engaging and altering the externality of the intervention, is not that easily accommodated and in fact requires more leadership initiatives on the part of educators.

For accountability to be effective, it must not be parasitical or punitive. Rather, it needs to become a contributory, participatory, and proactive partner. That means it cannot be shunned or scorned but must be welcomed inside the house. Moreover, it has to be invited to dinner. For accountability to be effective, it must be made internally proximate to and absorbed into the systemic structures of education. In other words, accountability should be the focused occasion for reviewing and perhaps altering the interfaces between input and output. Above all, accountability itself has to become accountable as an agent of value added. It has to become an ally, not an enemy; a partner, not a prosecutor. In short, it must become organic to the goals and processes of education as determined and defined by educators, not bean counters.

But that in turn requires identifying and strengthening existing weak links in the internal chains of accountability, and finding and implementing internal checks and balances so that schools become self-correcting. In other words, accountability has to be built into the process so seamlessly that it becomes the accepted way we educate.

For that kind of total overhaul to occur, distinctions need to be made between imposed and internalized kinds of accountability. That in turn requires the development of two major guidelines. The first is articulating a general principle of accountability; the second is describing the kind of accountability whose self-correcting contribution is inherently interfacing, integrative, and interactive.

ACCOUNTABILITY STANDARDS

The classic definition of accountability is taken from the Volvo factory experience. Unhappy with the number of cars emerging with major defects, Volvo was advised by consultants to introduce a quality-control team at the end of the production line. The new quality team was zealous. The number of car with defects immediately increased. It finally became clear via employee suggestions that quality control had to be distributed throughout the production line and become part of every worker's job description. Defects decreased dramatically. One month later the factory celebrated a no-defect day.

The key value of accountability is thus distributed quality control. But it does not work unless all parts are operational and in harmony. First, controls are inevitable. Invariably they are statistical. Data is thus the agent of control. What is counted counts. Second, checkpoints have to be identified throughout the process and consistently maintained. They must be meaningfully spaced. That rationale should be clear, even transparent. If possible, evaluation should not be overly intrusive. But above all, it must be able to accommodate the complexity of differentiation. Third, quality must be clearly defined. It should include both overall and disaggregated goals and paths in rubric fashion. That way quality becomes continuous and can be a total measure of the range of difference as well as common patterns of collective performance. In short, quality becomes a mirror match between macro and micro, totality and individuality, and minimally takes two forms.

SHARED ACCOUNTABILITY

So defined and promulgated, accountability must then be distributed and diffused throughout the school and the district. If it is not everyone's task, it is no one's task. Appointing an accountability or assessment czar or hiring an assessment consulting firm may be public relations tokenism. A one-size-fits-all external system is a hastily applied Band-Aid treating various symptoms, not causes. Requiring everyone to be accountable for the creation and control of quality, finding and focusing on the key bridge points in the process, and above all building in the rubric correctives and alternative growth paths to structure quality goals—such totality makes accountability educationally accountable.

ACCOUNTABILITY LEADERSHIP: SINGULAR, SHARED, INDIVIDUALIZED

To be effective and internal, accountability cannot become the monopoly, property, or focus of a czar of assessment. It must be multiple and multiply delivered. In particular, it first requires the kind of total overview administrators alone possess. Only they can orchestrate a total quality approach. Only they can establish the overall school targets and standards that all must accept as the basis for aligning shared and individual goals. Only administrators can monitor everyone, having the inclusive range of expertise that spans the entire process and can address the total structure and flow, and identify where it is broken or blocked. Only they can define and promulgate what and how accountability must now contribute internally to performance improvement. The creation of a series of common checks and balances that internalize accountability needs to be described.

But the leadership has to be multiply shared as well. Minimally, to encourage more extensive buy-in by teachers and staff, they should be invited to be directly involved in defining standards of student success. They also should be called on to help with the detective work of identifying weak structural links or information gaps. Above all, they should be advised that whatever changes they recommend must be built-in and self-correcting to be genuinely accountable. Teachers also have to share, design, and implement accountability standards and procedures across grade levels and subject matter. Finally, to insure individual buy-in, accountability has to be delivered to each teacher in each class in each subject. Prioritizing goals for alignment must start at the base with the individual teacher, then proceed upward through grade and subject-matter levels, and finally rest at the top, supporting school- and districtwide goals. Such a bottom-up approach assures that the emphasis remains centered on the classroom and student performance. To tie together all levels with common foci, here are five key fulcrum points for leveraging greater accountability and change:

1. What is separate should be joined.
2. What is unilateral should be shared.
3. What is held in reserve or hoarded should flow.
4. What is vertical should be leveled to the horizontal.
5. What is directive should be collaborative.

INTEGRATION AS ACCOUNTABILITY

One of the values of accountability is that it pays a great deal of attention to what falls through the cracks. It compels rescuing fragments from oblivion—bridging gaps between teaching and student achievement, and aligning school goals with externally assessed and mandated objectives. But at the heart of all disjunctive structures is the need to integrate administration, instruction, and measurement.

As noted earlier, accountability works only when all parts operate in harmony. Indeed, the value that accountability regularly adds is synthesis. The only way all parts can work together effectively is through the common holistic model of internalized and shared accountability. Not unlike the commonality of quality, it requires the acceptance by all of the integration of three foci: administration, instruction, and measurement.

The accountable teacher thus not solely instructs but also administers, manages, and evaluates learning. The accountable classroom becomes a miniature of the whole. Administration, instruction, and measurement are integrated into one seamless operation.

In summary, then, educators need to hearken to the wise warning of Robert Frost about building fences, in "Mending Wall":

Before I build a wall
I'd ask to know
What I was walling in
or walling out

In the process of walling out we also unfortunately may be imprisoning ourselves. In trying to keep out accountability or raising obstacles and objections to its coming, we may be devaluing our resources and limiting our options. We may become, in short, prisoners of our own fences.

Rather than bewail their lot and seek martyrdom, educators need to seize the day. They need to rally. They need to turn an enemy into an ally. They need to clean up their act with the broom of educational accountability and prove that they are in fact smarter and more resourceful about accountability than all the bureaucrats combined.

Instead of knee-jerk resistance, educators can offer enlightened compliance. That way the external gods of accountability can become internalized and institutionalized. Educators can serve and evaluate their differentiated students both qualitatively and quantitatively; create integrative structures that contain their own checks and balances; individually and collectively embrace a process of quality control that is organically faithful to the common goals of education; and, finally, honor their professionalism by still being masters of their own house. Who knows? Perhaps, in the process, education may even set the example for government and business.

CHAPTER 24

Research-Based Learning

In many ways, far from being understimulated or undernourished, education currently finds itself in possession of an embarrassment of research riches. Moreover, the utilization of such research has become de rigueur and professionally urgent. Research-based education has become the battle cry of federal funding agencies, foundations, curriculum developers, and educational leaders. Research has become a seal of approval, especially for new curricula.

The range of research is enormous. Studies of various ways to engage students have produced a wide range of options that go way beyond what was available just a decade ago. These options include the different approaches of differentiated education, project education, service learning, character education, inquiry learning, and so on. Part of that development is the effectiveness movement and its focus on finding the most effective way to teach reading, math, science, foreign languages, and so on. Indeed, the debate about which is most effective, especially in the area of math instruction, has really become a contest of research findings.

Electronic access has compounded the overload of research availability. It also has, in many instances, made the ignorance of and failure to use research increasingly inexcusable. Much or all of the content and process of the national certification of teachers by the National Board of Professional Teaching Standards is research based. Increasingly, an outstanding teacher is defined as one who is continuously more knowledgeable not only about his or her subject matter, but also about the research that will make the mastery and communication of that subject more effective. For example, in schools with a commitment to becoming learning organizations, knowledge of the research literature and its applications to teaching constitutes the weekly meeting agenda. In some instances such knowledge has been made part of teacher evaluation. In recognition of its contributory value, job descriptions have been amplified now to include research knowledge.

To demonstrate quickly the electronic availability of research, here is an admittedly incomplete sampling of research-based learning on the subject of educational leadership. For standards, there are those produced in 1996 by the Interstate School Leaders Licensure Consortium. The full text is to be found at www.ccsso.org. The National Association of Elementary School Principals (NAESP) just published its own guidelines, which include a strong call for instructional leadership. The association maintains its own website, www.naesp.org. The granddaddy of all electronic research sources is ERIC, especially its Clearinghouse on Educational Management (http://eric.uoregon.edu). A variety of viewpoints can be found on visionary leadership, servant leadership, facilitative leadership, ethical leadership, creating a learning organization, and so on. Refining the focus, for example, to instructional leadership, information, findings, and discussions can be found on the website of the Annenberg Institute for School Reform (www.annenberginstitute.org). Further discussion of the experiences of educational administrators as instructional leaders can be found on the organizational website of the NAESP Leadership Academy. The National Association of Secondary School Principals has developed and offers on its website a self-assessment tool to evaluate leadership skills (www.principals.org). The website also includes suggestions for growth activities and self-improvement based on the self-assessment.

Finally, current and cutting-edge leadership developments are also electronically available. Teacher instructional leadership, for example, was explored in a national forum sponsored by the U.S. Department of Education in April 1998. The forum included the ideas and experiences of some 120 teacher-leaders, all of which is available at www.ed.gov/pubs/Teacher. Additional practices redefining the teacher's role appear on www.icl.org and, of course, ERIC (www.ed.gov.databases.ERIC.html).

Often research finds its modest beginnings in the thoughts and questions of its researchers. For example, in his recent article on educational leadership, Richard Elmore (2002) was struck by the degree to which serious and probing questions about practice were not being asked. He noted, "People who work in schools do not pay attention to the connection between how they organize and manage themselves and how they take care of their own and the students' learning. The structure and resources of the organization are like wallpaper—after living with the same wallpaper for a certain number of years, people cease to see it."

Actually, the problem of micromyopia is not limited to education, but also characterizes business and government. Not acknowledging the generic nature of the problem being posed limits access to problem-solving research in other fields and sectors. In fact, the literature of high-performance corporations not only directly engages this critical problem, but also makes its solution a key condition and hurdle for becoming a high-performance organization. But whether or not there is an awareness of its wider use in other fields, the problem identified by Elmore is ripe for the picking. It undoubtedly will be studied and researched for many reasons. It is a serious and significant issue: "In the present political and social environment of schooling, this lack of attention is dangerous and irresponsible." Elmore is himself a major research contributor, and his reputation lends additional weight to the problem posed. Above all, his research goes to the heart of the problem and is linked to other reviews and definitions of the basic models of learning. In other words, research acts as the avant-garde, alerting practitioners to what will be studied in the future. Indeed, one of the key ways of evaluating research undertakings is by the extent to which they are presently directed or future driven. The best are both.

Not surprisingly, the application of research is often rightly the object of research itself. For example, finding ways of making instruction, administration, or evaluation more effective has taken the form of a number of add-ons or overlays. Thus, the concern with integrating evaluation and instruction has led to the formulation of instruction-based, assisted assessment, and test-based instruction. Differentiated instruction often is rewritten as rubric-based or driven instruction, just as project or inquiry learning become collaborative or team learning. Already noted is the basic mother lode of research-based leadership learning.

What all these add-ons and overlays signify is that education is in the perpetual process of playing catch-up. The problem is not that there is not enough research or that it is beside the point. It is that research is not integrated with practice. When it is shared across the board to attract wider buy-in, then what emerges is a community of best practices. What that means is that every educator, in addition to becoming knowledgeable about existing and applicable research, also has the task of integrating it with current practice. The goal is for all to be of a piece, and to negotiate the acceptance of research by the community of practitioners.

No area perhaps dramatizes the gap between research and practice more than the new research on the brain and the emergence of the new fields of cognitive science and educational psychology and genetics. The mapping of the centers of the brain has paralleled and occasionally crossed over to the process of cracking of the genetic code. The claim is that when blended together they represent the new sciences of human nature. Clearly, this enormously complex and fascinating subject is beyond the scope of this study, but its applications to education are not.

The key areas that have been researched and are now rendered with greater precision is how we learn; how we manage, retain, and enlarge our knowledge base; and how our development is programmed genetically and stimulated environmentally. The stakes are high. The old debate between nature and nurture is revived, but this time it is being viewed not as versus but as via. Each impacts and changes the other. They are secretly and openly interlocked. On the one hand, there are limits to what society and education can do to make people smarter and happier citizens. But, on the other hand, environment impacts and shapes genetics not occasionally but often, including while development is occurring. Continuous mental activity can delay and even prevent dementia and Alzheimer's.

Further, the traditional patterns of learning development established by Jean Piaget and Erik Erikson have been not just challenged, but altered, to mirror the new findings of brain research and cognitive science. Thus, the traditional taxonomy currently being taught to teachers in colleges of education is being not only questioned but even overturned. Given that claim, it is not surprising that one of the most insistent new add-ons is brain research.

Even the way we teach reading and employ imaginative literature needs to be reexamined to enhance its value. Imagination needs to be used not only as a major connecting force, but also as one that governs the way we think, behave, and even aspire. Imagination is amphibious. It inhabits the worlds of reason and fantasy, of the present

and the future. It also tricks us into embarking on difficult though ful-
filling tasks that we never would have undertaken if we knew better
or relied solely on reason. With its visionary power stirring us on, we
grow; and we take risks of growth that rationally we might shun.

What, then, are the implications and applications of this particular research for education? For example, based on research findings, teachers
may decide to make more extensive use of the arts to teach reading in
general, and employ biographies to enliven history, sociology, and political science. The arts depicting social and economic struggle need to be
blended with the statistics of inequity. Art tends to be holistic and thus
serves as an antidote to excessive specialization. Asking students to assume the roles of different historical figures or to reenact great debates
develops the scenarios of the imagination and anchors learning in dramatic constructs of historical meaning. Above all, the arts tap the capacity of the imagination to think around corners. In short, the new research
is explaining to teachers that the way we think is the way we learn; and
in particular the way we imagine is the way we grow and innovate.

One last yield from the field of cognitive science. Much of what has
been learned about the way the brain works and thinks has come about
through the research on artificial intelligence, robotics, and computer
programs. What rapidly has became apparent in the process is that although the computer can compute faster and more accurately than we
can, for example, the square root of 487, the apparently simple question of which door you would use to leave the room would drive a computer program brain to distraction. Even sophisticated programs have
difficulty with abstract notions of what is a door and what does it mean
to go out. The net result is that not only have we gained more respect
for the way the human brain works and learns, but also the attempts at
mechanical replication have led in turn to more precise mapping of
brain functions and behaviors.

What, then, is the upshot and impact of research on education now
and increasingly in the future? The following responses and adjustments seem to be justified.

The proliferation of curricula approaches presents particular challenges to older teachers unfamiliar with these new developments. It
also poses administrative problems of providing professional development and matching appropriate teachers to curricula. (This is discussed
separately and in greater detail in the chapter concerned with optimiz-

ing curricula.) The research on best matches of teacher and curricula can provide a critical contribution. Teachers have to become increasingly computer literate if they are not only to access research findings on the Internet, but also exercise critical judgment assessing the validity and veracity of what is available from various websites. Such research literacy is also needed to understand and make optimal use of the various electronic data tracking systems assessing performance.

Increasingly the problems or issues of education are not limited to education. Efforts must be made not only by educators but, more importantly perhaps, by researchers to broaden the base of their inquiry to include other sectors in which a given problem also exists and in which its solution may have been found. Eliminating or reducing the general isolation of education undoubtedly would help education and business, for example, to be allies rather than enemies.

Obviously, educators increasingly should become aware not only of what is being researched, but also what is not. Like Elmore, they have to have input into shaping the research agenda. Those who pursue the doctorate have the rare opportunity to actually do that research. Teachers occupy a key nexus for both implementation and integration. First, they preside over wiring the findings into place and making them a seamless part of daily practice. The classroom serves as their testing ground, and feedback is crucial for approval and correction. Second, all the add-ons noted above have to be integrated into a new more holistic complexity. Thus, instruction has to be test related, assessment driven, brain research compatible, rubric differentiated, and so on. No wonder that curricula developers are seeking to fill the gap by making all the adjustments in advance and delivering an already integrated or aligned product. Otherwise the complexity of factoring in all these elements might be so overwhelming that it would detract from teaching on the one hand and compel a kind of catch-up that might never be successful on the other.

In their most intense form, the challenges of research knowledge and application may bring about role and structural changes. If teachers, especially those who opt for national certification, increasingly are expected to know more about research and its findings, such that research expands their job description and becomes part of regular evaluation, their roles may accordingly have to change. They may wish to be also recognized as research-based teaching or learning leaders; and they may expect governance structures to be altered to allow them greater input into the decision-making process. In turn educational administrators whose curricula as well as subject-matter knowledge base may be strained to the point of inadequacy may opt for or support a more collaborative leadership partnership that would officially document and sanction such changes in role and structure.

Teachers would be required to become more knowledgeable about what teaching machines can do and perhaps, at this point, what they cannot do at all or as effectively as human teachers. Above all, teachers have to abandon the extremes of regarding educational technology as worthless or as a panacea. That would clear the field for them to be receptive to research focused on human-machine symbiosis. Finding and negotiating such interfaces would constitute a new mission for teachers and offer solutions to current educational problems that are crushing and even debilitating.

The mapping of the brain in terms of basic learning and higher-level knowledge transfer requires basic adjustments of fundamental pedagogical patterns of developmental leaning. Brain-guided and -compatible instruction is the obvious new order of the day, just as, perhaps, the new science of human nature replaces the old.

The surprising rescue of the imagination in general and the arts in particular has brought about a new add-on: arts-assisted or arts-enhanced instruction. Not only will the arts assist general learning; they also can affect aspiration and future dreams, especially those of disadvantaged or disillusioned youth.

There is little doubt that the driving force of educational research is convergence, especially of the human and the machine, of nature and nurture, of the aspiration of imagination and the determinism of genetics. Convergence finds its home in education, in which it acquires the force of synthesis. But that in turn requires educators to abandon the either-or for the both-and approach, and the false dichotomies and oppositions between teachers and administrators, teachers and students, public and charter schools, education and business, and teachers and parents. The ultimate contribution of research then may be to give educators a new vision of the unified nature of their task and role. Above all, it requires that teachers work together in learning and planning teams in which lessons can be shaped by collaborative applications of the latest research.

CHAPTER 25

Optimizing Curricula

Clearly parents cannot hope to understand, let alone master, the range of curricula choices available. In fact, many educators don't. But curricula choice is part of and is as important as school choice. Parents know that one size does not fit all. They know that what and how their kids study not only can make a difference in terms of their kids' general success, but also taps and optimizes kids' different intelligences and growth potential. Parents know what turns their kids on or off, what they are drawn to and what bores them. In other words, education is a matching game: matching kids to what engages them. That requires double knowledge; this chapter will discuss the curricula half.

Although what is presented here is not an exhaustive survey of curricula choices, it is representative of a number of challenging choices currently available. Equally as important, the curricula options have been matched with the kind of teachers best able to optimize such curricula and with the kind of students who will benefit most from their selection. In other words, the choices involve multiple factors and underscore the need for multiple planning.

Because of the pressures of accountability and high-stakes testing, the development of measurement appears currently to rival and perhaps even to have eclipsed the development of curricula. Knowing where students are and what they know appears more important than knowing how they got there. The end seems more important than the journey. In addition, technology has come to the aid of the evaluation of instruction by providing precise and rapid monitoring, tracking, and displaying of student performance data disaggregated by individual, class, grade level, and school. In some cases, evaluation has even crossed the line to drive scripted curricula, which, sadly, are sometimes called "teacher proof." As already noted, the danger is that such prescribed curricula generally are pitched to the least creative and independent teachers and students. Indeed, prescriptive methodology inadvertently may provide the transition to and offer the strongest argument for replacing such limited instructors with machines. Brave new worlds of Big Brother require and thrive on standardization and obedience.

What is lamentable about such trends of limited aspiration is that during the last two decades there has been such incredibly rich and robust curricula development that education seemed poised for a quantum leap. More comprehensive ways of organizing and reorganizing subject matter, and engaging student interest and involvement, have appeared. Here is just a partial list: differentiated education, service or place learning, project or inquiry education, character or moral education, school-to-work transition training, life skills training, integrated or holistic studies, whole school reading programs. Moreover, these curricula have been carefully researched and tested, and adjusted for different student populations. Publishers, often partnering with faculty and instructional designers, have produced the necessary materials, audiovisuals, and workbooks to support implementation. But the effort often fell short of comprehensive acceptance on the one hand, and of competent performance on the other. Why? The answer may reveal as much about education in general as it does about principals and teachers in particular.

The problem is the matching process, or rather the mismatching process. Generally, curriculum designers are silent as to the kind of teachers they would prefer to teach their programs. It is understandable politically and economically. They do not wish to alienate their customers or prematurely limit their market. Typically, they describe the special and unique features of their latest creation, tout its many applications, and document its successes. Even the few who provide professional development as a condition of sale seldom boldly and directly describe the kind of educators who would find this curriculum congenial and embrace it enthusiastically. The blurbs of praise from teachers in the field, a sample of administrators, and some professors of education are as far as the curriculum developers will go. Instead, they occasionally may offer a few observations that are indirect and usually mild requests for teacher adjustments of perspective, orientation, and temperament—most of which are so innocuous and generalized that they offer little guidance. And most unfair of all, it usually puts administrators on the spot to pick the best teachers for a new curriculum often mandated by the superintendent or the board for the entire district.

What are principals or directors of instruction to do? If the curricula are relatively new or innovative, the chances are that administrators also have little or no experience working with them. The blind are leading the blind. Then, too, because frequently a number of different curricula are being introduced at the same time, with typical haste and desperation, the principal and teaching staff may be stretched thin. Finally, at meetings of faculty, parents, community, and board members, principals are often expected to display the range of their curricula knowledge and to respond to many questions, especially from parents, that often exceed their knowledge base.

One possible way out of the dilemma is to tell the truth—namely, that this is not a one-size-fits-all process. Different curricula should be not assigned or distributed in an arbitrary fashion but matched. But before that can be done a teacher profile for each curriculum has to be developed. Such a profile would bridge the stated goals of curricula developers and reduce the trial-and-error chaos of assigning curricula without carefully selecting teachers and guiding them through implementation. What is needed is a column A and a column B. Creating a teacher profile that is shaped and defined by that curriculum and that also maximizes and optimizes its implementation may bring more precision, sanity, and focus to the selection process. In other words, an extracurricular task is required. A series of fused job-curricula descriptions has to be developed so that administrators can play the role of match-maker; such descriptions could guide administrators in the selection of educators as well as of appropriate professional development and evaluation. Below is a sampling in the form of want ads of the instructional demands for the implementation of three curricula: differentiated education, service learning, and project learning.

WANT AD: EDUCATORS FOR DIFFERENTIATED EDUCATION

Positioning

Teachers accustomed to being in charge and to occupying the center of the classroom may have difficulty implementing differentiated education (DE) (Simkins et al. 2002). Repositioning is required. Students occupy the center, teachers the periphery of the circle.

Monitoring Multiplicity

Control is no longer possible through singular, across-the-board assignments. Monitoring is the dominant management mode. Juggling many balls in the air at the same time is the norm.

Alternatives

DE requires constant alternative approaches—different strokes for different folks. No one way works for all. In addition, variety should also include hierarchy. Approaches should offer adjusted levels of performance and aspiration, ideally as a rubric (Exemplars Project 2002).

Assessment

No one form of evaluation should be used. In addition, the kinds of assessment should be adjusted by grade level (chronology and brain research), and pitched to different performance levels. As Blake said, "One law for the ox and the lion is oppression."

Progressive Levels

DE requires that students who display increasingly higher levels of potential be assessed accordingly. Thus, it might be helpful to follow the medieval four-part progression—apprentice, journeyman, associate, and master—and to develop assessments that match those levels.

Overall Composite

To be effective in a DE class with a specific subject matter, the instructor should be both a specialist and generalist. DE also requires extensive management skills. In many ways a DE class is not only taught but also administered. Keeping track of all the individuation taking place, generating multiple approaches to learning and assessment, and providing customized instruction require the flexibility and patience of an air traffic controller. Being able to operate a good computer tracking and monitoring system may save the instructor's sanity. Finally, DE enables educators to know their students more thoroughly and deeply than ever before. But they have to work hard to achieve that admirable goal.

WANT AD: EDUCATORS FOR SERVICE LEARNING

Philosophy

The key philosophy to embrace for service learning (SL), sometimes also called Place-Learning, is that of John Dewey. In the late nineteenth century Dewey lamented the gulf between formal schooling and students' lives in the community. His double solution was experiential and place-based learning. Students would learn by doing, and the doing would take place outside of school. The student would not only receive but also contribute.

Focus

SL is not community service. It is an academic program in which the community serves as the curriculum. There are thus always two subject-matter areas: traditional academic subjects, and the problems and opportunities the community offers to task those subjects. But the second drives the first. The challenges compel the acquisition of knowledge and skills. In other words, in SL the desire to learn is not imposed but chosen. The academics needed are learned in order to serve the needs of the community.

Case Manager/Social Worker

Ideally, teachers of SL should have had sociology as their second subject-matter major. That would have introduced them to the methodology of community needs assessment and provided the perspective to view the community as a learning and problem-solving lab. What would emerge is a community that offers a significant range of challenges: social, political, economic, cultural, demographic, ecological, and so on. As case managers or social workers, students gradually become aware of the dynamics of different needs. The choices are almost unlimited: monitoring local drinking water, escorting seniors to supermarkets to shop, finding or building places for the homeless to live, providing instruction for kids in shelters for battered families, and so on. The challenge is always twofold: how to engage and solve community problems and how to use academics in the process. The key question students involved in SL have to ask is not "What do I know?" but "What do I need to know to solve this problem?" The operative word is "need"—that releases the motivation to learn.

Team Building and Coaching

Virtually all SL tasks involve groups of individuals who need to work together collaboratively. Thus, an SL teacher has to train students to work together and introduce them to the group dynamics of conflict resolution and negotiation. Team leadership should be rotational and driven by varied competencies that can fulfill specific needs. Teachers do not chair or direct the teams, but serve as their coaches.

Researcher

Both the doing and the learning must be rigorous because SL operates in a lab environment. The first step of research is inventory: "What do we know about this issue or situation?" The answers come from experiential and research sources, in that order. Students have to be trained to observe, to gather information through questions, and to formulate hypotheses to be further tested. Once that process has gone as far as it can go, the stimulating and wider frameworks that often reside in previous research are tapped. The researcher-teacher introduces students to library and Internet research so that they can access what others have thought and said about this problem. Gradually and almost unknowingly, the students are brought within a community of scholars; the final stage of their efforts is to make a contribution to the body of knowledge. At that point they, like their teachers, are researcher-learners.

Managers and Arrangers

Many of the tasks of managing SL are mundane but critical. They include scheduling appointments, transportation, safety, parental approval and cooperation, legal and liability issues, and insurance. Teachers need to serve short stints with and be briefed by district-level administrators responsible for such logistics and legalistics. The care with which all the above are administered can make or break an SL program. Teachers who find this an unprofessional burden should not be involved in SL.

Colearners

Once the important tasks above have been attended to and hopefully mastered, the teacher of SL has to make one final major role adjustment. No one teacher could possibly possess a knowledge of the range of problems encountered in SL and the academics to help solve them. And so, in a sense, the teacher has no other choice but to become a colearner and experience with students the vulnerability of ignorance on the one hand and the final pride of contribution on the other hand. In short, students and teachers are on the same level and learn and develop together. Teachers must be able to confront and interpret the unpredictable nature of experiences with the same uncertainty and immediacy felt by students.

Satisfying Requirements and Meeting Standards

The greater the distance between a curriculum and standard, traditional academic practice, the more bridges have to be built and linkages established. Thus, a recurrent high priority of all SL activities is record keeping. Typically, students enrolled in SL activities write a great deal, as much as twice what students do in regular composition courses. Most SL projects easily can be linked to history, social sciences, and the sciences. Understanding quantitative methods and displaying findings requires knowledge of basic math plus graphs, pie charts, and matrices. It is the role of the teacher constantly to identify and track the degree to which SL is in fact an academic activity, hopefully at the highest levels of performance. Indeed, the positive findings of Lieberman and Hoody (1998) of discipline and self-growth and those of Cummins (1996) of documented gains in terms of GPA should bolster and inform the integration of academic and experiential learning. Those interpersonal and academic gains should be the forefront goals of both teacher and students.

Assessment

Obviously, assessment is one of the most difficult areas that SL teachers regularly encounter. Indeed, its complexity cries out for computer tracking and linking of the academic and the communal. Moreover, it includes a happy addition to normal academic assessment: community evaluation and the production of products. The initial process of community needs assessment finds its fulfillment, hopefully, in community evaluation of the extent to which the needs have been met, not met, or exceeded. In the process, SL routinely produces products of all kinds, including scientific data, written histories, multimedia documents, visual and audio records, articles and reviews in local newspapers and magazines, and radio and TV programs. All provide excellent grist for the mill of evaluation and affirmation. There is one final, although mostly subjective, assessment judgment. Spurts of growth and the realization of potential frequently occur in SL. This is particularly dramatic in at-risk kids. Their growth rate is often spectacular, in particular in the area of leadership. Such breakthrough developments, especially those of student leadership, can be dramatically presented and evaluated through before-and-after profiles.

Overall Composite

Teachers of SL must have a passion for problem finding and problem solving. They also must be savvy about communities, what makes them tick, and what makes them fail. Above all, they must always focus on what falls through the cracks. They must resist lamentation, exasperation, and cynicism, and develop an optimistic tough hide and sense of gradual change over time. Teacher attitude and outlook have to provide a key corrective model for students. Otherwise they may throw their hands up in despair and join the ranks of the apathetic and inert. What needs to be inculcated in students is a sharp eye for things that need to be changed; a solid feeling that the solution can be found through cooperation, community savvy, and academic smarts; and a desire to document the results so that the experience and research findings are eminently sharable and transferable.

WANT AD: EDUCATORS FOR PROJECT LEARNING

Positioning

In many ways project learning (PL) pushes differentiated education further. Not only the students, but also the projects, are differentiated. The constant focus on a single subject is not available as reassurance. It is not unlike the film about touring Europe: *If It's Tuesday, This Must Be Belgium*. The number of projects, like the number of countries— each with its own language, culture, and terrain—can be bewildering. The teacher is the calendar. He or she is also the sole contact person for individuals and their projects, and thus is responsible for the convergence of differentiation for both. Reducing the levels of variety through group-based projects is offset by the need to minister to team-based dynamics. As in SL, the teacher is inevitably a team coach.

The Amplified Teacher

Projects are often so multifaceted and even interdisciplinary that they regularly exceed the expertise of a single teacher. In addition, there is the practical need to provide some relief from being the only "go-to" person. Two solutions, separately and in combination, have emerged. Where PL is a schoolwide commitment or dominates certain grade levels, a project teacher team is assembled to minister to both the individual and project needs of students and student project teams. That teacher team ideally is a miniature of the whole, replicating all or most of the academic subjects of the school. In addition to offering expertise, each teacher of the instructional team is familiar with the state subject-matter requirements and standards that must be met; and hence is indispensable to the linkage process. The other solution is identifying and establishing working relationships with professionals outside of the school. They may be at nearby universities or working in project-related fields in the community in which the school is located. Where such professionals are not available, teachers can negotiate and compile electronic partners available on e-mail as advisors. Such outside experts also play a particularly important role later in evaluating projects. At that point, they bring a real-world expertise to bear on determining whether the projects exhibit validity and reliability. Combining teachers and outside experts provides the best of both worlds. It amplifies not only the teacher and the teacher teams but the entire school. It provides a second faculty, committed to the students and their projects. A small budget can be established to pay honorariums to outside professionals for undertaking project review.

Project Manager

The lead teacher is above all else a manager and administrator of many projects. The first step is the selection of a project focus. Marx, Blumenfeld, Krajcik, and Soloway (1997) have identified a number of difficulties. Teachers find it difficult to choose project topics that incorporate the required curriculum. Student interests are often nonacademic. Students also are inexperienced in working on their own and estimating how much time and work will be required to complete a project. The rule of thumb is that projects always take more time to complete than expected. Indeed, many are not finished by the end of the term and are prematurely rushed to conclusions. In general, teachers find that project learning involves more work than the traditional textbook-based curriculum. Project topic selection may thus, unfortunately, be influenced by workload. But to tap the full benefits of motivation and involvement, researchers and teachers agree, students should identify and pursue what interests them. Besides, some so-called nonacademic subjects, like video games, a popular choice, may turn out to be quite academic. The frequent lamentation heard at the end—"If I knew what I was getting myself into I never would have picked this topic"—is a critical learning experience, and one that is not often made available during the formative school years. The role of project manager is as complex as it is pivotal. It makes or breaks a project-based program.

Electronic Aid and Support

Project learning has attracted a number of project-based learning packages. All web-based, some of the best known are JASON Project, Journey North, ThinkQuest, and Classroom Connect's Quests. These electronic programs are completely self-sufficient. They offer virtually everything—curriculum, assignments, learning resources, assessment tools, and a roster of experts the students may question through e-mail. Although these electronic aides do not offer the full range of subjects students might select, they do make it easier for teachers who may be intimidated by the range of knowledge expected and may miss the re-assuring anchor that a program-based curriculum provides. But perhaps the most significant yield is why project learning, unlike other innovative curricula, has attracted such a strong and detailed electronic support system. The answer may be that project-based learning and operations are precisely the dominant mode in many businesses and professions. As such, they add a further career value to such learning.

Satisfying Requirements and Meeting Standards

Satisfying requirements and meeting standards are problems for PL as much as for SL, although SL assignments are even more often distant from academics. Nevertheless, it is the role of the project manager not only to establish the academic linkages, but to do so as the project evolves and thus minimize last-minute catch-up. Curtis (2002) of the Lucas Foundation, which funds many project learning programs, describes how an architectural project satisfied state subject-matter requirements: math (computation, measurement, graphing, and patterns), social studies (knowledge of different branches of government), technology (use of electronic information gathering and

communicating), and English (writing extensively for multiple purposes).

Range

PL has been effective with a wide range of students, from special ed
to gifted and talented and obviously to mixed groups. The three key
variables are student speed, depth of grasp and task, and the degree and
kind of interventions by the teacher. But again, as Curtis notes, students
involved in PL retain information, are able to apply what they have
learned to real-world problems, are absent less often, and have fewer
discipline problems. Such gains offset the constantly shifting role of the
teacher.

Managing Ambiguity, Overwhelming Complexity, Uncontrollability, and Unpredictability

In many ways project learning can be overwhelming for students.
The floodgates are open, and data and ideas may pour in without structure or limits. Thus PL may introduce them prematurely to experiences
that they have never coped with before. Indeed, many adult professionals might not manage these experiences well. It is the difficult and
delicate task of the teacher to provide not answers—there may, in fact,
be none—but antidotes to the temptations of despair, giving up, and the
general sense that the students are out of their league. The teacher has
to provide, as it were, intellectual therapy.

Interdisciplinarity

PL, like SL, offers the experience of encountering and working with
many disciplines, often at the same time. The first time students are
able to see connections between math, social studies, science, English,
and so on is a rare and heady experience for them; but it is not without
its problems for the teacher. Typically, students are not aware that the
differences of disciplines also involve their own distinctive methodologies. They naturally but wrongly assume that one way characterizes all.
Ever so gently and gradually, teachers have to apply brakes to that uni-

formity. If some students persist and encounter the inevitable differences of disciplines, then referrals to the appropriate subject-matter colleagues are necessary. Indeed, the teacher regularly is expected to make such referrals and to operate as an academic broker.

Assessment

Although PL shares with SL, and to a lesser extent with DE, the need for multiple means of assessment, special attention has to be paid to the fact that PL produces a product often created by divers hands and within multiple disciplines. Without an interdisciplinary in-house project team, evaluation would be fragmented. Therefore, the team has to craft a collective composite framework within which to nest each project for assessment. The framework needs to be made of rubber, not concrete, because it may have to be reshaped for each different project. The ultimate fallback resource is the outside experts who also may have been called on to assist in the project. Whether outside evaluation is done in person or electronically, the project manager teacher is required to preside and, if necessary, offer balance at this final stage of the process.

Composite

Of all three curricula, PL pushes the envelope of different instructional roles furthest. It probably offers the least opportunity for direct instruction and basic text-based learning. Typically, it starts early and runs late. As one ex-principal at an Ed/Visions school put it, "I used to worry about getting them here. Now the problem is getting them to leave." In addition to acting as a project manager and a team coach and facilitator, PL instructors have to regularly assume the role of academic broker. And that is both an external and internal task. Outside experts and ultimately evaluators have to be assembled and often nurtured; and an internal academic team usually requires the same managerial and velvet glove finessing. Increasingly, the project manager has to put on the back burner his or her academic expertise and substitute for that the role of administrator of knowledge.

SUMMARY

Hopefully, what has been demonstrated is that challenging new curricula require a precise and comprehensive understanding of what it takes not only to teach, but also to optimize, such programs. Materials and instructors need to be symbiotically joined at the hip. The realization of the potential of both is always mutual and interactive. Perhaps surprisingly, for all the individualization of both curriculum and its instruction, common denominators surface in all three curriculum-driven job descriptions. Such commonalities even may be predictive of the roles and job descriptions of future teacher and administrator.

The most obvious common role is that of the teacher as a constant intervener. All these curricula require teachers who are energized, love to take charge, and are constantly proactive. They are roll-up-your-sleeves types who are not afraid to get their hands dirty and who do not hesitate to go where angels fear to tread. They welcome the noise of busy student activities and conversation and are not put off by apparent chaos. Their enthusiasm is matched only by their curiosity.

What also emerges clearly as a common warning bell to principals is the degree of possible disconnects. The more a new curriculum departs from traditional or standard ones, the more adjustments in roles, resources, and job descriptions will be required. As noted, in this age of accountability and high-stakes testing, the gaps created have to be bridged by not one but various assessment strategies, always aligned to all the state and federal standards and requirements.

Another clear-cut pattern is that all teachers have to be managers. As noted often, the programs are often more administered than taught. Management skills also have to include electronic monitoring and tracking, the compilation of databases, and the creation and maintenance of academic and intellectual networks of expertise. A related additional common role is that of team management and governance, internally with academic teams and externally with outside experts and resources. To the standard need for knowledge of group dynamics and skills of conflict resolution has to be added collaborative governance, which also models the cooperative connections between disciplines. Finally, there is the role of the broker and dispatcher who negotiates connections and expedites delivery.

These are not the customary roles of teachers. They also are generally absent from most, if not all, college teacher prep programs. Indeed, to the oft-mentioned and -researched list of reasons why teachers generally resist teaching in such programs (more work, no standard textbook, lack of structure) should be added perhaps that this does not match their internal image of what a teacher should do or be. Classroom management for purposes of discipline and workflow is one thing, but the management of knowledge, process, and compulsory multiplicity is quite another. Purist teachers might conclude that is the task of administration; that is what the principal does.

And thus the circle unexpectedly but fruitfully comes back to the beginning. The dilemma of principals in selecting appropriate teachers was an initial concern that prompted the above compilation of job descriptions. Now the principal may emerge as the key agent to facilitate those role changes. Why? Because almost all the areas of common need are managerial in one form or another. Most administrators can tap their training and experience to minister effectively to each role change. Principals can model teacher growth. Where and when adjustments are required, principals can grow and change along with their teachers.

A POSTSCRIPT

New curricula, whether consciously designed that way or not, ultimately involve not only instructional, but also administrative, role change. The teacher as manager becomes increasingly the norm. That pattern of transformation brings principals into the center and compels a new role for them as well. They are best equipped at this point to guide teachers as administrative interns and to develop and perhaps be part of the staff to teach the necessary professional development programs. One plea though: use both column A and column B. Tie together the needs of the curriculum and the roles of teachers. That will not only anchor administrative training, but also perhaps produce the teacher-managers who shall optimize the implementation of such curricula.

In many ways new curricula embody or anticipate the future. Not unlike all innovation that, in effect, creates the future, new programs are often ahead of those who have to implement them. Still, they encourage significant growth and stretch. Clearly, the future task is to find ways to bridge the traditional and the new, the past and the future, the building blocks and the way to fly.

CHAPTER 26

Turnaround: What Education
Has to Offer Business

I don't know why the mere mention of business compels educators to become so indignant, martyred, defensive, and often incoherent. To request more light than heat evidently will not take us where we want to go. I am both a business and an educational consultant. There are not many of us who straddle both worlds and can view each from the inside perspective of the other. And what that double view suggests is, minimally, three issues.

1. Each world's view of the other is reductive. Business wants education to exclusively produce future employees who fit in and won't cost millions to train or retrain. Education wants business to provide its students with meaningful work and careers that reflect an educated sense of social and corporate responsibility.
2. There is incredible mutual ignorance. Recent discussions of education as a businesss have betrayed an incredible lack of knowledge about marketing. Comparing business operations unflatteringly to a factory production line expresses a total unfamiliarity with even the most basic manufacturing processes. When the Public Education and Business Coalition received a grant to train one hundred principals on business practices, surveys of the participants revealed that educators only read and talk to educators, and know little or nothing about increasing competition, balancing quality and productivity, Sigma VI continuous improvement programs, and so on. It is an ironic ignorance because these things are precisely what public education increasingly has to face. Although

educators rightly are upset by the ignorance of business about schools, they never contemplate how business professionals might react to similar distortions. In fact, one would be tempted to wish a plague on both their houses if it were not for the third issue.

3. Business and education have much more to share than their mutual acrimony would suggest. Indeed, a case might be made for their being allies rather than enemies. But such a prospect requires the balance of equals. Typically the exchange has been one sided or unidirectional. In an attempt to redress the imbalance, I focus here on what education has to offer business.

Business woefully lacks solid models and best practices minimally in five areas that have been evolving and, in many cases, achieving distinction in education.

1. LEADERSHIP SHARING

Increasingly, many principals have partnered with teachers (Lambert 2002). A combination of site-based management, principal-teacher partnerships, principal's cabinets and learning councils, and so on have shaped the sharing of leadership roles and enlarged jurisdictional relationships. Distributed leadership, advocated by Elmore (2002) and others, has found more of a home in education than in business. Teaming is the closest business comes, but that arrangement is usually confined to local, rather than companywide, governance. It is never extended to challenging separative divisional structures. In fact, education has pushed that envelope further by evolving governance collaborative structures that in some schools serve as the operating system.

2. MULTIPLE ROLES

The gradual use of cross training in business falls far short of what is emerging as crossover training in education. Teachers, education's version of middle-level managers, have taken on multiple roles and tasks. They are alternately case and project managers; facilitators and coaches; school-community liaison officers; school-home, schoolwork, school-college counselors; and so on. With some curricula, like service or project learning, they do not so much teach as administer the program. In short, education more than business is moving in the direction of 360-degree multiple role distribution.

3. BRAIN RESEARCH

Educational psychologists have partnered with neurological and cognitive researchers to identify with greater precision the basis and dynamics of cognitive learning and development. Five principal areas have been fixed and tracked, and applications to classrooms already have appeared in abundance. There are virtually no signs in business of awareness, let alone use, of this state-of-the-art research and its applications. This is particularly surprising given the vaunted celebration of business as the supreme example of the learning organization, à la Senge.

4. DIVERSITY

Nothing externally or internally in business matches the extent and depth of diversity in education. In fact, business customers are generally homogenous, thanks to the clever market segmentation of products or services. But it is public education's mission to implement the vision of the Statue of Liberty. Moreover, it is not enough for education to be inclusive; it also must provide multiple paths to differentiated success. No business determined to make a profit would ever accept as a customer base the combination of special ed, the range of ethnic and racial minorities, bilingualism, and all new immigrants and aliens. Indeed, without education as a rite of passage of diversity, business would be out of business.

5. ACCOUNTABILITY

The incredible pressures for accountability on all levels—local, county, state, and federal—have compelled educators reluctantly to become experts on assessment. That expertise is one that business generally lacks and increasingly and hurriedly has had to acquire in the wake of the Enron and other failures. In education the multiplicity of assessment approaches now rivals that of curricula development. One of the most impressive, which business lacks but needs, is the rubric of differentiated evaluation. Doubly flexible, it can be tailored to different levels of student ability as well as disaggregated adjustments of performance goals by subject matter and grade level. It is a marvelously dexterous matrix that can rival or even improve on the much-touted Sigma VI model perfected by General Electric. Indeed, as a business consultant, if I were asked for advice by a firm contemplating implementing the GE panacea, I would recommend the rubric approach.

Although additional areas of excellence can be cited, hopefully the argument for what education has to offer has been clinched. But I cannot resist citing another edge that education has, one that is reaffirmed by the incredible current pressures put on education.

With all the emphasis on diversity, the multiple roles of teachers, the changing position of administrators, greater demands by different interest groups, and so on, the focus of all levels of education leadership has remained the same: the commitment to commonality. In fact, that focus should remind business CEOs that in spite of, or because of, internal changes and external mergers, their perennial mission is the same search for common purpose. That alone holds the community of the company together. That alone gives coherence to work and purpose to vision. Education, in re-creating its future, is generating a common innovative spirit that has much to offer the future of business.

CHAPTER 27

Accountability and Role Change: Persuading Lone Rangers to Be Team Players

Unlike most professionals, who function in an interactive environment with other professionals, teachers are loners. Almost perversely, many cling to their isolation like a hair shirt. They proudly close the door of their classroom and reign supreme like a judge in a courtroom or ruler of all one surveys. At least doctors, who are notoriously tempted toward the same godlike self-aggrandizement, are always surrounded by nurses and technicians. Not so teachers, who pose as the solo king or queen of the hill.

That is the way it has always been, until now. Whatever the mixed effects of accountability, it is clear that it will have a profound impact on teacher culture. Moreover, the change is inescapable. There is nowhere to hide. Assessment is uncompromisingly invasive, ubiquitous, and totally transparent. In particular it is totally inimical to the traditional role of the lone ranger. Indeed, to facilitate an appreciation of how much teachers may have to change and what may be the extent of the behavioral modification, here are two profiles, before and after.

THE TEACHER AS LONE RANGER

Indispensability

The teacher may view herself as the key, the linchpin, the supreme commander. Learning is the exclusive province of the one up front. She determines whether learning takes place or not, what the standards are, and how they are applied. She may rule with an iron fist or a velvet glove, or use both to manage students, but she is the final authority and arbiter. Her word is law. She cannot ever be challenged. Her centrality and importance certify her indispensability to the learning process. The impression generated is that if the teacher were not there, there would be no learning.

Secretive

No one else really knows what is taking place daily and hourly in that classroom. Evaluation by principals is occasional and often perfunctory. Besides, the observation is of a class that is often rehearsed, even scripted, beforehand to show the teacher at her best and most benevolent. In other words, the image many teachers project to other teachers, administrators, and parents may be public relations. No one really knows the day-to-day truth except the students, and they may be compromised, bribed into approving silence, or typically not listened to.

Extremes

Many teachers are tigers in the classroom but pussycats outside. They are assertive or even dominating with students but cowering, obedient, and cooing with administrators. Although new governance arrangements have encouraged more leadership sharing between teachers and principals, many teachers uncritically support the indispensability of principals and cannot imagine a school functioning without top-down authority. The oscillation from the extreme of dominance to that of docility is a norm of most school environments and of the teacher culture itself.

Of course, the same characteristics can shape a best-case scenario. They can describe a teacher whose indispensability takes the form of being intensely dedicated; whose secrecy is really a prized form of privacy, so that nothing outside of her class is allowed to compromise her single-minded focus and commitment to her students; and whose oscillations really express her views of the legitimately different roles of teacher and administrator.

But the issue of transparency remains. We do not know what really occurs in every classroom. Besides, standards have been raised. Assessment is a new norm. Data tracking is increasingly mandated. No child is to be left out or behind. In short, the game and the rules have changed. For better or worse, accountability has become an urgent and intrusive agent of school reform. The sacred and separative preserve of the classroom and the role of the lone ranger have become subject to the revelations of data tracking. The focus has shifted from changing the teacher to changing the teacher culture, from the individual to the environment, from the singular to the multiple, from the lone ranger to the learning team.

What, then, will be the specific and expected impacts on teacher roles and the classroom? How will accountability alter teachers' relationships with their students, as well as with parents and administrators? Will the changes be so intrusive and altering that they signal and shape the emergence of a new kind of teacher—a hybrid combining individual and group identity? Here, then, are some of key drivers of change, as well as their dynamics.

THE TEACHER AS A TEAM PLAYER

Alignment

Teachers will have no choice other than to work together as teams, either for the first time or to enlarge the scope of previous collective effort. Teachers will have to hammer out the common goals and standards of their grade levels and subject matter as defined by the alignment of the school district with state and national outcomes. All must be in synch. A districtwide report card will be compiled that in turn will become part of a state report card, compelling teachers to function collectively within agreed-on parameters. The lone ranger will now be joined by all the other lone rangers to form a posse. The fiercely independent and the quietly incompetent may become strange bedfellows. Competence will be the dominant force, to the point at which it may upgrade the bulk but minimize the creativity and difference of a minority of brilliant and stirring innovators. But the serious loss of such irreplaceable quality will be offset by across-the-board quantitative gains.

Uniform Measures, Benchmarking, and Tracking

As a team, teachers will also have to focus on what areas are to be measured, when, and what forms the assessment will take. All subject areas and time lines will be defined. There will be little or no room for negotiation. The method of measurement will be tests. The nature and range of such standardized subject-matter tests will be generally known in advance. In addition, often the school district, through its principals, will announce the target levels and numbers that need to be met. Most of the teachers will teach to the test. More independent teachers will supplement testing with other, less draconian, measures. It will be difficult for them to hold their ground as schools strip the curriculum increasingly to that which is being tested. In addition, the installation of benchmarking and data-tracking systems will mean that teachers no longer can be secretive or private about what goes on in the classroom. The numbers will be invasive. Transparency will rule. Hopefully, no school district will install cameras in classrooms, although the paranoiac will expect that to happen any day.

Sharing Lesson Planning and Research

The experience of a common pressure cooker will compel group learning. Teachers will increasingly rely on one another and share their lesson plans and seek input. They will take turns investigating and reporting back on what the research advises. Teaching will become less isolated and more collegial. Teachers also will review and reflect on how learning is organized to determine to what extent current structures support or undermine individual and group effectiveness. The collaborative process will probably do more to shape and produce improved teaching and learning performance than any professional development programs. Collectively, teacher teams increasingly will be self-managing and self-governing, face inward in collective self-reliance, serve as a support group, mentor new arrivals, and constitute a research-based learning management team. Given the relentless permeability of accountability, they will redefine the vision of education in general and the professionalism of teaching in particular.

Critical Review of Student Work

More emphasis will be placed by the group on reviewing and evaluating student work. Help may be requested in massaging the numbers to be more diagnostic and less punitive. Rubric overlays and disaggregating of data will bring greater precision and focus to what needs improvement. Again, what the research shows will be tapped. Ideally, students will be brought within the fold not only to become more knowledgeable about the overall assessment process, but also to participate directly through self-assessment and the development of growth plans. The initial cold, hard, and impersonal face of assessment gradually will become personalized and humanized.

Parental Partnerships

Learning teams will increasingly value parental input and participation. In addition to having to communicate with parents about the new accountability system, teachers will increasingly recognize that without the cooperation of the home as an extension of the school they may not be able to meet their target goals. In fact, teachers may factor into student profiles and even report cards the degree to which families are involved. Including socio-economic factors might bring more realism and intelligence to the target goals and their timetable.

The two profiles above not surprisingly show a mixture of resistance and compliance, avoidance and engagement. Probably the most serious problem is the almost knee-jerk resistance to accountability. That will accomplish little except to normalize martyrdom and to make the public suspicious that teachers have something to hide. Besides, the forces of accountability are so tenacious and multiply reinforced and mandated that it is not the battle educators should pick to win. The real battle is the future one of identifying and tapping the promise of professionalism emerging from this comprehensive change in teacher culture. That is what needs to be addressed if the gains of the past are to be preserved, rediscovered, and recast in the future.

As important as class size is to performance, of equal or greater importance is finding the time and means for teachers to counsel, plan, and collaborate as a team; to review and diagnose student work; and to develop new collegial relationships with parents. These are the most positive and leveraged yields of accountability. These outcomes are what need to be recognized, preserved, and nurtured. In fact, they are so critical to the entire future of education that they alone may determine whether the entire accountability movement succeeds or fails. But such potential deep-seated gains will remain stillborn unless there is creative and bold intervention by visionary leaders.

Unfortunately, these new dimensions of teacher performance often are either assumed or killed with token recognition. Of course, everyone agrees teachers need to work and plan together; of course, they need to critically review student work; and everyone knows how important parental involvement is. But such predictable and rehearsed recognition does nothing to realize the potential of these three areas of professional growth and development. Unless they become driving priorities and something substantial is done to facilitate their incarnations, the vision of a new teacher culture will be robbed of its future.

The success or failure of accountability hangs on change on both sides of the aisle. The teachers cannot do it alone. Administration must exercise its instructional leadership to find the means, the time, and the training for team accountability learning and teacher-parent partnerships. Many options currently exist: extending the school day and/or year, reconfiguring course schedules, fusing face-to-face learning and electronics, teacher flex time for home visits, and so on. Time, space, and place have to be found to facilitate strategic conversations between teachers and teachers, teachers and students, teachers and parents. The stakes are too high on the one hand and the need to achieve target goals too urgent on the other not to recognize that the magnitude of the change in teacher culture requires an equal magnitude of change in the basic ways schools structure learning.

Accountability has brought to the surface the need for comprehensive changes to the basic teacher culture—more dramatic and deep, perhaps, than changes to any other agent of school reform. But if those changes are not to be lost or consumed in counterproductive arguments of them versus us, school districts cannot remain passive and just sit back and cheer on a mechanical parade of numbers. The school calendar has to change. Teachers have to be reintroduced to teachers so that they may realize the strength of collaborative intelligence and create research-based communities of best practices. Teachers have to become more adept at reading and diagnosing the accountability numbers of student assessment. Teachers have to treat parents as colleagues and to form partnerships of growth; for without parental backup the results either will not happen or will not be lasting. The stakes are so high, the gains so big and tangible, that not to seize the day and create new cultures of joint learning may turn out to be a major indictment of current leadership. When numbers alone rule, sadly, the favored structure is the production line.

CHAPTER 28

The World Citizen: Facilitating a Future Global Identity for Students

One hears disturbing reports of Palestinian children being taught to hate Israelis, of Muslims in general being programmed in mosques to distrust or vilify all Christians and Jews. Strange and uneasy links between radical Muslim and Christian fundamentalists have surfaced. Even though Russia is no longer the massive exporter of revolutionary ideology, its earlier efforts are long-term and deep-seated, and emerge regularly in Latin America. Recent national elections in France brought to the surface the age-old gaps between natives and foreigners, between whites and blacks over jobs and power. And so it goes.

Many have argued that none of this is new. The names and the games may have changed but it still reflects the same old diverse territoriality and identity of conflicting nations, religions, and cultures. It is an endless, unresolvable, ancient tangle that has always been with us and will remain so in the future. Such views have prevailed because sadly they have history, even biblical documentation, on their side. But circumstances have changed sufficiently to reopen the question and to attempt a fresh start. In particular, three developments compel reexamination.

1. LONG-TERM EFFECTS OF PROGRAMMING

The brainwashing of children to hate or distrust does not have to employ the most sophisticated techniques to have a long-lasting effect. Recall the double cultural turnaround that had to occur in the twentieth century in the Soviet Union. The first time was in 1917, when individual farmers had to struggle to work effectively on collectivized farms;

sixty years later, the process was reversed and Russians had to become capitalists and individual owners. During both transitions many Russians starved. Unfortunately, we have few examples of positive programming as a counterintelligence force leading in more positive directions. But a new legacy of hate is now being seeded. The future of world peace is at stake.

2. THE LEVERAGE OF PETTY TYRANTS AND ROGUE STATES

The small can take on the big, the rogue dictator can defy the United Nations, the playing field can be leveled by the leveraging power of mass destruction. The arsenal now includes atomic weapons, biological and chemical contaminants, and paralyzing gases. Most are easily transportable and deliverable by suicidal fanatics. The fear is that such destructive power not only can easily be acquired by crazy states, but also can be sold on the open market to other would-be fanatics. The search for stabilization is an endless process of putting out one fire after another. There is no preventive medicine approach.

3. INTERNATIONAL EDUCATION AND GLOBAL LITERACY

Currently there are 860 million illiterate adults and over 100 million children without access to schools worldwide. UNESCO and other groups have joined forces to sponsor Education for All, a coalition whose goal is to enroll all primary-age children in poor countries in school by 2015.

4. INTERNATIONAL VACCINE PROGRAM

Although food programs are critical, they sometimes offer too little, too late. They also often pose both logistical and financial difficulties. But what has emerged as perhaps an equal or greater priority is preventable childhood diseases. Even children who have enough to eat can die of measles. A vaccination costing about 80¢ could spare their lives. And so there is now an international campaign to vaccinate all the children of the world, including, right now, those in Iraq.

5. SOURCES OF COMMONALITY

Happily, there are a few positive signs of emerging common cause. The most compelling is ecological. Pollution does not respect borders. Smoke from the forest fires of Indonesia drifted and caused breathing problems in Singapore. The exhaust from cars has collectively brought about global warming and the greenhouse effect. There is a global shortage of drinking water. In order words, the common global situation itself provides a collective focus and rallying point for a more collaborative future.

But if the above mixture of fear and promise is pushing us in a new direction, what is pulling us? What is spelling out in detail our beliefs, hopes, and even action agenda for the future? The answer is a vision—a positive expression of hope and action that takes the high road of commonality. One approach is the goal of acquiring an additional and official identity—of becoming a world citizen as well as a citizen of one's own country. The passport of a world citizen might look something like the following.

Passport of a World Citizen

Name:

Address:

Country:

Preamble: Declaration of Interdependence

Whatever the situation of your individual country, this passport addresses what we all hold sacred and common in the world: our dependence on one another for world peace, health, and fulfillment. It thus addresses and celebrates the bond of interdependence as an equal and hopefully overriding partner in global negotiations with separatist national, religious, and cultural causes and countries. Hopefully, what holds us together can be strong and deep enough to bridge the gulfs that separate us. Below are five principal goals that provide the rationale for and constitute the agenda of the world citizen acting in concert with other world partners.

1. To preserve the fragile ecology of the planet
2. To heal the sick and to protect the future health of all the children of the world through inoculation
3. To educate everyone, everywhere, every way
4. To embrace and value difference and global diversity
5. To fix what is broken, old, and punitive

Oath and Pledge of Allegiance

I pledge allegiance to the United World of Planet Earth and to all the people it embraces now and into the future.

I promise to support with my whole being the causes of world peace, security, and fulfillment.

I also vow to do everything within my power to preserve, heal, educate, embrace and fix the world so that its future will be brighter and more hopeful than its past.

I swear by all that is commonly holy and valued by all the peoples and cultures of the world that I will honor in my life, work, and belief the ethical code and behaviors of a world citizen.

I pledge to devote my time and energy to persuading others to share the vision of a world living together in peace, harmony, and mutual respect.

Perhaps this vision of global citizenship should be incorporated with the unfolding new vision of education itself. Is it not interesting? Whenever something big—in this case global—has to be tackled, we naturally turn to education. No other national resource or avenue is as pervasive and persuasive. But perhaps that is not so surprising after all. Education has always occupied the nexus where aspiration and vision meet, and where unity and diversity are harmonized. We need to remember that unique double role when we are tempted to be critical of education.

Part VII

TEACHER SCENARIOS

CHAPTER 29

A Major Change Takes Hold

"It's going to be another busy day," Bill Edwards thought as he dropped his heavy briefcase in the space alongside the driver's seat. A social studies teacher at the middle school in Westside, Indiana, for four years now, Bill was close to being granted tenure. As he drove to school, his mind went back to the way things had been just two years ago and how everything had changed so dramatically.

He joined the faculty in September 2020. Two years later he was ready to quit. The workload was overwhelming. He stayed up late every night marking papers and preparing lesson plans. Often the work spilled over into the weekends. He was always tired, and he sometimes was short tempered and impatient with his students.

The worse part was that he never had any time to meet with his colleagues. Only one department meeting a month was squeezed in, and that was spent listening to directives from above and being told what the textbooks and software programs for next year would be. They already had been selected at the district level by Mrs. Twombly, whose bibliography did not include a book or article with a date later than that of her master's degree. And she had not been in the classroom for over ten years! That was not all. Dr. Honerer, the principal, regularly exhorted—"scolded" would be more accurate—the teachers to involve parents more. Fat chance—they did not even show up for parent-teacher conferences. Bill concluded that he was going up a down escalator and things would only get worse. Then, two years later, a drastic change occurred.

Bill could not be sure who initiated it. The impression he had was that many were involved, although each person had his or her own agenda. Probably it was the union survey of working conditions, hours, and pay that started it all. There was a new head of the local, Harry Zou, who had come to the school with a master's degree in labor relations. He believed the union had to do its homework first before getting involved in negotiations. And that meant research and data, so he set up an elaborate survey.

Its findings surprised everyone. The teachers all knew they were working hard, but the average number of hours, factoring in time spent after school, at libraries, and at home on the computer, was sixty-four per week! And that did not include an additional five to ten hours spent doing administrative and clerical work and checking the database that monitored student test scores and performance. Bill's office mate, Sam, who has a quick sense of humor wisecracked: "Now I know why I have become increasingly celibate."

The response to the report was immediate and hot. The school board and the administration challenged the findings and questioned the research design. Parents were somewhat stunned. They did not know what to make of it. The students were indifferent: how hard or long teachers worked was none of their concern. The media had a field day. The newspaper ran a series of articles on individual teachers and their typical workweek, and what it meant in terms of student access and quality time.

The local TV set up panel guest shows featuring different points of view. There was one devoted to parents, and what emerged was the strong need to expand teacher involvement in parent involvement. School board members and the superintendent deflected all discussion to the issue of costs, just as they had done two years earlier when a reduction in class size was proposed. Union officials were firmly focused: hours would have to be reduced, working conditions would have to be altered, and salary would have to increase. Reps from student government were properly indignant in defending their oppressed teachers, but managed in the process slyly to introduce some of their pet peeves about cafeteria food and poorly equipped labs. And on and on it went without apparent end, full of sound and fury but signifying nothing.

The controversy became wearisome after a while and even boring, because nothing kills interest like stalemate. Then unexpectedly, from out of nowhere, the governor announced that he was assigning three members of his fifteen-member state commission on education to study the union report and to form a fact-finding investigative group. The governor was proactively worried: "I am concerned that if what this survey shows is accurate then what we have in Westside is but the tip of the iceberg. This may be not only a statewide, but also a national, problem." One commentator wryly noted that the governor was using this issue to toss his hat in the ring; he too wanted to be an education president.

Quickly everyone turned to examine the three-member group. One member was from business, another a professor from the education department of the state university, and the last a retired plant manager. It was anyone's guess what this motley group would come up with.

The town did not have very long to wait. Three weeks after their arrival the group called a town meeting to give a preliminary report that had initially been shared with the governor.

The three sat together at a small table on the stage of the high school auditorium. The retired plant manager stood up. Mr. Zageski was tall, wiry, and direct. He explained that the purpose of the meeting was to tell everyone what the group had found, what needed to be changed, and how that might be done. They were not going to take questions but instead a local committee that represented all constituencies had been put together and briefed; and they would take the stage to continue the discussion. We now knew why the first row had been roped off and who was sitting there. Zageski announced that he had five points to make:

1. The survey design was proper and its findings were accurate.
2. The problem was time, not money. Whatever solution was put forward, it should not increase costs.
3. Reducing teacher time should not be solely a quantitative problem but also a qualitative issue. Namely, what should be done with the time saved?
4. Four time needs emerged as urgent and important: more time for teachers to plan with their colleagues, more time to critically review student work, more time for teachers to plan with parent partners, and more time for teacher professional development.
5. The time for all would come from the following changes: subject-matter classes would be reduced from five to three meetings a week; students would be grouped into small study teams for col-

laborative learning and peer tutoring, including online time specified by teacher work assignments; teachers and students would receive training in the team dynamics of negotiation, conflict resolution, and setting team learning goals; and, finally, the performance levels of all teachers and students would be benchmarked and set up against measures for the next five years, the length of the proposed changes.

The three members then gathered their few papers, got up, invited the representative committee on stage, and left the hall. You could hear a pin drop. Everyone was stunned. No one was prepared for such basic changes. Besides, it all seemed to hang together and make sense. It did not seem that they had forgotten or left out anything. But the proof of the pudding is in the tasting. How did that solution play out?

The reverie over, Bill arrived at school. Today was Tuesday. He had taught his classes the day before. He now met his classes three times a week, Monday, Wednesday, and Friday. His first meeting that day was with his social studies colleagues who taught at all three different grade levels. That range nicely facilitated the discussion of continuity from one grade level to the other. The conversations always followed the same format, which the group had dubbed the Janus system after the two faces of the month of January, one looking back and the other forward: retrospect and prospect.

It was a good system; it kept everyone on track. Each teacher reported on yesterday's lesson: what worked, what did not, and why. One member of the group was in charge of keeping a running log on action research topics to be undertaken by members of the social studies group. Because time and energy were limited, the topics selected for research were reserved for the teachers' spectacular successes or flops. So far, three topics had been undertaken that year. In at least two instances the results had been designated not only as correctives, but also as best practices. In fact, both were scheduled to be presented at the state education conference. Westside had an impressive research track record.

Next, each teacher presented his or her lesson plan for the next day and the week. Actually, three lesson plans were presented: one for the class, the second for parents, the third for student study teams. Discussion was lively, sometimes heated. Books, articles, websites and software programs were suggested. Another member of the team maintained an inventory of resources and developed a system of rating each on the basis of teacher feedback. This turned out to be invaluable when monies became available for purchasing and when new teachers came into the system and needed help to get started.

Bill then left for the first of his meetings with five sets of parents for fifteen minutes each. Those not free during the day were scheduled either in the evening or weekends; and the back-ups were always the phone and, when available, e-mail. Bill always looked forward to meeting parents, whom he regarded as having the same status and value as his colleagues. Bill knew the research: without parent involvement and a supportive home environment the gains of the day would not be consolidated and carried over to the next learning stages. Bill also had developed a lot of respect and admiration for many of these parents, and often their hard lot.

The first topic of each teacher-parent meeting was the mutual checklist, one half of it maintained by the teacher, the other half by the parent. It ranged from the basics of attendance and tardies, to TV monitoring, to family time together, to study time and homework completion, to performance in study teams. And then together the teacher and the parent would put together the learning goals for the week, including a discussion of overcoming certain obstacles or resistance. At the end of the hour with four parents (there was one no-show), Bill felt exhausted and exhilarated. For the first time he was part of a real teacher-parent partnership program. It was specific and targeted. It factored in all that was being monitored, and above all it worked with the variables of different kids and families. In effect, it was the best and most holistic version of differentiated education: it was applied across the board but adjusted for each family. Bill therefore did not mind taking the extra time and effort after each meeting to record any changes in the parental assignments as well as the reasons for those changes. The results sometimes bordered on the spectacular; and Bill had to concede that they could not have been achieved or sustained without the time being found to make parents an integrated part of the learning. As one parent put it, "You and I put together the best of both worlds: the school and the home school."

Lunch was a good time to relax and socialize. In the past he had hardly ever had time to eat; he would snack at his desk during prep time. After lunch the next hour was devoted to professional development. Workshops were scheduled regularly at the school or district. Unlike in the past, most of these were now teacher selected. In addition, teachers had their own development budget, which combined matching funds from the district and the parents' fund-raising foundation.

Happily, professional development opportunities were not limited to attending workshops. Electronic options were allowed and even encouraged: a number of teachers were enrolled in online seminars; others examined and discussed taped programs developed by vendors or educational associations; a few were taking advanced or graduate courses online. The professional hour in short was busy and noisy, with a lot of happy chatter afterwards.

The final task of the day was meeting with student study teams—sometimes with all of them and sometimes with individual teams. Which team received the most attention depended on whether a team had become bogged down or its members were at odds with one another. If all were managing reasonably well, then Bill had a number of options: introduce another team-managing and team-building set of exercises; offer a crisis situation recorded on tape in which a plane has to make an emergency landing in the desert and the passengers have to pool their resources and work together if they are to survive; tap the school psychologist to lead a discussion on techniques for getting along with difficult people; examine the range of decision-making processes—from one person as boss, to majority vote, to consensus—and list the tradeoffs and gains and losses of each system; or schedule a trip during that hour or after school to a nearby manufacturing plant that works exclusively with teams. The topics were endless. In addition, often Bill would distribute short readings from different team experts at one meeting for discussion the next time. These were carefully chosen to be not only stimulating and provocative, but also from diverse fields and professionals.

The study teams were successful. They followed up and consolidated classroom discussion and textbook assignments. When problems of understanding arose, they were noted and brought up first thing at the next class meeting. The teams functioned like a one-room schoolhouse in which collective responsibility was the order of the day; they also were self-help groups. Peer tutoring was always available and usually effective, often proceeding in round-robin form. Kids good in math and kids good in English took turns helping each other. It turned out to be an excellent way of using school time and building greater self-reliance, as well as group learning.

As he left the school after this last session with students, Bill was tired, but in a good way. He was not drained or depressed. Rather, he felt a quiet exhilaration born of satisfying hard work. He felt stimulated and alive. He did not count the numbers of hours at school anymore. It was now a qualitative, not a quantitative, experience. That group of three experts who had come out of the blue two years ago had given education not only a new day, but a new lease on life and learning. As Bill drove off, he returned friendly waves from some of his students and their parents. He felt good that he was contributing to their lives and they to his, in the give and take that makes for community.

CHAPTER 30

"Who Is in Charge?"

The McBride Elementary School on the south side of Philadelphia was a relic. Built in 1923, it was a dingy, dark, brick school that had served successive generations of immigrants for more than 125 years, and it was still going strong. For the last ten years the make-up of the neighborhood had been largely black and Hispanic families. The Title 1 stereotype prevailed: most were on food stamps and received welfare, and the kids were entitled to free lunch. The McBride school historically had served as an anchor of the community. It was strongly supported by parents. In fact, a parents' volunteer patrol more than any other factor kept the school exterior free of graffiti and its community garden free of vandalism. But trouble had been brewing as early as 2019. That was when Ms. Mebley and more than ten other teachers retired.

For the next three years it was catch-as-catch-can. An interim-appointed principal lasted one year; she opted instead for a school in the more affluent north end. But worse than that, the school could not attract new teachers who showed the old commitment; and the few who came did not stay. At best the school had become a baby-sitting service, at worse a prison. The neighborhood was up in arms. Something had to be done.

The superintendent asked the principal of another high-minority, high-poverty school to transfer to McBride. Her name was Rachel Gonzalez. In the system, she was called the triple hitter: black, Hispanic, and female. As it turned out, none of these factors determined what later happened. Her real gift was her independence and her determination to change the way things were done. In fact, she started off that way. Although she officially did not start her new assignment until September, she came on board in June after school was over and arranged to have all the teachers paid for one month.

It was a busy summer. Three big projects got started. The first thing Rachel did was announce a summer school and camp set up by teachers but run later largely by parents and aides who were paid. It was a community-focused improvement program with service learning as the essential curriculum. Next she asked the most outgoing teachers to form a recruitment team to fill eleven openings by September. Rachel gave them the salary parameters and a flexible range of qualifications, nothing more. They were free to take some chances with candidates who were not the most traditional. They were on their own, and whomever they selected was it—no second-guessing by the principal or the district. But they had to live with their mistakes. (Later on they were given the task of mentoring the teachers they hired.)

But the third challenge topped them all. Collectively the teachers were to use the summer to review everything in the school, and to come up with new operating plans for the fall. After these were presented and discussed and decided on, Rachel requested that the teachers elect a nine-member learning council to run the school. Like the recruitment committee, the council had final decision-making power. It did not make recommendations to the principal but decided what was to be done itself.

She defined her role as principal as primarily a protector of their autonomy. She would report back to the council the debates and requirements of the district and suggest ways the council's decisions might be couched so as to be more easily acceptable. She also would bring before them reports and priorities from the community, so that there, too, the council would better be able to navigate troubled or political waters. Finally, she would be a fund-raiser. She would go after grants and, more important, try to find businesses and corporations that would serve as sponsors. She combed the files to put together a list of graduates from over the previous fifty years. Many were doctors, lawyers, and other professionals who would be asked to contribute to and attend reunions at the school. How the money was to be spent also was left in the hands of the learning council.

Did Rachel's plan take hold by September? It did and it didn't, progressing by fits and starts. First off, some of the new hires were totally green. Two had never been in a classroom. One was a retired engineer who saw himself as Dr. Seuss coming into la-la land; his fourth grade quickly straightened him out. But with time and patience he turned out to be a splendid teacher and a much-needed male role model.

After a trial period of about three months, and with some intense mentoring and brokering, the new staff settled down and began to work well together in harness. There were two exceptions: a new kindergarten teacher who was too permissive and a second-grade veteran from another school who was too punitive. In fact, the recruitment committee already was looking for their replacements and had arranged for student internships in both classes. Two out of eleven was not bad. Having to live with their choices made a big difference to the teachers on the recruitment committee. Besides, teachers knew what to look for.

The learning council got off to a bad start. They missed deadlines, overspent the budget, and spent an excessive amount of time arguing with each other. Rachel realized that she was asking for a total change in the teacher culture. They had been brainwashed into thinking that only father or mother knows best and that they really could not make decisions as teachers that only administrators were supposed to make. And they were not trained to be administrators.

Rachel quickly arranged for two weekend retreats. She called up her favorite two professors, Drs. Brown and Sedley, under whom she had studied. She met with them for over two hours. She presented the challenge she and her council were facing and asked them to help design and participate in the two retreats. (She had to change the date of the second retreat to accommodate the schedules of her two collaborators.)

Rachel found their conversation to be a fascinating encapsulation of where things were in the real world and in academia. Both professors were members of the Department of Educational Leadership, which was just what was being called for, except that such leadership had been limited to administrators and never applied to teachers. Brown started: "This is a tough one for at least two reasons. First off, the research does not generally deal with teachers as leaders. Second, these teachers evidently do not even have the mind-set or ambition to be a leader. They are used to taking, not giving, orders, to deferring always to a higher authority. For example—and I know this is not what you want to do—but if you took over the council now and ran it as a site-based management team with you still in charge, they would feel right at home. They have, in short, an authority complex."

Sedley broke in: "I see it a little differently. I think it is more of a paradox than both of you suggest. Teachers are schizophrenic. In the classroom they rule like judges in a courtroom. They close the door and there they are totally independent, the masters of their world. Outside on committees or in public they seemed cowed, almost totally dependent. So you have two extremes: excessive independence and excessive dependence. Rachel, you seem to be asking us to help you tap the first and minimize the second so that they can be more assertive. But even if we could do that, which is doubtful, that still would not solve the other problem, which is how they can work together as leaders."

Brown injected: "I think I know where my colleague is going. And it is rather a novel, even sensational, goal. What is needed is the creation of a new synthesis that comes out of the thesis of independence and the antithesis of dependence. We cannot abandon what in fact constitutes their double reality but we can move toward creating a third reality—that of interdependence. We have to make them, if possible, interdependent leaders."

Sedley quickly chimed in: "And the research we would tap would be that not of conventional educational leadership but of team dynamics and leadership, even though that would tip us more into business than education. You see, Rachel, what you are trying to do for the most part follows a business—and even more so a manufacturing—model. To be sure, there are a few educator researchers, like Roland Barth and Richard Elmore, who have called for teacher leadership. But it has been mostly understood as a metaphor, not as something that should happen. Even Elmore's much-quoted notion of distributed leadership never envisioned a group actually doing the leading—acting as if they were the principal or, worse, the principal was no longer needed."

With that suddenly everyone was quiet. Rachel was intuitively aware that the conversation had led her former professors into uneasy waters. She saw them contemplating the prospect of betraying or straying too far from their programmatic homes. She quickly rescued the project by saying: "I am not in the business of starting a revolution or going off the deep end. After all, I am a product of your education. And look how terrific I turned out to be as an administrator!" The laughter cleared the air and averted any threat of subversion.

Then Rachel buckled down and weighed in: "But here is my problem. I can't do it all: lead the charge, provide ownership, maintain morale, and raise our sights. I need teachers to take up the slack. It is like you both taught me. You cannot have a quality program or operation if only one person is in charge of quality. Everybody has to take up the cause or it won't happen. So how do I help my teachers not to need me? How can they acquire the authority that they see solely in the principal? What training do we offer during the retreat?"

The professors both thought. Finally, Brown said: "You created part of the problem with your sink-or-swim approach. Change has to be gradual. You have to move from being indispensable to gradually becoming dispensable; and that will probably take a year. You have to model the behavior you want and then, piece by piece, turn leadership over to them. If you thought we could put together a quick fix in one or two retreats, you were mistaken."

Rachel said: "OK, I agree. So what we are talking about is a year-long professional development program to train teachers to take over administration, not as principals, but as an interdependent team of leaders. And it is my task to gradually turn over the reins and to take off the training wheels. Is that our plan?" The professors both nodded. Then the three turned to developing a team-building retreat.

Before the year was over Rachel had almost totally disengaged from the learning council. Sometimes it involved deception; she would pretend that she was ill or unavailable, and decisions had to be made without her. One time, when she was absent, the group changed its name to the executive learning council (ELC). Rachel swallowed hard on that one and did not advertise the new name at the district level. She already was taking enough flak from her fellow principals about giving away the store. By the second year the ELC was firmly in place, had added a few new members to insure new blood along with continuity, and, under Rachel's prodding, had agreed to run a summer training academy for teacher leadership teams open only to teachers who also agreed to stay in the classroom.

Although Professors Brown and Sedley were not officially sponsors of the academy, they agreed to speak on "The Research Agenda of Distributed Leadership." Rachel talked next on "Best Practices of Distributed Leadership"; but the spotlight was reserved for the members of the executive learning council, whom Rachel happily allowed to steal the show.

CHAPTER 31

The Teacher Leadership Collaborative: A Structural Scenario

It was a cold January morning when the car pool pulled into the snow-covered parking lot outside of what once had been a supermarket. Three adults, two males, one female, stepped out and hurried toward the entrance doors. Their breath formed strange shapes as they looked up above the door and saw the makeshift sign: "Charter School #264, Brato, Wisconsin." They quickly stepped inside, their glasses frosting over. They still found it odd that this was the high school setting in which they taught.

The school had opened three years ago, in 2022, one year after the lease on the building was acquired. It was a barn of a place. All the shelves on all the aisles had to be removed. Partitions about three feet high then were put in place to divide up the enormous space into cubbies or learning centers. Up front, room was left for two donated couches and two armchairs for parents and visitors. Off to one side was a small, enclosed area equipped to serve babies and toddlers. There was no central office; off to the other side was a secretary at a desk. Past her was a lunchroom equipped with picnic tables and surrounded by vending machines. Further down was an open area for ceramics, followed by woodworking and drafting studios. In between were a small TV studio with media equipment, as well as a print and silkscreen shop.

There was no separate computer room. All the cubbies had at least ten computers and their own software library and printer. Each one was designed to be self-sufficient and comfortable, like a home away from home. A student computer squad that called itself The Flying Geeks maintained all the technology and answered calls for help from both faculty and students. Heat and air conditioning came from exposed ducts suspended from the ceiling. The concrete block walls were covered with student-designed murals, woven wall coverings, flags of nonexisting countries, and banners bearing the names of fictitious science fiction or medieval domains.

For some reason students and parents visiting the school for the first time to gather information about enrolling had opposite reactions. The kids loved it. The parents could not believe that this was school, although after the first shock they were amazed by how quiet and industrious it was, like a busy, well-run factory. But what usually persuaded them was the reaction of their son or daughter. They had not seen such enthusiasm, ever, about school.

Since there was no principal, visitors were greeted by the designated "go-to" person of the week. Teachers took turns at that role. The tour and commentary took the form of an agreed-on format:

- This charter high school first opened three years ago.
- Charter schools are not private but public schools.
- They are funded with tax dollars, the same way all public schools are funded.
- We receive $5,376 per student, which is the per-capita amount the state gives to all public schools.
- The one difference is that each charter school has the additional cost of providing and maintaining its space and paying utility costs.
- This particular charter school has no administrative staff—no principals or assistant principals.
- We do have a secretary, and we outsource most financial and record-keeping functions.
- Everything else is run and done by teachers, students, and parents.
- You ought to know in advance that your role is important. We mean that.
- Our school enrolls families, not just students.
- The curriculum is individualized with project learning.
- Each student works on an individual project or a team project.
- Most of the teachers are state certified, and they range in age from twenty-two to seventy-three.

- Three teachers are former principals; four are retired professionals from fields other than education.
- All our students have passed the required state exams, and all who wish to go on to college will be able to do so.
- Our student guides will now give you a tour and answer any questions you may have.

Of course, the brief summary could not do full justice to the extent to which the school also was self-governing. It democratically involved all. The school was run as a collaborative in that teachers, as leaders, along with students and parents, decided collectively all issues; and they did so through consensus, not majority vote. A town meeting was held every month to discuss the recommendations of various collaborative groups; dissent was sufficient to send recommendations back to committee.

Above all, everyone involved in the school recognized and accepted that running the school was everyone's responsibility. There were no free rides. Teachers had to spend extra time and energy to administer and manage what they taught, and to sustain the optimum environment for that teaching. Students similarly had to shoulder administrative chores such as serving as rotating custodians of the cafeterias and toilets, providing breakfasts and lunches, and maintaining the computers and all the equipment in the studios and workshops. They also were responsible for teaching and tutoring others and preparing the agenda for leading parent-teacher conferences. Parents were asked to sustain a continuation of the school at home—in effect, a home school version of the regular school. Parents also were asked to open their home to students who, for various unhappy reasons, needed a place to stay for a short while. In short, the school sought to be both a learning and a caring community. Learning was to be reconceived collectively and collaboratively as what all did together. And how it all held together and worked was also reconceived as the common task all had to assume for such learning relationships to happen and to be sustained.

Strong teachers favored charter schools because administration was not a separate fiefdom. Things did not come down from on high. Wisdom was not a monopoly of the top. Nothing was prescriptive. There were no bosses. Teachers could be leaders without leaving the classroom. Administration of education thus was not distant from learning; it could be inside the gates. Above all, it became an ally of instruction and evaluation. As far as meeting quality targets went, teachers as leaders happily accepted such accountability, because they had a direct say in what determined student success, and because teachers hired, evaluated, and fired other teachers. They knew better than principals who were not in the classroom on a daily basis what it takes for learning to occur. They also knew better than principals, who rule generally by dominance, what it would take to run a democratic collaborative, so that students could better understand that one cannot have freedom without assuming responsibility. In short, the school's graduates were both effective learners and good citizens. One cannot have one without the other. Besides, they were generally happy, and pleased with who they were and what they had accomplished.

CHAPTER 32

TMs (Technology Managers)

Juanita Rogert, a registered TM, was always an early riser. The alarm was set for 6:00 AM. The date was Saturday, September 6, 2020. Weekends were part of the workweek. Indeed, as TM, she had no choice, for she managed a cohort of 104 high schoolers, ninth through twelfth grades, on a 7-day, 24-hour, 365-day schedule. As she turned over and slid her legs from under the covers, as gently as she could so as not to disturb her partner, she reached over and pressed two buttons on the console on her night table. One turned on her battery of computers and monitors in the next room, and the other turned on something just as important: the coffeemaker.

Juanita spoke her name and password and logged on: the screen acknowledged who she was and her title: "Technology Manager." The first screen she brought up dealt with security and behavior. As it filled in, she thought to herself: "It's amazing, but until these security and discipline problems could be resolved no learning could take place." The system used simple but elegant technology. All students wore electronic metabolic bracelets that tracked their whereabouts. The Big Brother critics objected to treating students as criminals. But the TMs had asked the parents to grant permission, and they had all agreed when two things were explained: "We are not and do not want to be the thought police. If a kid strays outside his agreed-on parameters, the first ones we call are the parents. You decide what to do. But the real reason we need this is to support their freedom to become involved in learning situations without constant supervision. Do you know how many good ideas have been wrecked by the question 'But who will supervise them?' This way supervision is noninvasive but assured."

But there was another function of the bracelet. It was a metabolic monitor and dispenser. Pharmacology had reached the state at which it was possible to develop the optimum metabolic profile of each individual and, having that in hand, to set up via the bracelet an automatically dispensing set of medications to correct any imbalances and restore optimum behavior and intellectual functioning. If a particular student required, for example, special doses over and above the standard range, there was an established procedure for medical prescriptions to be filled. Depression was virtually eliminated, and illegal drug use declined dramatically.

The students referred to their bracelets as "Mom and Dad." That was exactly the symbolic role also provided by the TM and her staff, who collectively represented the students' loyal family. In this connection, it should be noted that a great deal of learning took place not only off school grounds but also in the home. In large part, the phenomenal success of homeschooling in the first decade of the twenty-first century led to the notion that new experimental designs for education should incorporate homeschooling within the school. The goal was a continuum—an unbroken line of learning from school to home and back again. Reinforcement was total. Ideally, no one fell through the cracks.

There were no blips of deviation on the security and behavior screen, although more than half of the students were already up and away, working and learning. Juanita surveyed the computer scene with satisfaction. She mused out loud: "If a case could be made for freedom and trust as the ultimate control, the evidence is right here." Juanita then turned to her favorite monitoring activity: "student flight plans."

Each student was required to file a flight plan of study, testing, internships, work-study, and community service each week. Because there were no formal classes, only learning modules that were technologically available and tutor supported, students were free to design their own learning life. To be sure, it was done in consultation with members of the learning team, who signed off on each activity within their purview. Indeed, the face sheet of the flight plan took on the appearance of an elaborate checklist before takeoff. Probably the most important consultation and plan had to do with the decision to take modules beyond a student's official age or grade level.

The school was a school within a school. An average of one hundred students from grades nine through twelve were grouped and put under the guidance of one TM and her instructional and career staff. This multiage and multirange cohort was small enough so that everyone knew everyone else, but large enough to preserve variety. Above all, study levels were not rigidly determined by grade level. Thus, if a ninth-grade student could do eleventh-grade math, all he had to do was put it in his flight plan; if he received the OK check, he was allowed to move ahead.

Because all instruction was technological, evaluation and feedback also were constantly tracked. If a student faltered it would become immediately apparent and trigger the intervention of the tutor corps (a mixture of members of the instructional staff, students, and certified parents and community volunteers). In the first year of operation (some three years ago) 90 percent of students enrolled in AP courses had passed. Juanita looked on the screen for the current running total: 96 percent. And even that was not totally accurate, for some students take longer to finish, and the self-mastery approach allows progress to be self-paced. Because of the incredible feedback and evaluation system that technology offered, and because progress was tied to mastery and quality standards, the elaborate information base provided the best guarantee of outcome attainment, on the one hand, and knowledge totally shared by all parties, on the other hand.

Juanita spent the next two hours reviewing the weekly flight plans that would become operational that Monday. She typed in questions about some; students would have to respond to the questions before going on. Other issues she directed to members of her staff. That done, she was about to log out when a red light icon came on. She clicked and what appeared was an urgent reminder about an upcoming Autonomy Day, one of four yearly celebrations at which all students, parents, and members of the learning community gathered together.

She looked over the program for the day. The common theme was student autonomy. There were a number of student-led parent-teacher conferences. The students had decided four years ago to revive the medieval guild system and apply it to their educational program and progress. Thus, all students entered as apprentices, then progressed to journeyman, then to associate master, and finally to master. The progression was designed to structure development from dependence to independence and finally to interdependence, the supreme goal. The leadership model students selected was that advocated almost fifty years earlier by Robert K. Greenleaf: servant leadership, or the leader who leads by serving.

During Autonomy Day, each student's progress toward autonomy and mastery was officially announced and applauded. Special students were singled out by the TM and her staff, a task facilitated by the fact that each student maintained an electronic portfolio of activities and achievements. It was always a great day. The highlight was the culinary products produced by the AP chemistry class.

Juanita pulled up the format so that she could put together her notes as to what she had to do that day and what remarks she wanted to make. The format recorded what she had said every year for the last three. The last item had to do, surprisingly, with costs.

One of the major causes of the decline of public education in the past had been constantly increasing costs. Tax payers rebelled. School referenda to build schools often were turned down. Budgets were reduced; teachers were let go; class size was increased. It was a disaster. Teachers' unions volunteered to freeze wages. School administrators followed, but it was too little, too late.

The downsizing first hit Oregon, of all places, in 2014. The school system of Portland was exemplary: student performance consistently was in the upper percentiles, teacher morale was high, parent involvement was strong. But then the financial bottom fell out. Suddenly the issue of teacher shortages was replaced with that of teacher excess. An economy in recession, continuing stock market declines, falling tax revenues, class size reductions, and an increased number of students killed the goose that laid the golden eggs. School systems just fell under the weight of their unsupported and often bloated budgets. What had happened to many manufacturing plants and businesses now happened to the impregnable school systems: the dreaded downsizing.

In Portland over 250 teachers were let go, class size jumped from an average of 26 to 42 students, and free school bussing was discontinued. Typical of all downsizing, termination had nothing to do with individual performance, just number of years of service. It used the faceless neutrality of across-the-board treatment and numbers. Once the unthinkable actually happened in one place, the domino effect took hold. What occurred in Portland began to happen in every major city and small hamlet across the country. No state was exempt, not even Nevada, with its gambling revenues. Calls went out to the president to declare education a major disaster area, like an earthquake or hurricane. But he had earlier indicated to state governors that they would have to solve their problems on their own. Besides, he had by then already spent his surplus and was racking up record, triple-digit deficits of his own.

The media had a field day. A number of stories zeroed in on hundreds of teachers applying for jobs in Asia teaching English as a second language. The plight of students current and future being treated en masse was highlighted in stories that described their being herded into large lectures in auditoriums capable of holding one thousand students. A number of commentators noted the special irony of history: ten to twenty years earlier, when the United States and Russia had gone head to head in terms of military spending, capitalism had finally outspent communism and brought it to its knees. But now we had outspent ourselves; we had beaten ourselves. The wisdom of Pogo, of the Walt Kelly comic, prevailed: "We have met the enemy and he is us."

Emergency commissions and blue ribbon panels were formed. Solutions ranged from the predictable to the incredible. A federal commission sought to nationalize teachers and make them all federal employees, not unlike what had been done earlier to airport security guards. A number of parents' groups volunteered to work but asked for tax credits and even rebates for doing so. Groups turned on each other in the blame game. Administrators took the scalpel to the teachers, who in turn performed surgery on administrators. The situation became increasingly grim, ugly, and martyred. Each group took turns displaying its stigmata and exhibiting the degree to which its ox was being gored. Finally, it was all summed up when a group of education professors convened a conference entitled "Economically Driven School Reform."

As the new school year approached, what gradually began to emerge was that whatever solution was offered had to confront one overwhelming financial problem: namely, almost 80 percent of all school budgets was earmarked for the wages and benefits of a labor-intensive workforce. No problem solver could avoid that fixed fact. Finally, desperation, not enlightenment, brought forth from the wings the prospect of technology closing the gap.

Dubbed by some the Machine Teacher, the virtual classroom gradually took over both regular and homeschooling, serviced an increasing number of students without a corresponding increase in costs, and also provided the kind of accountability tracking and monitoring of student performance required by current testing protocols and federal legislation.

Naturally, the transition was neither smooth nor uncontested. Many recalled the Luddite revolution in England in the nineteenth century, when steam-driven textile mills were built to replace home and cottage spinning jennies. Charges of dehumanizing an entire generation of young people were leveled. Others claimed that teaching to the test would become the norm because machines were essentially drill sergeants. They never would be able to inspire students to an aspiration and a dedication to learning and leading.

Those in charge of instructional technology did not respond. Whether they had no answers, did not wish to add fuel to the fire, did not wish to trade accusations—or, now being at the top of the heap, did not have to—was never established. Schools opened the following September with the technology firmly in place. But what remained as an overall and constant reminder was that the midwife of this radical change was not educational philosophy but economics; and it could be just as easily be undone the same way.

So Juanita could not ever escape the final and recurrent test of her own managerial autonomy—cost containment. She was required regularly to demonstrate that she had not exceeded budget and that no additional funds would be required; in fact, there would be once again a small surplus that year. As she ran her budget through the format, she thought to herself, "Isn't this odd? The last word of the day and of my report is money. Gone are the sentimental exhortations of educators about producing public citizens. Absent is the waving of the intellectual banners of lofty inquiry, scholarship, and research. Instead, in the most mundane fashion we conclude by saying to those who pay our way: 'We have not acted excessively, unwisely or injudiciously. We have been good stewards of your trust and taxes.' But above all, we shall be judged by the autonomous achievements of our students, who also have been taught not to be excessive, unwise, and injudicious in their studies, relationships, and aspirations."

CHAPTER 33

The Future May Be in the Past: Creating a Universal Curriculum

It was just coincidence (unless you believe in fate) that three of the ten new teachers hired at Avery High School in the fall of 2025 had been educated with the best books curriculum created more than a hundred years ago at the University of Chicago. That approach had spread and been adopted as the core curriculum by many, mostly liberal arts colleges. In fact, in the last decade of the twentieth century the notion of a more traditional core curriculum was once more put forward. Our three best books purists, Ben Taylor, Sarah Pitts, and Paul Zagino, had been part of that revival but did not know of their common background until the high school was given a major grant to design an interdisciplinary curriculum.

The problem was familiar. Avery High School, like every other, operated with a departmental structure that fragmented knowledge. In addition, the school had different tracks and agendas associated with each department: white-collar career, college prep, and blue-collar vocational. The issue was how to bring all the subject areas and diverse tracks together in some reasonable harmony. What made the task harder was that many did not believe the departments should be brought together in the first place. The departments were strong and preserved their identify by being separate. But the district, which had secured the grant, pushed ahead and began to form different committees.

Our three novices, who did not know one another and not much about their common background, were assigned to the textbook committee. The goal was to find interdisciplinary textbooks. It rapidly became clear that except for a few general arts and humanities textbooks the pickings were thin. The committee seemed to be going toward a dead end. Then the group suddenly rallied, except for our threesome, around the idea to create their own textbook.

Ben spoke up first: "I think you're reinventing the wheel. The work already has been done for us. It is called the best books program."

Sarah added: "And it's often updated, therefore not limited to the ancients by any means." Sarah also noted that by crossing countries and cultures the curriculum almost could be universal in its coverage.

Then Paul chimed in: "And it doesn't have to be limited to books. It can also include films and the arts." But the rest of the committee was so seized with the glamour and prestige of creating their own opus that they ignored Ben, Sarah, and Paul and began distributing assignments.

The three met after the meeting and decided to have a cup of coffee and talk. They quickly discovered and were consoled by their common best books background. They better understood why they all had raised objections at the meeting. But then, because commonality breeds scheming, Sarah suggested, "Why don't we form an unofficial subversive subcommittee and develop an alternative plan of our own?"

Ben quickly agreed, but added: "It can't be just what we studied, and it certainly can't be dominated by the classics. The kids won't read it and the administration won't buy it."

Paul added, "I agree, but we can't eliminate all the classics. Maybe what we have to do is reorganize all the books into themes or driving ideas, then select the books and films and whatever else to illustrate those themes. And if they are old but fit in, so be it."

Sarah agreed: "I think themes are the way to go. But we need some students in our group. We have to know what grabs them. It may be what also involves us, but the language and content choices are critical. What is the point of all our efforts if students do not take to the program? Suppose we come up with 'leadership,' for example, as a theme. We have to put it in the students' language."

Paul added: "We also have to find a way to integrate the different tracks. We have to find crossover ideas—bridges between business, manufacturing, and the liberal arts."

They all looked at one another and evidently thought the same thought, which Sarah articulated: "Maybe we are creating an interdisciplinary textbook, but in a different way." She paused and then added, "But that may make all the difference."

They then all agreed on the next steps. The first step was for each of them to compile a list of books and films that had the capacity to become courses in their own right. The books and films also had to be able to stop know-it-all, bored students in their tracks, making them go quiet and sink into thought.

Then the three teachers had to test those books and films according to their bridging capacity—their ability to cut across disciplines, classes, and cultures. And finally, the teachers had to distill from both steps a checklist of criteria for selecting which works would be used. Here is the list of ten bridging elements the three conspirators developed.

1. HISTORICITY

Significant books should have not only a sense of history but a historical sense—a recognition that matters of the urgent moment are linked to previous momentous urgencies, that we are not alone in the universe or singular in time and place. A paradoxical stance to adopt is the image of Janus—the two-faced figure that begins the year and that simultaneously faces back and forward. The constant perspective of retrospect and prospect—of genesis and terminus—even may impart to current problems of productivity an understanding of what the Egyptians faced in building the pyramids.

2. PHILOSOPHY

Often the study of history is wide but one inch deep. It needs to be supplemented by depth, and there is no better partner for descending to the deep than philosophy, the original discipline of archetypes and paradigms. Her sister discipline, epistemology, supports understanding cognition: How we know what we know, and how we know what we don't. It may be philosophy more than anything else that will help us understand and ultimately make peace with the machines we create, which may be more intelligent than we are.

3. CROSSCUTS

Books that surprise cut across not only time zones but also borders and even academic disciplines. Unexpected connections are all the more reinforcing for being so. Art, biology, agriculture, politics, technology—all provide the context needed to supplement the depth of singular focus. Above all, questionable gaps need to be bridged, such as the unfortunate separation of politics and economics. We need politicians who are not ignorant of markets and economists who understand the process of compromise. The best books do not pass off halves as wholes.

4. SQUARE ONE DISCONTENT

Conventional moorings and traditional underpinnings are undermined by works that shake foundations. A seminal book disturbs the universe. A calculated discontinuity and even dizziness may reign, as transition becomes a new norm. Reflection compels a return to basics and reconfiguration of the new basics of square one.

5. RADICAL VISIONARIES

The book must not hem and haw, apologize for boldness, hold its vision in timid reserve. Rather it must attempt to see the unforeseeable, know the unknowable, and always go where angels fear to be proactive. Above all, in its most radical moments it must read like science fiction. If instead it is self-protective, tentative, and cautious, it will fall short of being part of the history of the future.

6. PRACTICAL

A best book must not openly or secretly despise this world and its imperfections. The failure of leaders should not be explained away by the fact that their followers are not angels, that rumor mills mess up communications, and that unions make difficult demands. Best books live in this world. They relish problem solving and overcoming limits, and they value the innovation of ordinary workers. In short, they love to work with people who love to work and make things happen.

7. FALLIBLE

There is a difference between being fearful and being fallible. Best books are bold and speak their minds but they are not cocksure. Their world, like reality, is not absolutist. They allow for being wrong or missing the mark here and there. They are open to being corrected or amplified. Further data and research may alter their findings, but their thesis should still dislocate the status quo.

8. LIKEABLE

The book should have a personality. The author should be a likeable colleague. The book should not just be read but convened like a seminar, with the author as its benevolent curmudgeon. Accepting the challenges and dislocations of a work often is eased if the audience is persuaded that the messenger is neither uncaring nor wishes them ill. He or she is in fact a winning companion on a journey that author and audience are taking together.

9. HUMANE

This is a request not for a bleeding heart on the author's sleeve but for a hard-nosed approach to empathy. The ultimate paternalism of leaders is to worry about what worries their employees. Transforming an organization so that research and development, like quality, becomes everyone's job has a better chance of happening if the environment is not ruled by a blaming mentality. Scott Adams, creator of Dilbert, claims that the worst thing about work is a boss who messes up your ability to do a good job and then blames you for your failure. Eighty-five percent of all workers claim that their bosses are bullies. Best books are smart about caring; so are best leaders.

10. THE UNFINISHED AGENDA

Best books keep alive the incredible creativity of humanity and its unpredictable solutions. They describe and are open to new amalgams,
hybrids, clusters, and so on—combinations that put together people and
structures that depart from the familiar. At best, seminal books are always threshold works. They make us hold our breath in awe. They help
us understand why we are still here, why we are likely to be around for
quite a while, and, finally, that the adventure is not over—as always,
the best is yet to come.

Given the above, is it a little more understandable that best books can
both become courses in their own right as well as shape and bridge the
curriculum. Reading them may be the best form of both initial and lifelong learning for the students at Avery High School, and perhaps for all
students everywhere.

Part VIII

ADMINISTRATOR SCENARIOS

CHAPTER 34

The Principal and Strategic Conversations

It was an exciting but different graduation. Shirley Samson had invited all her family and her friends to her house at 1:30 PM to help celebrate her graduation. She was to receive her PhD in educational leadership. It had been a long haul. She had started five years ago and now she was finally finished, a member of the class of 2026. During that time she had worked as director of curriculum and instruction in the superintendent's office of Northern High School, then as assistant principal, and now, within two weeks, Dr. Samson was to assume the principalship.

People started to arrive early, bringing presents and potluck contributions. Soon it was so noisy that no one could hear what the speaker was saying on TV. Shirley quickly donned her robe, shushed everyone, made sure her tassel was on the left side and ready to be switched to the right side, and stood still waiting for her name to be called. Finally, she was next in line. She stood still and serious. Then, the president solemnly said, "International Online University is proud to award the degree of Doctor of Philosophy to Shirley Samson, magna cum laude, and to bestow on her all the rights and privileges thereto and pertaining. Congratulations, Dr. Samson, your degree is being faxed to you now as we speak."

Everyone started to scream and yell so loud that no one could hear the slight whir of the fax as it printed out her degree. Shirley's eighty-two-year-old mother whispered, "I know all about online education and how special it is. But a TV graduation—isn't that a little tacky?"

Later in the day Professor Philips, who had been one of Shirley's favorite teachers at the master's level and her biggest champion, sidled over to her and gave her a present. It was a clearly a book. He said: "It is a big step up. Things will get crazy soon. Remember the basics and let them guide you." He kissed her gently on the cheek and slipped away. Shirley intuitively knew that the book was Plato's *Dialogues*.

Professor Philips regularly had reminded Shirley that the most important activity in education is listening. He could predict the kind of teacher someone was by the noise level of students' talking. Quiet classrooms were obedient but deadly. He also claimed that he could determine teachers' intelligence by the degree to which they asked questions. Listening and questioning—those are the key tools of educators, especially for administrators.

That stayed with Shirley and shaped her observations and her awareness. She noticed, for example, that there are basically three kinds of exchanges that take place in schools. The basic one was between teacher and students (including now the machine teacher); the other was between teacher and coteachers, colleagues, and parents; and the last was between administrators and teachers. What concerned her was not so much the quality of those conversations, but that they were always separate. Three dialogues were going on, but they were like parallel lines that never meet. As a result, linkages that should have occurred never did. The whole thing lacked coherence. There was no real integration of instruction, evaluation, and administration. Each one floated free of the others. Shirley thought to herself: "It is bad enough we have the separation of academic disciplines and the inevitable turf wars that accompany it, but this is downright stupid and counterproductive. We should not be creating more gaps than normally exist—and serious ones at that—but bridging them."

Shirley ticked off three serious arguments against separation. First, she believed that teachers need to link the way they learn with the way students learn. Second, learning should take place within an organizational and administrative structure that optimizes the convergence of all the learning levels. And third, the sign of all that occurring should be the gradual appearance of the interdependent educator. Shirley began to brood over how, as a new principal, she could start a different set of conversations—one that would be more reflective of the common focus that they all share and that somehow could bridge or at least narrow the existing gaps.

But although she was a principal now, she could not order professionals to talk, let alone on certain subjects. Besides, such conversations do not take place in a vacuum. They require structure. As she brooded over the challenge, three kinds of structure, each with its own focused strategic question, began to surface:

Horizontal, or the interface conversation: How can teachers, students, and parents be more interactively and collectively effective?

Vertical, or the alignment conversation: How can that coalition of learners align and prioritize its objectives so that they are in synch with those of the school district?

Circular, or holistic conversation: How supportive are our structures and processes of collaborative learning and conversations? If they are not supportive, what needs to be changed to optimize shared purpose and common goals?

Shirley sat back and smiled: she was pleased with what she had outlined. The PhD was beginning to pay off. She then picked up the gift of Plato and wondered: "Will you be enough to carry the day—to implement my plan of change through conversations and questions? I am not sure Plato is enough. He assumed what I cannot: namely, those professionals ask and answer tough questions candidly. No, I need a Plato-plus factor."

One of her other favorite professors always had berated students for failing to take the next step—for stopping short of where something could go. They exhibited what he called leadership shortfall. He defined that as a premature and predictably safe state. As such it defined the general failure of leaders to allow themselves to be led to wherever the problem or their passion takes them. He called all the next steps not taken "plus factors"—they symbolized everything that was not being pushed to the next stage. It was not unlike Robert Frost's two roads diverging in the wood; choosing the one less traveled makes all the difference.

The plus factor in education was the way teachers became leaders without leaving the classroom; or factory workers become managers without leaving the production line. The professor's favorite example of shortfall was not asking the next question, which distinguishes Nobel Prize winners from others, and which leads to original and seminal research and publications in all fields.

The plus factor Shirley needed to supplement Plato was the work done on strategic conversations by van der Heijden. He also created the model within which Shirley needed to nest her planned and structured Platonic exchanges.

The model of structured conversations was simple and elegant and rested on three principles:

1. All organizations are communities. Conversations sustain communities because interaction generates common purpose.
2. Strategic conversations take place at all levels. They may be big or small, short or long. But as long as they occur regularly and meaningfully they maintain all the interactive facades and the informational traffic of the organization.
3. Strategic conversations become action through strategic planning. That planning is designed to intervene in the evolution of the organization. In the process, the future nature of conversation itself becomes part of the planned change.

Dr. Samson was now ready. She had fixed in her mind the three key directions and their appropriate questions. She also remembered the principle of next steps. Finally, she had the right model that held everything together. All she needed was a good way to start. She did not want to be prescriptive and tell everyone her visions of change. Work still had to go on. She decided on the approach of a double agenda.

Her first meeting was with the school team steering group. The principal began by quietly saying, "I would like to make part of all our regular meetings an ongoing agenda item of self-examination, in which we talk over with each other the nature of our work together, what makes sense, and what does not. In fact, I thought we would start with this meeting and agenda—indeed, with meetings and agendas in general—and list what is worthwhile, what is questionable, and what may be dispensable."

She paused to survey the faces of her colleagues and read their body language. Most were leaning forward. A few had crossed their arms over their chest. She continued: "This is a genuine no-holds-barred approach. There are no sacred cows. There is only one absolute: everything said or recommended has to have the same targets of effective teaching and student achievement. OK? Let us divide up into smaller groups of three each. You know the drill: select a spokesperson to record and report on the group's conclusions and recommendations. I think we have enough time to put them all into priority order. Now remember the focus: you are going to evaluate both this kind of meeting and its current agenda. I suggest at least three categories: worthwhile, questionable, dispensable. You may come up with more and even change the terms: but what I need to know from you is what should we keep, what should we delete, and what we need to sort out and perhaps redirect. Your evaluation of the action items on the agenda at the same time will accomplish what we were supposed to at this meeting. OK, go to it!" The noise level would have pleased Professor Philips.

The reports of each group achieved more consensus than anyone thought they would. Dr. Samson compiled the reports and distributed them to all committees at the high school. She also developed a discussion format, based on the first meeting, that she asked all committees to follow and that was distributed both in hardcopy and by e-mail. One of the witty members of the original steering group had put together a listing of wanted criminal types whose crime was driving committees crazy at meetings. Dr. Samson quickly shared that profile. That was followed by an anonymous list of various ways of achieving agreement through exhaustion. Dr. Samson commented, "The fact that we can laugh, especially at ourselves, is a good sign."

The process of reflection and review of each committee and its characteristic agenda lasted three months. It involved everything: the current evaluation system, mentoring new teachers, resource allocation and budgeting, state-mandated testing goals, parental involvement, and so on. The process was taking hold. Discussions were lively and candid. Nothing was left unaddressed. There were no buried agendas, no dirty laundry hidden. Above all, the recommendations for changes essentially engaged the key obstacles and removed most of them. The reports and findings of all the committees were compiled into what came to be called "Our Change Book." Shirley concluded, "We are becoming a community. It is time to go to the next stage."

Dr. Samson announced that right after the end of school the entire faculty would go on a two-day retreat. It would be held at a summer camp for kids that would not be operative until a month later. It was two hours away in a beautiful setting near a lake. The goal was threefold: to review the mission of the district in light of the committees' discussions of what constitutes student success and faculty effectiveness; to use the affirmed and perhaps redefined mission to align individual and school goals with those of the district; and finally to produce a series of success scenarios and plans to change the way the faculty, students, and parents worked together to raise student performance and teacher morale.

It worked like a charm. Teachers were so enormously pleased that finally they had the central say in defining student success that they pushed hard for structural change to make it happen. Shirley had invited Dr. Philips and others as observers and recorders. They could not believe how productive the faculty were and how intelligent and well-thought-out the planning scenarios were. Indeed, one observer questioned their using scenarios rather than going directly to planning. Shirley responded, "Plans have a way of heading for pie-in-the-sky. Scenarios of real people doing their real work in real time serves as a reality check. It keeps the plan anchored in the familiar and thus makes the prospect of what is being planned more likely to happen."

Dr. Philips commented: "Well, you deserve the credit for pulling off this incredible series of changes and in the process forging a collaborative learning community." But for a change in their relationship, Shirley had the last word: "It was not me. It was the process." She added: "My role was that of Plato, the means strategic conversations, the goal creating teacher managers."

CHAPTER 35

The MBA Principal

Victor Rollins was enrolled in the MBA program at Penn State, class of 2015. He had completed all his class work and now was scheduled to begin a six-month, on-the-job internship. One of the most popular internships was that of directing a signature school. Victor had applied and been accepted at the Communications High School in New Orleans, where the entire reconfiguration of high schools into career schools had first started, in 2006.

The school superintendent at the time, Tony Amato, was also referred to as the CEO, the new popular term for school administrators. In 2006, he announced that these new high schools would not be "elite schools. There will be no IQ tests, no entrance exams. The students would be selected by lottery." These career academies would combine academics and career training. Each one would partner with an existing company in its career field.

The Communications High School had an affiliation with New Orleans Public TV and Radio. Perhaps the most famous and dramatic partnership existed between the Restaurant Management High School and Outback Steakhouse. The Aussie-themed restaurant chain had spent almost $450,000 building an actual, functioning restaurant as part of the high school. Students were trained at a facility that actually served the public, and when they graduated they were offered a position as a manager of one of the Outback restaurants. There was no need in this case to go on to college.

Amato claimed that these new career high schools had three aims. First, they were to demonstrate that not all good professional and well-paying jobs require students to go on to college. Many of the older brothers and sisters of those who reenrolled in one of the career academies related sad tales of finding no jobs or being underemployed after graduating from college. In fact, many had to enroll in the local community college to pursue a career program. Second, Amato wanted to go in head-to-head competition with the private schools that had drained off a number of students from the public schools. He hoped that these career academies would lure many of the students back. Third, he wanted these new schools to be run as a business. Instead of hiring principals with education MAs he would hire MBAs with managerial training. Each career academy would operate not only as a training ground, but also as a profit center. It would generate income, never be in the red, and constantly update its equipment using its own resources. In other words, it would be an autonomous operation run in entrepreneurial fashion. Oversight would be provided by a governing board drawn from outstanding professionals and companies in the field to insure that the training would be state of the art. Such directors would also help to attract partnership companies.

Viewing the history and development of these signature schools on the New Orleans Public Education website, Victor, from his perspective in 2015 and with his MBA training, was able to perceive how at least two other factors were operating that fortunately favored Amato's vision. Both were economic, one national and the other global.

In the first decade of the twenty-first century, public schools were in serious financial trouble. Budget shortfalls at the state level, declining tax revenues, the cost of building new schools for anticipated larger school populations, competition from charter schools and private management companies that drained funds, the increasing use of school vouchers—all combined to compel schools to be run as a business—a public business. Almost every school board began to attract a majority of its members from the business world. School-to-work programs gained momentum. Business partnerships with schools increased. Many school operational services were outsourced. It was all capped with the hiring of MBAs as the new principals, followed by the hiring of CEOs as superintendents.

A number of universities were doing a land office business retrofitting education MAs into MBAs. In short, Amato's commitment to career academies benefited enormously from the trend that was transforming public education in general into being essentially business run and business centered.

The other trend was equally profound, although more abstract. It was the increasingly visible impacts of the global economy. The principal one in developed countries was the radical change in the nature of employment. Ironically, the global economy provided more employment to developing countries than to developed ones. Creating products and services at lower costs kept prices down but it also shifted jobs abroad. Struggling to offset higher wages with greater productivity became the daily challenge. Only two ways were found to be effective: technology (robotics) and downsizing. The latter eliminated many jobs, including the better-paying ones that had sustained the middle class. The thinning of the ranks of middle-level managers was accompanied by their replacement by employee managers. A slow but steady management metamorphosis took place. The end result was that the economy was not able to generate the number of jobs requiring advanced college training that it had previously. Is a college degree required to run a McDonald's or a car rental agency? In short, the goal of Amato's career academies was to help their graduates maintain their status as members of the middle class. In the process, the academies also helped to preserve managerial roles for university graduates by opening the field of educational leadership to those trained in business.

Victor had no difficulty conceiving of education as a business. The teachers were middle-level managers of learning. The product produced and the service provided were career training. The customers were the students, their parents, and the businesses that hired them. Productivity goals were multiple:

- zero defects, or no dropouts
- quality outputs, or number graduated
- quality control, or scores on state- and federal-mandated tests
- longitudinal data, or longevity at work and positive evaluations
- advertising, or word-of-mouth satisfaction

To be sure, unlike in earlier arrangements, which permitted poorly performing schools to continue, there were penalties associated with failure. Because the budget was tight, students who dropped out, failed to graduate, or failed to offer satisfactory performance to employers reduced income, which only could be made up by reducing salaries accordingly. With precise electronic monitoring of both student and teacher performance, it was possible to determine precisely the weak links and to identify whose salary would be reduced and by how much. On the positive side, a substantial pot of money was reserved as a bonus for reaching all productivity goals. Those bonuses were substantial and could average between $15,000 and $20,000 each year. Moreover, because in most cases they were contributions by participating businesses, encouraged by legislation, they were tax free. Thus, for the first time accountability and incentive worked together to hold teachers responsible for what they produced and to reward them when they did well.

Victor found newer teachers the most cooperative. He had to take extra time and effort with older teachers who were unfamiliar with the more entrepreneurial and motivational aspects of education as a business rather than as a public bureaucracy. Fortunately, the monitoring process and its penalties help to winnow out weak teachers. Weak students were another matter.

One of the major objections of educators to a business approach was that educators had to work with whatever hand was dealt to them, but business could be selective and thus, in effect, guarantee its achievements. What was at stake politically and economically was whether the concept of No Child Left Behind could really be applied. The concept included kids from broken homes and dysfunctional families, kids living in poverty, kids in special education or with learning disabilities, kids who came to school poorly prepared or performed poorly on tests, recent immigrants and others with poor English skills, and so on. In some schools, that combined population could total 60 to 80 percent of the students. How could teachers be held legitimately responsible for raising all those students to acceptable levels and, failing that, be penalized by cuts in wages?

Victor explained to the faculty how the supplements to the NCLB legislation would work. First, a catch-up track for students would be created. Those admitted would be diagnostically screened. This track would have a heavy emphasis on service learning and electronic instruction and drill. Second, social promotion or moving ahead by age would not longer be used. Graduation or completion requirements would remain, but there would be no time limit. Students who dropped out of the program at eighteen or earlier would not be eligible to receive unemployment benefits for at least two years. If they could prove that their family needed income to survive, they could stay in school and graduate and the family would receive unemployment benefits for not more than two years. Third, all students in the catch-up track and those who dropped out or were on unemployment maintenance were factored separately so that teachers were not unfairly penalized for working with special populations. On the other hand, those teachers who worked with students in the alternative track received a substantial additional bonus for each student who graduated and was hired. Fourth, all students were profiled according to a highly differentiated matrix rubric so that every student was multiply benchmarked. That permitted not only the precise monitoring of progress, but also the triggering of interventions as needed. Fifth and finally, monitoring of on-the-job performance was to be given the same weight as academics and used to help motivate study and learning.

Did it work? At the end of his two-year internship, when Victor accepted the job of running that school, he answered quickly, "Of course. But that was because it had to work. There was total transparency. The numbers were there for all to see and compare. They did not lie. The numbers do not play favorites. Then too no one in the total process was treated unfairly or unevenly. Teachers were not expected to be magicians pulling rabbits out of empty hats. Students who could not cut it were given a second change, sometimes a third and fourth. The combination of carrot and stick worked, with almost all teachers opting for the carrot. And those who could not hack it, or take being whacked by the stick, left. Turnover of both teachers and students was an acceptable 15 percent. Most of the teachers were from the old school; and frankly I preferred training new ones in the system from scratch. In short, it was in everyone's best interest to make it work. And it did. We did get negative feedback from some employers about graduates. So we did a two-year follow-up study on graduates at work. What we found were gaps in knowledge and skills that needed to be addressed. So we revised the curriculum accordingly."

Victor paused and mused: "But what really made the difference was that no one was left out of the equation or left behind the eight ball.

Everyone had an equal stake in the outcomes. Everyone had to be part of the mix. The teachers had to be treated fairly and professionally, and rewarded accordingly. Parents were entitled to a return on their parental investment. And businesses deserved employees who were responsible and knowledgeable. Everyone had to make it work or it all would have fallen apart. The changes probably could not have happened if left solely in the hands of educators. There would have been too many competing ideologies, too many adversarial mentalities, too much martyrdom about whose ox was being gored, and so on. The business focus is single-minded and tyrannical: produce or leave; produce and get rewarded; produce and watch students get rewarded. The name of the legislation should be changed to No Student, Teacher, or Parent Left Behind."

CHAPTER 36

Principals as Futurists

Don Savage, Naureen Donnelly, and Paul Zvi always had been close. They had been principals together for many years in the same school district. They all had started in the same year, 2023. They met every Tuesday for breakfast at 6:00 AM to brainstorm and console one another. They took turns functioning as a coach to one another. They also had obtained their doctoral degree online from the same university, been in the same chat rooms, and studied together for the comprehensives. In short, they all felt free to say whatever was on their mind to the group.

Lately, their griping sessions were becoming longer, angrier, and more inclusive. Finally, Naureen brought them up short: "What's happening to us? We sound like a bunch of old and cynical whiners complaining about everything. It's tiresome." Silence followed, the weary silence of agreement. Finally, Paul spoke up: "I will tell you what set me off this week—that invitation to go to our PhD class reunion. You got it also. Well, two things sent me into a deep funk. First, the gap between what we thought the job of principal was going to be like and what it has turned out to be. We have become whipping boys and janitors. But the second thing, which hit me harder, is that over half of our doctoral graduating class are no longer administrators or even in education. They have jumped ship. They sell insurance; own small businesses, many online; are self-employed entrepreneurs, and so on. Most are doing well financially, some just getting by. But they all saw no future in being an educational administrator. So the question is: What the hell is wrong with us? How much more loss of role will we take before we disappear altogether? How many more schools and responsibilities will be asked to assume? Why wait for the inevitable ax to fall?"

The sun was beginning to rise. That was the signal to break up. They all pushed back their chairs and shared the check. Suddenly, Naureen grabbed both men and hugged them: "I love you guys. You are my best friends. And we are all smart enough to put our heads together and think our way through this. What do you think? How about meeting this Saturday for breakfast? The agenda is: our future. Same time, same place?" Don responded, "OK with me. Same time, but not the same place. If we are going to change our thinking, let's at least change the environment. How about the restaurant at the Hilton?" They all agreed and shuffled out.

They met three times and argued and proposed all kinds of options. At the fourth meeting some light began to dawn and a direction began to emerge. It began with the group asking two questions: What does education need? What do we have to offer?

The needs were so great in 2027 that one did not where to start; Paul jumped in with the beginning of a laundry list that ordinarily would have taken up all their time and consumed their intelligence, but he stopped himself and asked simply: "What did education have when we decided to become principals that it does not have now? I will tell you. It had security, it had respect, it had value. In other words, it had a future. And that's what education does not have now—and need I add what we don't either—a future."

Don replied: "Great! Was that supposed to make us all feel better? It is bad enough that the present sucks. Now you have upped the ante and invoked a bleak future. Now I have no illusions left."

Paul was relentless: "You missed the point. What I am saying is that we have to use our situation as symptomatic of education itself. And then we have to give education and ourselves back what we both lack: a future."

Naureen piped up: "But where is that happy future going to come from? From thin air? We are not magicians pulling rabbits out of an empty hat. If we could do that we would be able to solve our own problem."

Paul patiently answered: "You both have forgotten our training in forecasting and trending—those two great courses given in conjunction with the World Future Society. Well, if you remember that you also will remember that futurists always surface historically when the future is in doubt. Indeed, their function is to define the dilemma of the day as the lack of a future. What they offer are two things: projections of future conditions when things may be less draconian and when present insurmountable problems may be solved; and jumps to ten to twenty years ahead, when what is currently urgent has been resolved in unexpected and often easy ways."

Don mused: "So if I understand correctly, what you are suggesting is that we help education recover its future by becoming futurist consultants. Is that it?"

Paul tantalizingly answered: "Yes and no. You are right. We should become futurist consultants to education. But our task is not to deliver futures, happy or not; but to facilitate educators' thinking ahead. We need to serve as guides on the side rather than stars on the stage. Above all, we do not want to presume that we have the answers; we only have most of the questions. The worst thing we could do would be to limit creativity by maintaining that our own projections are the best around."

They all warmed to the idea. Naureen, the supreme organizer, stepped in: "OK, here is our homework assignment for next week. Three lists. First, list all the reasons educators will give why they would not want to use educational futurists and how those obstacles might be overcome. Second, put together a list of all those decision makers who know, trust, and like us and would be willing to hire us for an assignment. Third, and finally, list what specific services and activities we would offer to whom. Oh, and by the way, do not quit your day job."

During the next three months, the threesome began to put together a business plan and a program prospectus. Naureen designed a website, Don made the contacts, and Paul set up the services to be offered. They called themselves simply Education Futurists Collaborative (EFC). Then they received a call from one of their old school classmates who was a superintendent of a large district in Kentucky. He wanted to know if EFC could run a retreat for his administrative group of some fifteen professionals. The goal would be to build a collaborative team that would be not just reactive but also proactive. The dates given conflicted with some personal commitments of Don, Naureen, and Paul, but after discussing it with their families they called back to say that they would do it.

Then they huddled and talked over the task. Although they were anxious to make a good first impression, they decided that the goal had to be realistically adjusted if they were to be successful on the one hand and the administrative team was to benefit on the other. The first thing they therefore did was to designate stages of accomplishment or comfort levels. In a process not unlike the threefold one of introducing a new methodology in the classroom, they classified organizational stages into future oriented, future directed, and future driven; and they developed a taxonomy for each one. The goal of the retreat would be the first stage, although all three would be shared and defined. Similarly, group stages were designated progressively as cooperative, cohesive, and collaborative, and ranged from group to team to community.

Don, Naureen, and Paul all were excited by what was emerging. They found future expectations to be unexpectedly realistic and accommodating. They were not being pulled into reaching for unrealistic goals, with their feet planted solidly in the present and the next gradual steps beyond that. The futurizing and the interfacing of the group would be gradual but decisive; and they would always also know where they had to go if they desired to go beyond that.

Paul was excited: "This is great stuff! If they are only half as enthusiastic as we are now it will work. But we have also to develop day-by-day ways of implementing both goals. We have to find the things that are familiar to administrators, things they routinely and mechanically do every day, and change them ever so slightly to be more proactive and group oriented."

Naureen, who had in front of her a calendar-planner, said, "Why don't we start with the calendar? Why don't we ask them all to bring their calendars to the first meeting? Ask them all to review their calendars for the last three months and identify two things: how many items were future oriented and how many were group oriented, and what were they. In discussion, then, ask why some of the administrators designated events or meetings as future or group oriented and others did not. Then finally ask them to identify items for the calendar for the next year. What would be different?"

By the end of the first planning session, the three friends had more material than they might have time to introduce. It included reviews of calendars, agendas for meetings, professional development plans, vacations, attendance at professional meetings, and magazines, journals, and books routinely read. Don, Naureen, and Paul also planned to give each participant a future trends diary and a scenario projector. The first was to be used to record trends that they believed had a high probability of happening and would have a significant impact. There was also a section reserved for wild cards. Second, at the end of each week the participants were to select one major trend and write a scenario of how that would play out in a day-to-day situation in the future. The diary and accompanying scenarios could also include what their retirement career might be and what would be written in their obituary.

The retreat was an unqualified success. EFC was invited back three months later and three months after that. Word got out and the company received three invitations within the first two weeks after the retreat to undertake similar assignments. Unfortunately all were scheduled for weekends. After a full week of regular work, Don, Naureen, and Paul might be exhausted, and that might compromise their effectiveness. They decided to align their summer vacations and to take some extra time if necessary to schedule and accommodate assignments. Since summer is when educators are free and typically pursue professional development, it worked.

What EFC had not expected was that often during the team-building sessions, other future issues and configurations emerged. Some involved curricula, others teachers and parents; a few were focused on local communities and another on the global situation. It was heady. Although EFC could not possibly undertake many, let alone all, of these projects, the suggestions were too good to lose. The company's brochure and website were expanded to include a new section entitled "The Futures Advocacy Agenda of EFC." It included the following:

1. FUTURES LAB

One school in a district should be designated as a futures magnet school. It would be an experimental, state-of-the-art, and cutting-edge learning environment.

2. FORECASTING 3000

This would be an elective track in the high school. Its goals would be mastery of trend-gathering and forecasting, with particular attention paid to student careers. Student-compiled scenarios would be distributed as a senior project to the entire high school community each year.

3. THE DEMOCRACY PROJECT, 2050

This would involve projecting ways democracy could work more effectively in the future, measured by greater voter turnout, use of electronic town halls, greater access to information, and so on. Each year a different country aspiring to a more democratic process would be adopted, studied, and made the object of phased recommendations.

4. THE FUTURE COMMUNITY PROJECT

Using service learning, students would redesign the community in which they live by using the survey input of its members and by setting a strategic plan to realize that new design.

5. THE COLLABORATIVE LEADERSHIP PROJECT

This project would bring together teachers, students, and parents and explore the individual and the collective leadership options of each, as well as how they interface in collaborative terms. The goal would be to find what all constituencies have in common and what structure could best enhance such shared goals.

6. THE WORLD CITIZEN PROJECT

This project would be based on the future of dual citizenship. Each person would remain a citizen of his native or adopted country but also become a world citizen. What the latter identity would entail, its rationale, the nature of the passport, and so on would be explored, as well as its creed—a declaration of interdependence.

Don, Paul, and Naureen looked over their new brochure, looked at one another, and then went into their favorite three-way hug. Paul murmured, "I am glad we found a way to stay in education. But who would have thought that looking ahead would also give us back our own future!"

Part IX

PARENT SCENARIOS

CHAPTER 37

The Coffee Network

Stephani Caputo slowly sipped her coffee and lingered over dinner. It was her only time during the hectic week to hold onto her family before everyone went their separate ways. Her husband John, a UPS driver, slyly slipped the newspaper under his arm and retreated to the living room. He would drop into his favorite chair, rearrange the pillows, click on the TV to the news, and settle back to read, and usually nap. It was John Junior's turn to help to clear the dishes and put them into the dishwasher. Stephani's father, who had lived with them for the three years since Grandma died, also offered to help. The other two kids, Mary and Rose, went into their shared bedroom to begin doing their homework. Stephani then loudly barked her standard after-dinner announcements: "Girls, no TV, radio, or phone calls. And I will join you in a half hour to look over your work. John, don't fall asleep: I need the living room for my parents' group meeting at 8:00. John Junior, I know it is pushing your responsibilities tonight but I also need you to set up the big coffeemaker and set out eight cups and saucers. Pop, can you help me with the cookies?"

Stephani stopped and thought to herself: "Did I cover everything? Well, I think so." She went into the hallway to get the cookies she had bought on the way home from her job as a truck dispatcher at one of the big home supply centers. Her father and she chatted about the agenda of the upcoming meeting.

As she was arranging the cookies on a large plate, Stephani thought about what her mother had been like as a parent. She had been just as active; the apple does not fall far from the tree. Of course, that had been more than twenty years ago, when Stephani graduated from high school, in 1999. The Parents Teachers Organization then was 99 percent parent and 1 percent teachers. Everyone walked on eggshells so as not to intrude on what was clearly designated as the teachers' preserve. Parents could raise money to buy new curricula materials but only the teachers could decide what those materials would be. All that had changed. Now parents and teachers were really partners.

Stephani marched into the girls' bedroom. It was unusually quiet. Both were listening to music on earphones. Stephani deftly reached over and removed the earphones and slid them into the pocket of her apron. The girls were about to launch a protest, but when they saw their mother's stern face, they decided not to. "OK, you know the drill," Stephani said.

The "drill" consisted first of pulling up on the computer screen their workweek. It displayed the details of all the reading and homework assignments and their respective due dates. It also contained any special comments or guidelines from teachers and tutors about the current projects, taking into account the girls' past performances and grades. The girls and their mom talked about this information for the next thirty minutes.

Stephani, like all the other parents, had received extensive training as a parent-mentor and learned how to probe and ask facilitating, not accusatory or fault-finding, questions. She also had been taught not to be lured into the trap of trying to pass herself off as a subject-matter specialist. Subject-matter mastery was what their kids had to acquire and demonstrate. If parents stayed within the inquiry mode, those dialectic skills could carry over into every area, and kids would still be comfortable and unthreatened. Stephani remembered that the first training she had received was about the role of the home and the contributions of parents. The girls were just starting elementary school; John Junior was going into the middle school.

The top five student success factors based on research were listed on the board. The fourth one was parental involvement. But then a few of the parents pointed out that "time on task" and "monitoring" were activities that took place not only in school, but also at home. The presenter from the central office of the district was a little discomfited by the parents' self-aggrandizement but pressed on.

Three things were particularly important, she argued: parent training, parent work partnerships with teachers, and setting up the optimum home environment. The last engendered a lot of discussion.

The first mistake that she made was her assumption that everyone lived in spacious homes in which each kid had his or her own bedroom and computer in addition to the one supplied to each family by the district. The second mistake was assuming that the mother would be the only or primary parent implementing the partnership. A quick poll of the class indicated that over 80 percent of the women worked; that another 10 percent also were enrolled in advanced degree programs; and finally that aging but still vital grandparents lived in over 40 percent of the homes. (Legislation passed in 2010 had extended the foster child act to include senior parents, making the households in which they lived eligible to receive the same financial subsidy.)

What emerged clearly was that many homes were multigenerational, involved two and in some cases three or more adults who held full- or part-time jobs, and finally that gender and age were no longer the predictors of participation and involvement, as they had been in the past. But perhaps what was the most dramatic discovery was that learning was no longer the monopoly of the school. Every home had in effect become a homeschool. The incentive here, too, had been financial. Every household that met the minimum requirements of being a homeschool partner, and also submitted an acceptable time and work log that monitored parent involvement, received a substantial tax credit on a portion of its home costs. For the first time families who paid rent received the same tax benefits as those who could afford single-family homes. This legislation, like the one on caring for seniors, was part of a new proactive approach that factored in the later social and welfare costs of school dropouts and crime. It also followed the double principle of delivering services at the most basic level and of strengthening families.

Parents learned that there were three basics of an optimum home environment: work space, time, and supervision of both. Parents' input quickly expanded the designation of work space to include the kitchen or dining room table, especially if space were limited and there were more than one kid. Parents also realistically complicated the next matter of how much time students should spend studying. How much sleep should they have? Time to shower or bathe at night or in the morning had to be included, as well as time to eat before studying at night or going to school in the morning. Clothes had to be picked and laid out the night before; and they had to be clean and neat. In short, all the necessary nitty-gritty details of living together as a family constituted the basics. What also became clear was that whatever was involved in parent participation, it would require not only functioning as a homeschool but also managing a homeschool. In fact, the class requested that homeschool management be the subject of a future workshop.

All the training workshops were parent centered, and many of the parents quickly put their powerful stamp on them. A graduation was held after eight weeks of training and each parent received a certificate. John, Stephani, and Grandpa showed the diplomas to the kids. Mary groaned: "Now they all have certificates to boss us around officially. And now there are three who will grill us!" Everyone laughed, and Grandpa added: "But everyone knows who is the boss of all the bosses!" Everyone looked at Stephani as she blushed.

But what was the reason for the meeting tonight of a group of parents? The workshops on parent-teacher partnerships drew heavily on the research done on homeschooling. One of its strengths was overcoming family isolation by becoming involved with other families. That struck Stephani as a good idea. She had proposed it three months ago at a general meeting, and lots of hands went up as parents volunteered to start up a parents' group.

The assumption was that the group would be primarily geographical. That was immediately challenged. Arguments were made that it should be based on common interests or talents. Others argued the opposite: it should feature diversity. Still others argued that it should be primarily driven by families taking trips or vacations together, especially realizing the lower costs and preferences given to groups of twenty or more. And on and on it went. No common agreement surfaced. Finally, the convener ducked the whole matter by telling everyone to think it over and to discuss it next time. But the last word typically was that of a parent: "Yes, and talk it over with our kids and find out what they would want or prefer." Everyone muttered: "Of course."

When the trinity of Stephani, John, and Grandpa posed the general problem to the kids and listed all the choices mentioned at the parents' meeting, the kids all looked at them like they were stupid. "All of the above," was their collective answer. Mom and Pop were exasperated and looked at each other, but Grandpa was intrigued: "What do you have in mind and how would it work?" John Junior, who loved to be theatrical and academically pompous at times, began by proclaiming: "It is regularly a mistake to look for a solution close to the problem. It is also a mistake to come up with a solution that is either too rigidly narrow or too expansive to be manageable. Finally, you don't want to come up with a solution that is too permanent. We were taught you have to take a total systems approach. For example, the reason the train is late in Paris is that there is a snowstorm in Sofia." Mom interrupted impatiently: "We are not running a railroad here!" John Junior, unperturbed, went on: "You are right, but that was the example we were given about systems in general. But if we do not become hung up on railroads and look at the problem in a systematic way, what do we find? Two things: options and ways to offer choices."

Stephani then piped up: "The only way you can find that is to ask those involved to put together their wish lists. Priorities have to drive this thing, not what is easy." Her father muttered to himself: "Out of the mouths of babes . . ." But Grandpa persisted: "But what is the point of making such wild and crazy lists and then frustrating and disappointing everyone if their preference cannot happen?" John Junior responded: "But we don't know that it can't happen until we know what we want. You can't put the cart before the horse." Mom wanted closure: "OK, let's discuss what you want and what we parents want." Rose interrupted: "I would rather take some quiet time to think it over and put together my list. I also can number them in priority order. We kids can discuss our lists and see if there are any common denominators. You guys can do the same." Mom conceded: "OK, that sounds like a plan. But suppose Grandpa is right, and, when all is said and done, we can't work it out? What then?" Rose, catching her mother's eye, repeated what her mother always said: "Well, then, maybe it was not meant to be."

The next week when all the parents again got together to discuss what they might do with one another as families, they were all amazed at how alike the problem-solving process had been at home. In every instance it had been proposed by the kids; they all had used that stupid railroad example to stop the parents in their tracks; and they all had insisted that if what was wanted could not be worked out, then we would be better off not having any official set of exchanges, but should allow exchange to happen on its own and according to its own momentum. The parents all marveled at how the parallel curriculum, as it was called, of systemic and holistic thinking had taken hold of their children and benefited their grasp of solving problems. Above all, as the parents pooled the lists, five clear-cut patterns of priorities emerged: social, service, travel, events, and interest groups.

The social included parties, dances, picnics, and forming friendships. Service was payback—to the community, the school, one's religious group, the sick or elderly, and especially children suffering from incurable diseases at Ronald McDonald House. Traveling together for short trips on weekends or longer vacations was attractive because of the economies of group travel and as a way to broaden horizons. Events included going together to attend local and distant concerts, festivals, and even professional meetings, like service-learning conferences, that accommodate and welcome young people with sessions of their own. Finally, kids and parents wanted to be with other kids and families who had the same interests and even hobbies, and to be able to deepen their understanding of what interested them.

The obvious complexity of all the preferences was turned over to the computer, which sorted everything out and provided access through a menu of the five areas of interest. Matching became an easy process. For example, the meeting scheduled for 8:00 that night in Stephani's home was of a self-selecting group that wanted to combine service and travel. They elected to go to the southwest, where they had never been, and to be involved with Habitat for Humanity, building two homes on an Indian reservation. The group worked on details, blueprints, logistics, and expertise. Grandpa, who was a former mason, was in charge of the foundation of the building. He could not wait to get there. He felt like a kid again. Stephani hid her excitement: "We will see how it all works out. After all, this is only a trial run."

CHAPTER 38

The Educational Planning Clearinghouse

Things were becoming increasingly complicated for twenty-first-century parents, some in good ways, others in not-so-good ways. Here is the short list:

- Complexity of school choice
- Differentiated tracks and rubrics within choices
- More knowledgeable and multiple intelligence profiles of individual students.
- Increased costs of attending college
- Career options in an increasingly global economy

In the first decade of the twenty-first century parents floundered. There was no real planning or counseling being offered, especially to middle- and lower-class families. The wealthy, of course, could always buy such services. But no one institution in the public or private sector stepped in to fill the breach. Then, in the second decade of the century, the Gates Foundation and a few others funded some experimental programs. Most were connected with the central offices of school districts, but a few also enlisted the participation of some for-profit tutorial and test-prep organizations that had some of the expertise needed and also were interested in expanding the range of their services to clients and increasing market share.

The Morehead family of Tulsa had read about a new service available at the central office of the school district. One of their older kids was enrolled in a subsidized tutoring program with a national for-profit tutoring and testing organization; that program had just advertised in the local paper that it was also offering an education planning service. The Moreheads decided to try out both and compare the two.

The central school office team was headed up by an assistant principal whose title in fact was director of school choice and planning. He was supported by a team of two counselors (one career, the other a family service social worker) and an expert in testing and evaluation. Not all were involved in the sessions with every family or at any given meeting. In fact, the planning process relied heavily on initial family input. The first step was preparatory. Each family was given a copy of the most current handbook and video produced by the non-profit, Washington-based Public Education Network (PEN). Funded by the Annenberg Foundation, the first handbook produced by PEN was entitled "Using NCLB (No Child Left Behind) to Improve Student Achievement: An Action Guide for Community and Parent Leaders." It was a clear, detailed account of what the legislation required, accompanied by a glossary of education terms; it also listed various ways active parents could best use that legislation to hold schools accountable on the one hand and to benefit their kids on the other. For example, many parents learned for the first time that under certain conditions their kids were entitled to tutoring without cost. Over time and with additional legislation and amendments to existing legislation, PEN had to revise the handbook and expand it from its initial size of 80 pages to over 120 for the most recent version, issued in 2021. Two years earlier PEN had wisely also produced a video, which provided both an overview of the handbook and highlights of latest legislation.

In addition, each family was given a planning kit. It consisted of three major items. The first was a list of all the educational and school choices available to parents in that school district and beyond. The second was a profile of the minimum federal and state competency requirements at three graduation points: elementary, middle, and high school. Finally, a number of copies of forms for working out or drafting plans were provided for each kid in the family. The forms were designed as road maps going from preschool to kindergarten and on, through twelfth grade. Each major graduation stage was presented as a fork in the road. Footnotes factored in the minimum competency standards to be met for each stage. Optional future paths were shown at each fork in the road.

There were a number of places on the map to fill in test results, extracurricular activities, awards, citations, and so on. It was a wonderful visual tracking device that the Moreheads thought might be put up on the wall in the kids' rooms next to the markings on the door jamb that recorded their growth in height. It was suggested that students maintain an electronic portfolio to accompany the longitudinal plan. The composite was a comprehensive monitoring system that maintained past progress while focused on future goals. Many students submitted their portfolios and planning forms directly for admission to college.

Some parents at first were startled by the projections. For example, their two-year-old was listed as a member of the high school class of 2050. But after a while they became more comfortable with the entire planning process and living in the future. What was particularly striking was that each of their three kids could have his or her own individualized plan. Thus, Amy, the youngest, could be homeschooled at least through the third grade. Amos, the middle one, could shift from elementary school to a charter or magnet school that featured project or inquiry learning, at which he would thrive. Andrew, currently a sophomore in high school, could switch to the service learning track in his junior year to tap his desire to do community service; in his last year he could enroll in a cyber school and take college-level courses that also satisfied high school graduation requirements, and thus enter college with the freshman year nearly completed and with a year's tuition saved. "Wow! This is as much fun and challenge as a good board game," the kids exclaimed.

The Moreheads submitted their drafts to the central office. The team examined the three plans, discussed the specific choices in detail, and made notes for sharing with the family. It took a long time, almost a month. There was a heavy backlog. Finally, a meeting was arranged with the team and the entire Morehead family. The director of the team explained the purpose of the meeting: "We are here to discuss your plans, not ours, and in the process to raise certain questions and issues which you may not have raised or given as much weight to as we have. Naturally, we welcome your views on each of these points. After all, our common goal is to help you decide on what is best for your offspring and therefore what is the best learning plan for their future. The next step is for you to consider our input and suggestions. A written summary of what transpires here will be sent to you in two or three weeks. After you have given thought to altering your plans, a final revised version is to be submitted for action. We will then prepare a final document to implement the first stages of each of your plans. That should take another month. But we need to add that we are always available to you for consultation at every stage. A member of the staff will be assigned to your family as the contact person. The implementation plan will also contain dates for meeting again and for reviewing the plan at critical stages. It is important to remember that monitoring is part of good planning. Do you have questions on procedure? Good. Then let us first look at the plan for Amy."

Mr. Morehead leaned over and whispered to his wife, "It is a good thing we started this over a year ago, because with this speedy group we might have missed the first implementation for all our kids."

Mr. Morehead was also contrasting the approach used here with their earlier experience with the for-profit tutoring service, which also offered a planning service in conjunction with that of the public central office. There were three big differences between the for-profit service and the public schools' central office. The first difference was that the for-profit service offered college-planning funds. These were monthly set asides with tax deferral benefits as long as they were used for college expenses. Some were even called "legacy funds" to encourage grandparents to contribute and even to accept inheritance gifts free of inheritance taxes.

The next big difference was speed. The for-profit service did not have a team. The Moreheads met with only one person throughout. She was called a "planning officer." She gave the same PEN handbook and video and the same road map planning forms, except hers had the name of the tutoring service displayed across the top. She indicated that this was to be collaborative arrangement in that she, the parents, and the kids would collectively fill out the forms with erasable markers. Because three kids were involved that would probably take a total of three hours, one for each kid.

Finally, the for-profit service offered a unique service called "Interventions for Success." This was their proactive version of monitoring. It included the basics of tutoring for catch-up, test prep for understanding and mastering test design, AP courses online, and finally internships after school and especially during the summer. It was an impressive combination of early warning and early opportunity systems designed to anticipate and optimize each planning stage before it occurred. It was described as an insurance policy for student success.

The Moreheads decided to combine both services and told each one that they would do so. Neither one was overjoyed, but the parents decided that they had to do what was best for their kids; and, given the uncertainty of the future and the global economy, they needed as much help as they could get. Besides, Mrs. Morehead sighed, "If they had this service when we were kids, what different choices would we and our parents have made?" Her husband indicated that he would have made a number of different choices. The two became involved in a long conversation about what might have been; but they were pleased that they were thinking ahead so that hopefully their kids would have fewer regrets. At this point, the enthusiasm of the kids for the entire process was thanks enough and augured well for their future.

CHAPTER 39

Electronic Partnerships

By the end of the first decade of the twenty-first century, teacher-school-parent communications had become increasingly electronic. The extent was limited only by the availability of computers at home, the commitment of the school to enhance communications and relationships, and sufficient teacher time to spell out parental follow-up homework assignments and feedback. In other words, home environment was regarded as indispensable to student achievement in general and to higher levels of performance in particular. Even the best of teaching could fall short if the home was dysfunctional or compromised. Conversely, a supportive environment could enhance and even extend schooling. In fact, in some families, homeschooling was a way of life way before it became a more official educational option.

But for Esmeralda Diaz, single working parent, living in the city projects in 2015, it was not an easy matter. She was unable to attend most PTA meetings or even parent-teacher conferences because of work and baby-sitting costs. Although Esmeralda had dropped out of high school at the tenth grade to go to work, she intuitively knew that electronic linkages would make an enormous difference. In the fancy downtown apartment hotel where she worked as a maid, they used computers to keep track of inventory. "You would not believe," she confided to her oldest son, Reynaldo, "how much rich people steal!" The hotel taught her the basics of computer entry via push-button icons on the screen. She took that activity very seriously. If she could not account for everything, the cost of the missing items was deducted from her salary. She watched her manager, Maria, "do the numbers," as she called it, at the end of every day. It was beautiful. Maria even offered to show her how it was done in case she needed someone to help her.

Although Esmeralda agreed and learned the basics, when she listened to her kids and their friends talking about what they did on computers in school, she felt like she really knew nothing. But she also knew that having and using a computer at home would be a godsend. So with Reynaldo's help she applied to the school Computer-at-Home Program, which would supply each home with a basic PC, software, a printer, and, best of all, a linkage communications program with the school.

There were many Internet companies now providing schools with the service. The one the school had chosen and that Esmeralda used was called EdConnect. When she learned that it was based in Chicago—and here she was in Philadelphia—she realized that distance no longer mattered, only time. With Reynaldo helping her, she used her password to log on and to access both general information and her kids' individual pages, even though the three of them were in different grades and even in different schools. She was amazed at what was displayed.

First, there was the school page. It showed all the upcoming events, including test dates and vacations and school or grade trips. The principal had a regular column of news about the school and future plans. New hires were shown with a picture and a background profile. The PTA had a separate section for news about parents' events and activities, especially fund-raisers. The local group, like many others around the country, had formed a school foundation to attract grants and funds. In fact, the funds for the free computer program came through the foundation.

Then, Esmeralda clicked on her son's name and his page popped up. Alongside his name was his picture, taken at the beginning of the year. The screen displayed all his homework assignments for the entire week, as well as any tests coming up or papers due. Kids could no longer claim that they had no homework or that they had done it all in school. Esmeralda's friend Maria called this the "Gotcha!" section. The screen also displayed Reynaldo's attendance record for the month and any time he was tardy. Teachers' comments on his last report card, as well as evaluations of his test scores, were there too, going back to the beginning of the school year. Esmeralda turned to Reynaldo to ask him why this section was called "Archives."

Esmeralda learned that that was as far as most programs had gone about five years ago. Then gradually three additional sections were added. The first one to come on board was called "Benchmarks." That was followed by another entitled "Rubrics." The last was called "Interventions." Fortunately, a glossary link enabled her to understand what each word meant—but more important than definitions was an explanation that preceded the three new sections. The title of the introductory paragraphs was "Feed-Forward and Feedback." Here is what it said:

> The high value placed on parental involvement requires building two exchanges: informational with the school and learning interventions with teachers.
>
> The school is mandated to track student performance on five levels: by individual student, by grade, by subject matter, by teacher, and by school. The benchmark establishes the beginning point from which progress or the lack of it is measured. That data initially was shared only with the board and the state, but then the PTA pressured for its being shared with all parents on the website. That way parents could better understand where their kids stood in the larger picture and could observe the extent of their development from shared benchmarks.
>
> Parent discussion and questions about the data patterns led to the development of the rubrics section. Rubrics individualize student goals by subject matter. Usually five categories or levels of performance are described and laid out horizontally. The first describes an A performance, the last an F performance. But because each subject has a number of competencies—as many as ten—a spread of achievement is given to each competency. So at a glance one can quickly observe what is strongest and what is weakest, what needs the most work and what can be soft-pedaled. But to really tap both these additions for the benefit of student performance, the fundamental relationships between school and home, teacher and parent, had to change.
>
> The software was reprogrammed to accommodate two-way exchange. Teachers and parents could now talk to each other. They also could be more mutually diagnostic, each one inputting what he or she knew about the student's learning habits, styles, and behaviors. Most important of all, they could identify not only each kid's individual performance goals, rubrics, and foci, but also what each of them—parent and teacher— would do as part of that new learning partnership.
>
> The section of "Interventions" was thus introduced to specify particular activities in school and how they should be reinforced and extended at home. In effect, for the first time, parents are being given homework.

Esmeralda felt overwhelmed. She was not sure she was up to that level of partnership. After all, she was a high school dropout. Reynaldo knew so much already about computers and a lot of other subjects. How could she ever be his home teacher? It was different story for the little ones. But a high school kid and benchmarks and rubrics, that was way over her head, thought Esmeralda. Then she noticed a link at the end to FAQ. Reynaldo told her it meant "frequently asked questions." Esmeralda quickly clicked on the link. The first question floored her; it was exactly what she was worried about.

Q: How can I as a parent hold up my end of the partnership when I do not know the subject matter involved?

A: You do not have to know the subject matter. Your contribution is a series of questions; you use what is called an inquiry mode. For example, you select one the subgoals of the rubric and ask "How have you addressed and accomplished that goal? What grade would you give yourself, from one to five?" Then you talk it over in a nonthreatening, nonjudgmental manner. You will be surprised how well it works.

Q: How do I handle specific interventions recommended by the teacher?

A: You handle them the same way. Suppose the teacher recommends that you monitor your kid's reading and it involves a subject that is beyond your knowledge. In a textbook there will be questions and discussions at the end of the chapter. Ask your son or daughter to discuss his or her answers with you. Ask also after each one whether your son or daughter thinks he or she really understands the main idea. If it is a work of fiction, ask him or her to describe the narrative and to write down what questions he or she would ask on a test.

There were a lot of other frequently asked questions. As she read through them Esmeralda felt more and more comfortable with the process. The final section was "The Range of Parent Participation." It explained that there was no one role parents should take at any given time with any given child. This was not a one-size-fits-all model. Parents should select what suited them and their situation best. It could vary with different kids and progress over time. The chart of options in table 39.1 was provided as a guideline.

Table 39.1.

Range	Parental Roles
Minimum	Observation and assessment
Moderate	Supervision and guidance
Maximum	Participation and encouragement
Optimum	Partnership and colearning

Esmeralda looked intently at the chart and thought to herself: "I should have three charts, one for each kid. Because I think I am at a different place right now with each kid. Also, maybe it is not accidental that I think I am further along with the younger kids than with Reynaldo. But that is OK, the guidebook says. Besides, I can gradually change, and though I start at the minimum with Reynaldo I can move beyond that to other roles. And all the time, while I develop, so do the kids. Who knows? I may go back to school myself or put in for the job as assistant manager. Isn't it what the kids always say as they high-five each other? It is a win-win situation."

Part X

STUDENT SCENARIOS

CHAPTER 40

Tiny Tot Independent Learning

Jeff finished work at 4:00 and was on his way to pick up Devon and Kira at Kidee Academy. Kira, who was three going on thirty, spent the entire time there in pre-K. Devon, who was a bossy five-year-old, had morning kindergarten and then the school bussed her and other kids of working parents to Kidee Academy, where they would be picked up later. The academy stayed open until 6:00 PM.

Jeff, like his wife, Jessica, had a full-time job and was routinely overscheduled, just the way their kids were, with Daisy Scouts, gymnastics, dance classes, play dates, and so on. Jeff and Jessica did not see anything changing or getting any easier later on. In fact, it might get worse as the kids got older. It was now 2010. By 2020 Devon would be a full-fledged teenager. Jeff groaned and thought: "Why can't these kids just go out and play? Why don't they just ride their bikes like I did and not have to be driven here and there?" But one thing had changed for the better. He did not have to police the use of the TV when the kids got home; they both promptly went online. So did Jeff. It was nice: all you heard was the reassuring chatter of keyboards.

Three- and five-year-olds, some may think, don't go online—that must be an exaggeration. But the numbers do not lie. In 2000 only 6 percent of children aged two to five had Internet access. In 2002 it jumped to 35 percent. Now in 2010 it was up to 83 percent. Unlike earlier parents, who had been uncomfortable with computers, this generation of parents was tech savvy, and so were their kids. In addition, schools increasingly were using technology to boost test scores, serve as drill sergeants, and sustain Internet research. Many school districts also now had electronic communications programs linking the school and parents and the community.

What was equally surprising was that Internet access by Hispanics and blacks generally matched that of whites. Actually, minorities made more use of computers at school. The past gaps between the groups had closed dramatically, at least electronically. In addition, because kids spent more time at home online than ever before, TV watching had decreased so much that many kid shows had disappeared. To be sure, clever marketers shifted their products online, but they had to be educational to survive. More than 45 percent of the kids were getting better grades.

Jessica, Jeff's wife, came home with a bundle of groceries. She called out, "Jeff, are you home? What are the girls doing?" There was no answer. "Jeff, please answer me if you are here." Finally, Jeff replied, "Up here on the computer. So are the girls." Jessica looked at her watch and did a quick calculation: "I know what they are doing—homework or research. That gives me almost two hours to unpack, change into jeans, and put up dinner. But first . . ." She quickly prepared a peanut butter sandwich, cut it in half, put it on two plates, grabbed two juice boxes, and went upstairs. She kissed each of the girls on the head and slid the plates and drinks alongside the computers. Neither one looked up, but both mumbled, "Thanks Mom." Jessica went into the bedroom, and Jeff, in a martyred voice, said: "Where is my snack?" Jessica threw him an apple.

Electronic education, or e-learning, had come along just at the right time. Standards for performance were higher than ever before. And the consequences were serious. If Devon did not get a score of at least two out of a possible three when she took the state tests in math and English, she would not be allowed to go on to the next grade. And because schools had eliminated social promotion by age she might have to stay at that grade level for more than one year. Looking far ahead, both the opportunities and choices for college and work were determined early on, and competition for both had increased substantially.

Then, too, budget shortfalls had reduced the number of teachers. The only way class size could remain manageable and individualized instruction could be maintained was with e-learning. And because school e-learning was extended by home learning, in effect every home was involved in homeschooling. But other changes were even more dramatic.

Although e-learning forestalled making the school day longer, what was encouraged was having kids start school at an earlier age. Pre-K became more than a baby-sitting service. Kira, although only three, already knew her alphabet and could count to one hundred. She knew her address and phone number and could write her name. She was beginning to read. Devon, although only in kindergarten, was reading at a first-grade level and doing second-grade math. On her own and online she was taking a beginning science course. Required to develop an electronic portfolio, Devon already had four stories, three math papers, and two science pictures included. These portfolios followed students throughout their school years and were sent off as part of their application to colleges.

The advantage of a head start was no longer limited to a few but extended across the board. In 2000 there were 822,000 children enrolled in public pre-K programs. By 2010 it was over two million. The average pre-K class size was fourteen. Of the students enrolled, 68 percent had half-day schedules, 32 percent full-day schedules. Pre-K teachers had to be certified and were public school employees. Their primary area of expertise was e-learning.

Jessica called everyone down for dinner. The evening meal together was a command performance with no exceptions unless you were sick. It was the only regular family time. Both girls came down with papers they had printed out. One set of papers was their tests, already scored by machine and accompanied by an analysis of areas that seemed to need improvement and suggestions on how that might be done. Devon asked her mother to sit down with her after supper for help in math. The other batch of papers dealt with what was called "growth spurt work." These were advanced assignments that kids could choose once they had satisfied the basic requirements. The papers were passed around the table along with the food. And the busy family chatter of the day began, with questions and answers about school and work, vacations or trips planned, visits by grandparents and cousins, and so on.

After dinner the kids watched a half hour of TV and then went back to their computers. At 7:30 they were in the bath together. By 8:00 they were in bed waiting for Mom or Dad to read to them. They listened and gradually drifted off to sleep. Some things happily do not change. Reading to kids and stirring their imagination rivals the best of e-learning.

CHAPTER 41

K–16

"What's this K–16 program?" Jack's father asked, looking over the announcement his son had brought home from the middle school counselor. "I know about K–12. But what is 12–16?" The year was 2020.

"It's college, but the idea is not to make it a separate step. It is supposed to be all one continuous process," Jack answered. His father quickly asked, "What's the advantage of that? And suppose you don't want to go to college at all, or decide that is what you want to do later?" Jack replied, "Look, I don't have all the answers. They have called a meeting of parents to explain it all to you and Mom." His father read over the entire page. "They scheduled the meeting at 3:00 PM. Who can go to that? Your mother and I both work. Oh, wait, there's an evening date also, the week after. We'll both try to go to that and then talk it over. OK?" Jack nodded his thanks.

There were about one hundred parents at the meeting that night. On the stage was a big banner: "Work, College, Service." The principal of the middle school welcomed and thanked everyone for coming and then turned the meeting over to the K–16 coordinator, Ms. Hoffman.

Hoffman began by telling some stories about kids dropping out and displayed on a screen numbers about their limited job opportunities. She described how difficult it was for these kids to come back to school and often how much time they wasted trying to catch up; they also had trouble meeting college entrance requirements and finding a good job. She then summed it all up: "The goal of K–16 coordination is to start planning early and to avoid such breaks and gaps in college prep and work training. Besides, students can start earning college credits before they graduate from high school. The kids call it a "twofer": they take college courses that also count as high school courses. In fact, they can start as early as the freshman year of high school if they have a minimum 3.0 GPA. Some students even wind up with the equivalent of one full year of college while still in high school. That saves not only time, but a year's worth of tuition. Best of all, because our local community college is online, many of those courses can be taken without even going to the campus. It is a win-win proposition. Questions?"

A lot of hands were raised, but all the questions came down to the fact that the parents could not believe it. It was too good to be true. There must be a catch somewhere. Why would the high school give up its high school courses? Why would the college give away its credits for nothing? What became clear was that meeting higher standards and higher costs were calling the shots. The reasoning was that students in high school would work harder and aspire higher in the company of college-level students and in college-level courses. Cutbacks in spending for teachers' salaries at both the high school and community college levels also had forged this partnership: course sharing cost less.

At the end of the meeting, all the parents were advised to make family appointments with the K–16 counselors to set up their own road map of the next ten years. They all were given a planning kit that included a number of copies of road maps. Key tests mandated by the state were already logged in at the appropriate grade levels. A separate legend at the bottom of each page described what the test tested. The recommendation was that kids draft their own plan first and then sit down at home with the family to review that plan. After families had completed together the final plan they were to call and schedule a special meeting with one of the K–16 counselors.

When Jack's parents got home, they explained it all to Jack and gave him the planning kit. They asked him to work on his version of the plan, and then they would all talk it over. Jack looked at the road map and found he had more questions than the kit explained. So he did what he always did: got together with a small group of his friends to work it out together. The first idea, which everyone liked, was to set the road map up like a board game. They had been taught that sometimes it is smart to plan backward—to start from the end points and work back—so they began by leaping ahead. They designated certain points, like part-time jobs or certain courses, that would support their work or college goals. Each of those points was designated a branch point at which certain decisions had to be made and more information or data was required. Branch point cards asked Jack and his friends what they knew about certain careers or courses before they were allowed to make decisions. The cards also introduced other choices, such as switching completely to a cyber school, or enrolling in a career academy for one year, or working full-time for six months or a year while being homeschooled.

Meanwhile, Jack's parents could not understand why he was taking so much time to develop his own plan. They were anxious to go over it as a family and to make an appointment with a counselor. When Jack finally finished and showed them his road map, they could not believe their eyes. There was hardly any white space left. Everything had been filled in great detail—courses, work opportunities, community service, and so on. Additional pieces of paper were attached all over the place, keyed to different stages, that provided further options or explanations. Finally, all the different options of school choice were color-coded so that at a glance you could see what choice was being made, why, and when. His mother finally confessed, "Jack you will have to guide us through your map. Otherwise I will be lost." His father was amazed: "This is incredible. It is so much better than what they put together. Why didn't they come up with a board game?" Jack quietly said, "Because they did not ask us."

As Jack began to walk them through the complexity of his road map/board game, his father thought: "You know, it's amazing how our generation missed the boat. We lived by trial and error. There was no system to help us out. Boy, did we make some dumb decisions. Of course, things are more complex today. There are so many choices, so many opportunities and constraints, and, to boot, things are getting harder and harder. Kids today have to score higher, know more. Before, the only books on parenting that were recommended were books on psychology. That's important. But now we need books on parenting successful kids—kids who have to plan far ahead, beyond K–12 to now K–16. It's a new world for a new future. Jack is probably better able to mange that future than I am. But at least educators are looking ahead, and giving students the tools they need to make good choices."

9TH–12TH PLANNING OPTION: THE COMMUNITY MUTUAL BENEFIT HIGH SCHOOL ASSOCIATION

It started small. It began in the first decade of this century with high school students in ten communities throughout the country being given start-up grants by the Gates Foundation to be involved in community projects. But this was different from general service learning projects for two reasons: first, it focused exclusively on health in the community; and second, this project was the curriculum. The goals were to make students more aware and knowledgeable as future citizens about local health issues, to give serious consideration to health careers, and, finally, to develop an action program on behalf of the community and raise the level of health care and health education.

Initially, many educators were skeptical. They were not convinced that such a project outside of the school could cover and accommodate the required subjects. Parents were generally pleased because careers in the field of health seemed to offer security and advancement. Townspeople welcomed the support.

The first step was curriculum integration of study and service opportunities. The initial draft encompassed 90 percent of what was required. The rest was included in diverse ways. Students were reminded that they were still students and had to take and pass standard exams mandated by the state.

They also had to pass the same graduation test required of all students to receive their diploma. The next phase was to identify work-study programs in the health profession. These involved shadowing supervisors of hospitals, insurance companies, clinics, emergency and trauma centers, veterinarian hospitals, and so on. Another critical piece had to do with culture diversity. Many of the students who enrolled in the program, as well as many of the patients served, came from different ethnic backgrounds. Many even had different traditions of healing and different attitudes toward health professionals that often dramatically affected care. Another important area was environmentally related illness—the impact of lead and asbestos, air pollution, and so on. Inevitably, this generated an active cleanup campaign initiated and led by students. Of course, there were regular workshops on career health options. A number of the sites focused on a particular major disease that seemed to dominate an area. In some cases it was cancer, in others it was heart disease. Whatever the case, students in effect majored in that disease and studied its biostatistics, epidemiology, and nutritional and environmental causes. Special attention was given by rural students to rural health delivery and the increased use of electronic delivery of information and diagnostics.

Initial evaluation was positive in all areas. There were few dropouts, excellent attendance, higher rates of college attendance, passing grades on mandated tests, and positive parental and community evaluations. In fact, members of the health profession in each community developed a supplementary diploma that was awarded at graduation to the students who participated in the school-community mutual benefit program.

In the next ten years the experimental model of the school outside the school became a major option of most high schools. Some parochial schools shifted the focus to religious impacts and services. A number of urban programs developed early education opportunities from birth to kindergarten. A few rural programs researched total electronic delivery of learning—the one-room schoolhouse electronic program.

Who and what benefited? Obviously, the benefits went above all to the students, who chose to exist in a real-world and real-time situation and to recognize how much they had to learn to be effective. It was truly service learning. Students also often were offered significant career exposure that led to major career and education choices later. Teachers found such students highly motivated and even eager to learn. Parents generally were amazed at the turnaround. Their kids got up in the morning without a struggle, watched what they ate, were regularly involved in exercise, watched less TV, and even spent weekends on project activities. The attitudes of many members of the community toward young people made a 180-degree turn. And the community itself experienced a kind of transfusion and pointed proudly to improvements that came about as a result of this community-rebuilding program. A slogan adopted by one of the earliest programs soon became the banner for all such programs: "Competence, Career, and Community: The Student as Future Citizen."

CHAPTER 42

Small Is Better

It was strange countertrend, in a way. Everything seemed to be moving toward standardization and consolidation. Mom-and-pop restaurants, groceries, general stores, and drugstores were gradually disappearing. Every major intersection had one of each major fast food operation. Super Wal-Marts and Home Depots were everywhere. No matter where one lived, shopping malls were 90 percent the same. To a large extent education followed suit. The regional unified high schools were like enormous K-Marts. Students hardly knew one another. A crushing sea of faces and bodies filled the halls when periods were changing. Security was a nightmare. Many high schools contracted with outside security firms for guards and metal detectors. And then suddenly, out of nowhere, a series of countertrends surfaced.

A number of big high schools decentralized and created smaller academies, or schools within schools, numbering 100–150 students. That seemed to be good compromise because it balanced the advantages of smaller with larger. But some schools went further. Buffalo, of all places, startled everyone in the state by creating a number of district-sponsored charter schools for its forty-four thousand students. As is often the case, desperation motivated enlightenment. The superintendent of schools, Marion Canedo, confessed: "We are at the end of our rope. I might as well put a padlock on the door. And if we don't help ourselves, who will?" The chairman of the school board, Jack Coyle, agreed: "If we can do more with less, then shame on us for not looking at it. It is a very radical change, but it's logical."

At the time Buffalo was the only school district in the country contemplating such comprehensive decentralization. What did they envision and what did they hope to accomplish? The charter schools would all be small, averaging one to two hundred students. They would be at all levels: elementary, middle, and high school. A few could be crossover schools combining two or all levels. Each would be independent and essentially run itself. It would accept total double accountability, fiscal and educational. It had to stay within budget and facilitate the passing of state exams. In other words, these entrepreneurial charter schools would follow the "risk and reward" model of all charter schools: produce or close down. This was a total departure from traditional practice. Failing public schools not only were allowed to continue, but also were propped up with extra support. The squeaky wheel got the most grease. An alternative had to be found that was more legitimately competitive on the one hand and more accountable on the other.

Meanwhile, Canada, facing the same double challenge, elected a different approach to achieving smallness. They moved junior and senior students out of overly big and crowded schools into cyber space. The Calgary school system implemented a multiple delivery system that combined electronic with traditional means of teaching. Students took courses online at home or at a cyber facility at their own pace. The school continued year round. Each student had to remain regularly in contact with teachers and tutors. Failure to be in touch for three days or more resulted in a phone call to parents and a possible meeting. Textbooks were used to supplement online materials. There were five official intakes per year when evaluation, testing, conferencing, and planning for next phases took place. "Onliners," as they were called, elected their own student councils and student advocates, arranged face-to-face meetings with teachers and tutors, and held their own graduation ceremony. In Calgary's case, smallness took the form of individualization as the antidote to standardization.

Finally, California joined the ranks of supporters of smallness, except in this case smallness was focused on salvaging at-risk students who had fallen through the cracks. Some fifteen community colleges in California created early-college high schools on their campuses. These small programs, combining high school and college, were designed to absorb high school dropouts who wanted to secure a high school diploma and go on to college. The goal was to provide a second chance for those students who had not been motivated to complete high school, persuading them with the double incentive of securing a high school diploma and an associate degree at the same time.

In the final analysis, then, small is big, at least in education. In various different ways it restores proportion to learning. It is intimate enough to involve knowing many well. Often it offers, especially through cyber space, the only real individualization of learning. It builds community between students and teachers and between students and members of the community. It is generally more accountable, because smaller is more transparent; there is no enormous bureaucracy in which to hide or bury failure. Students and teachers are directly and visibly responsible to each other for being mutually successful. To some extent it is a lovely throwback — to the one-room schoolhouse and the mom-and-pop operation. But then the future sometimes resides in the past.

Part XI

SOLUTION SUMMARIES

CHAPTER 43

Open-Ended Conclusions

A book focused on the future is never really finished. It is ultimately open ended and intentionally incomplete. It does not so much end as just stop—*media res*—in the middle of things. It is essentially a work in progress. Its finality is thus artificial but necessary. Such inconclusiveness may also be one of the reasons authors are reluctant to look ahead. Staying with current problems is more comforting than pushing for future solutions.

As a professor, one of my regular consolations at the end of a semester is the illusion that a few of the students will keep alive and active some of the ideas that we have shared. But in a book there are no students to carry the arguments further; and it would be presumptuous to expect readers to assume that role. But a certain kind of future reverberation may be available and possible. It appears in all the many and various solutions that have been advanced in the course of this book. They separately and collectively embody and hopefully advance the future. Thus, perhaps the best way of concluding and summarizing this book is to bring forward in one place all the solutions that have been offered to the problems examined in the course of this book.

To be sure, I can imagine some readers picking up this volume and flipping immediately to this last chapter of solutions, not unlike readers of mysteries who hope to find out by checking the last page who the murderer is. Although that may not be the ideal way of following the various developments traced here, it is an understandable curiosity. We are desperately seeking solutions. Here, then, in more condensed and summary form, are the major solutions and reconfigurations I propose to help change the future of education for the better.

1. THE SOLUTION OF THE FUTURE ITSELF

I hope by now the future as a creative point in time has proven its leverage and problem-solving power. Taking the next step delivers educators from the bondage of time and space, and from roles that are questionably adversarial and often punitive.

2. THE SOLUTION OF HOLISTICS

Fragments will not tell the whole story. Focusing on teachers or parents alone leaves out all the other members of a dynamic and interactive cast of characters. Rendering the challenge of change in piecemeal and limited terms leads to partial understanding and solutions. Only by assembling the big picture can totality be approximated. Only then, for example, can the labyrinthine, imposing, and apparently intractable educational system be appreciated as a formidable obstacle to change. Only by shaping that macro can we appreciate the minor miracles of the micro: homeschooling and charter schools. William Blake proclaimed, "I must create my own system or be enslaved by another's."

Holistics also tells us that we are not alone. There are many major players who collectively have the capacity to exercise shared leadership. Challenge is thus not unconnected. Larger patterns drive change. Putting together the total cast of characters and their multiple environments offers the promise of concerted action, which alone can give education back its future.

3. OPTIMUM UTILIZATION OF TALENT

Use the best of what you already have, not only to attract more of the same kind, but also to optimize their talents. Allow outstanding teachers to recruit outstanding teachers. Talent responds to talent. Then use them afterward to mentor the new hires. Finally, optimize the optimizers; multiply the few you already have into the many. Employ outstanding teachers as learning managers of small teams of teachers, tutors, techies, parent assistants, and so on. Master teachers are always master managers.

4. INDUCTION MODELS

Much has been rightly made of the need for induction programs for new teachers. In the past, novices were not treated with kid gloves; the approach was sink or swim. It worked for those who could float until they finally learned to swim. The rest drowned; as many as half of all new hires left within the first three years. Aside from its being wasteful of and perhaps even traumatic for those involved, this approach subjected students more often than perhaps necessary to green teachers. Then, too, in districts with shortages the loss was particularly acute, especially if fees had been paid to teacher recruiting firms.

The standard remedy is to develop a special induction program for new teachers. Although the evidence is not all in yet, we have learned enough to know what works, somewhat, and what does not, at all. All findings fall into three categories: what the teachers brought with them that helped, what kind of further help they needed, and, finally, what kind of support they actually got. In general it is not a happy story.

What helped was sound preparation in subject matter, good teacher prep programs, and, for second-career teachers, past experience of weathering storms. What the teachers needed was year-long (not one-shot) orientation programs, mentor support, a helpful and welcoming teacher culture, and administrative and district support. What they actually got was an initial single orientation session that was overwhelming; token or occasional mentoring; generally hostile, unhelpful, or indifferent fellow teachers; and virtually no administrative or district support.

There are many reasons why this occurs. First, aside from providing invitations to welcome new teachers, principals generally have not been required or empowered to acculturate new teachers. Moreover, they don't have the classroom experience to do it well. Second, the teacher culture itself is separatist and unsolicitous. Teachers ask, "What's in it for me?" and then go their own way. Third, those assigned to be full-time mentors are perceived to have an easy ride. Besides, full-time mentors cost too much, especially if their mentees leave after the first year. Fourth, grade-level or subject-matter supervisors are so overwhelmed in general that slippage is normal. The irony of course is that they also are busy recruiting replacements for those they have failed to retain. To all this add the special new pressures and environments new teachers encounter.

Some are doubly unlucky: the subject and the grade level at which they teach may be the focus of state and federal high-stakes testing. Even if this is not the case, the general testing and accountability environment is often oppressive and dislocating. Classroom management—a euphemism for control—is usually jeopardized easily by disciplinary problems, which may include direct threats of violence. Many new teachers struggle just to get to, let alone through, the curriculum. Sometimes, the physical logistics are exhausting: teachers are assigned classes on different floors, often in totally different parts of the building. Many teachers, like homeless bag ladies, put all their equipment on a trolley that they push from classroom to classroom. Jammed or nonfunctioning elevators mean they are regularly late and walk into bedlam.

When asked finally what they needed to succeed, all new teachers said the same things: time, consultation, and classroom management skills. Clearly, current induction programs are failing. What else might work?

The first thing to be done is to change the arrangement and range of the induction period. The key may be coteaching. It should not be a one-year, fast-and-dirty fix but a three-year program, which happens to match the time period of maximum vulnerability. For the first year, two teachers—one experienced, the other new—would be assigned to the same class or subject matter. They would partner or coteach, but the experienced teacher would dominate; she would occupy the foreground, the new teacher the background. The new teacher in short would be an apprentice. In the second year they would be equals. The apprentice would now have graduated to being an equal partner. In the third year roles would be exchanged; the new teacher would occupy the foreground, the mentor the background.

Depending on the background and experience of the new teacher and what he or she brings to the task, the three-year program can be reduced to two. In some instances, quick studies can combine all three phases in one year. The program is elastic. It does not dictate but only insists that if some need more time, it is there for them. Treating time as a variable rather than a constant makes optimum use of the limited number of excellent mentors. But perhaps the major stumbling block is costs— finding the money to pay the usually very high salary of a full-time teacher serving as a mentor who does not teach.

But other options present themselves. Use retired educators—teachers, administrators, education college professors, and so on—who only want to work part-time. Train them in the last year before retirement so that they can hit the ground running. Review the list of approved classroom substitutes. Many there also would be happy with an adjunct status. Finally, a number of parents are former teachers who decided to take time off to raise a family but would welcome getting back into the fold part-time. Such mentors do not cost as much as full-time employees and do not require benefits. A full-time commitment to a new teacher even part of the time may overcome the obstacles that cause failure.

5. OPTIMIZE CURRICULUM

Help both teachers and administrators understand that instruction can be optimized only through careful matching of teacher and curriculum. Curricula, especially new ones, have to be self-defining. They have to describe in specific terms what kind of teachers and what kind of teacher styles best optimize their implementation. Without such fits of column A and column B, principals often have no basis for assigning faculty, with the result that often the blind are leading the blind. Fortunately, evaluations of such new programs can be mined for developing profiles of teachers who find such curricula minimally congenial and optimally challenging. That results in a curricula win-win-win: designers of new curricula find their best champions; teachers find an outlet for their special talents; and administrators finally are provided with a checklist for precise matchmaking.

6. CHANGING THE TEACHER CULTURE

Excesses dominate in teacher culture, with most teachers showing extremes of independence (in the classroom) and dependence (outside of it). Then, too, no one really knows what is going on in that classroom. Observations by busy principals tend to be occasional, superficial, and staged. Two solutions present themselves. First, a new goal of interdependence, brought about by extensive lesson planning with colleagues on the one hand and consultation with parents on the other, needs to replace excessive independence and dependence. Second, teachers' excessive privacy, bordering on secrecy, already is being invaded by electronic data tracking of both teacher and student performance. Transparency thus increasingly will reign. Data tracking already has yielded two results. Teachers are now provided with diagnostic tools to improve student performance. Parents are now provided with information on which schools and even teachers they should choose for their kids. Data may be transforming education into a market-driven, competitive institution.

7. COMPETITION AND CHOICE

The monopoly of public school education is no longer the norm. Competition has created choice, not only for parents and students but for all the other major players as well. Teachers have more external and internal choices. Externally, they can join charter schools or seek employment with one of the many educational vendors servicing education. Internally, they can become teacher managers or leaders and administer learning while remaining in the classroom. Principals have the same external options; in addition, they can significantly alter their role to become brokers or coaches employing a less directive style. In short, choice not only now dominates education but will continue to expand in the future.

8. ACCOUNTABILITY

Accountability is unavoidable. For better or worse it is now a permanent fixture of education. It has been enshrined and mandated in the federal legislation NCLB. Rather than resisting it, educators have to put their own mark of ownership on it. Above all, they have to internalize accountability so that it does not remain an external punitive set of rules and regulations. In short, the cure has to be cured. Education has to become not the object but the subject of accountability. It has to develop its own quality control system.

9. LEADERSHIP SHARING

Nothing, perhaps, more typifies the drama of educational change than leadership sharing. And nothing, perhaps, better sums up the nature of those changes than the linkage between school choice and leadership choice. The monopoly of top-down leadership is over. The vertical has been leveled to the horizontal. School teams and councils with principals now lead schools. In some charter schools, teacher leaders have replaced principals altogether. Parents and students are increasingly part of the empowerment of leadership sharing; students are increasingly being asked to lead teacher-parent conferences, and parents are being asked to partner with teachers. Parents of homeschoolers are not just teachers and tutors; they are also learning managers and inevitably learning leaders. In short, leadership options and styles have become so varied and distributed that to perceive leadership as still a single factor restricted to a single constituency is to pass off a half as a whole. No matter how messy and overlapping, the mix has to be recognized, preserved, and supported, for it has about it the strong diversity of alternatives required for the future.

10. EVALUATION SHARING

Probably the most important exchange between teachers and supervisor has changed the least. Evaluation is often dreaded. Teachers find it general perfunctory or punitive—in either case unhelpful. Supervisors are often frustrated by their inability to use evaluation to change the behaviors of poorly performing tenured teachers. Such adversarial limitations are now compounded by mandated performance goals and by the new electronic performance tracking systems, which bring new transparency to the evaluation process. Teachers and supervisors are thus being driven more and more into each other's arms. Both are even being offered incentive pay for high levels of performance. In short, it is time for the evaluation process to change.

It must become collaborative, not unilateral; focused on and linked to professional development; aligned to schoolwide, state, and federal goals; and structured to accommodate teacher-directed, mid- to long-term growth plans. In short, we need a twenty-first-century evaluation-sharing process.

11. MULTIPLE PARTNERING SOLUTIONS AND HYBRIDS

As the lone ranger leaders or teachers of the educational mythical culture pass away, they are being replaced by increasing teacher-teacher collaboration, teacher-administrator cooperation, teacher-parent partnerships, teacher-student colearning, and, perhaps most surprising of all, teacher-machine symbiosis. The singular and the solo are gone. Hybrids now reign.

12. E-LEARNING

Time, place, and even space are no longer fixed coordinates of education. Subject-matter delivery systems have changed the range and even the depth of subject matter. In most colleges, economics, for example, is now e-economics; English is now e-English. The time of technology is every hour of the day and every day of the year. The space of technology is everywhere. The problem in many homes today is not watching too much TV but spending too much time online. Students are already far into the twenty-first century. Education is generally still in the twentieth.

There is a pressing need to review teaching technology and electronic learning, to assess their value, cost benefits, and human-machine relationships. It is expected that during the first three decades of this century, twenty thousand years of progress (relative to earlier human progress) will unfold; and it will be largely technology driven. That is the world in which current students will live; and education needs to give them the tools to survive and to grow. It is time to make every school in part a cyber school, and connect via technology school and home, homework and homeschooling.

13. NEW SCHEDULE AND NEW DAY

The focus on dramatic supersolutions such as doubling teacher salaries and offering performance bonuses to teachers who raise student scores—and thus wooing talent away from the professions and into education—is naive. It won't work; and if it does it won't last. Attracting and keeping are not the same thing.

What teachers need is more time to do their job. More money is always welcome, but it will not buy time. Specifically, teachers need time to share their lesson plans with other teachers, to undertake together critical reviews of students' work, to meet parents and develop with them a program of cooperative follow-up learning, and to be involved in professional development and growth.

Sadly, finding teachers the time to do such key work is not a current administrative priority. If teachers were asked to solve the problem, they would immediately identify the villain of the piece. It is the schedule. Change often begins by taking a constant and making it a variable. Specifically, have classes meet three times rather than five times a week. Teachers would provide weekly learning plans for the two days of team and individual study. The two days gained would be used to partner with colleagues and with parents. Changing work conditions to help teachers be successful may turn out to be a more attractive way of acquiring and keeping new teachers than offering them big bucks.

14. PLANNING SCHOOL CHOICE

At present, the competition of school choice has sown seeds of discontent. Public school teachers and supervisors have attacked charter schools. In Ohio the teachers' union took charter schools to court to force their closure. Even homeschooling, which does not drain off per-capita dollars, is being subjected to calls for greater regulation and oversight by state departments of education. The system demands its pound of flesh. But while all this sound and fury are going on, and charges and countercharges are being leveled, students are the losers.

With so many options available now, and perhaps more available in the future, students and their parents need planning help. They need a structured way of optimizing their choices; they need guidance about positioning. In short, they need the services of educational professionals who can counsel and advise parents and students as to their future options. For that to happen, acrimony must be replaced by advocacy, bitter exchanges replaced by taking the high road. No better use of government grants or foundation awards could be found than to fund the development of a pilot model of a districtwide planning clearinghouse for local parents and students.

15. EXPANDED PARENTS' ROLES

Already noted is the important role of parents as learning partners with teachers. Teachers, in fact, will recognize that without such parental follow-up, they may not be able to reach their performance goals or student achievement may not last. Teachers will be required to invest more time, energy, and planning expertise in parent training, which may be equal in importance to collegial relationships.

Parents are also becoming more active and aggressive fund-raisers, in some cases creating foundations to funnel funds raised to education. Recently, parents in a small town in Oregon raised the equivalent of a favorite teacher's salary to save her job from downsizing. But a future agenda of parents is still evolving. Although its outline is not completely known, what is clear is that parents will become education's principle advocates, but only if they can become its principal partners.

16. TELLING THE TRUTH AS A SOLUTION: THE CASE OF NCLB

Although the legislation of NCLB has much to recommend it and probably will accomplish much, it rests on a false rallying cry. The claim that no child will be left behind is as absolutist as zero defects in manufacturing or the zero tolerance school policy toward violence that followed Columbine. The truth is that fewer children will be left behind, but many still will. Higher standards and heavy testing will force many students to perform at higher levels. But the same tests will also result in failures — such as the six thousand students in Massachusetts who, having failed the graduation test five times, will not be granted a high school diploma.

Some may argue that maybe that is the way it should be. Those six thousand students had a chance to pass five times and they failed each time. Why should the diploma be cheapened by giving the same recognition to those who succeeded and those who did not? But there are related issues not so easily disposed of.

First, let us not lie. Let us admit off the bat that some will be left behind, maybe fewer than before, but still some. So honesty compels us to be less absolutist and to change the name of the law to Fewer Children Left Behind, or FCLB. That may not have the political clout of the original, but it at least is honest.

Second, there is something disturbing about those six thousand students. Who are they? Why did they fail five times? Why were they allowed to fail five times? By the third time, at least, did not some warning light of intervention go off? Why did we allow the predictable to happen? If we believed if was inevitable and that many of these students could not be reached by schooling, then at least they should have been allowed to go to work. Indeed, the irony is that some of those six thousand may in fact later succeed at work or at least be able to live sustaining lives.

Third, we should be worrying about those who fail. They could engender major social costs of considerable duration. If they change their attitudes and goals later, will the lack of a diploma be an obstacle? To be sure, there is the alterative of the general equivalency diploma, but passing that recently has been made harder. Besides, it is still regular schooling—at which they have failed, and which perhaps has failed them.

Education does not have the resources or the expertise to become a social welfare organization. It should teach all those who want to learn and try to reach all those who apparently do not. But what always falls within its purview is diagnostic ability. It can identify and profile those who do not appear to profit from schooling and therefore should be offered a separate track. That separate track should not be the so-called alternative schools, which in reality are largely holding pens for future criminals and should be abolished. Rather, the track should connect directly to the social welfare mechanisms and resources of local, state, and federal agencies on the one hand, and to work opportunities on the other. However, an open-door policy allowing students to return to education at any time, totally or in part, should be maintained. Perhaps that way the total of six thousand might be reduced, and, equally as important, the stigma of failure might not be attached to those students for the rest of their lives.

17. AT-RISK LEAPFROGGING AND INTERVENTION

A somewhat unpredictable, but highly productive, solution to preventing the six thousand problem is being implemented in the North Oakland High School. There, a number of at-risk students come to school an hour early to take a college-level course in sociology. The rationale is twofold. First, higher-level learning may be more interesting and succeed where lower-level has not. Second, sociology is focused in large part on the lives these kids are living and/or will be living. Why not make the field's insights and research available to them? Why not show them their possible futures?

It has worked. Dropout rates have been reduced. All students involved in the intervention graduated. Fifty percent are going on to college. There are at least three reasons why this form of intervention succeeded. First, expectations were raised. In effect, these kids were told they had the intelligence to undertake and pass college-level work. Second, the material had great and immediate relevance. It directly engaged their current lives. Third, the intervention was proactive. It looked ahead to lives that were often compromised and unfulfilling. It thus invited life-changing decisions.

18. STUDENT CENTERED

Demanding that students do more without giving them the opportunity to run their lives and to experience the self-worth of self-management won't work at all; or, at best, it will produce temporary mechanical successes. Student-centeredness has to go beyond hype and embrace empowerment. Students must be given the chance to lead parent-teacher conferences and to plan their educational and work futures. The reason service learning deepens student involvement is that it fuses work and school, real problem solving and academics.

19. COMMUNITY SCHOOLS

The greater involvement of students in the community via service learning is enhanced when the school itself becomes a community school that is open when school is over and that accommodates community activities. That double use of facilities has brought town and gown closer together and in some communities has reduced or eliminated much of the opposition to school funding and the authorization of new construction. Sometimes, community use has been extended to include religious buildings, which are routinely underutilized.

20. ECONOMICALLY DRIVEN SCHOOL REFORM

Generally, educators, except for in some charter schools, have never been asked to run schools as an economic unit with a bottom line. As a result, teachers and administrators have not had to assume financial solvency and continuity; and being fiscally responsible and staying within budget has not been part of their jobs. That is a major oversight, especially given the insistence on general accountability on the one hand and current budgetary reductions on the other.

What would happen then if gradually financial accountability were made part of all job descriptions, and councils of teachers and administrators were empowered to review and prioritize all expenditures? I would predict major turnarounds, including economically driven school reform.

21. NEW REPORT CARD

Electronically driven data tracking and evaluation of performance ultimately will result in new report cards. They will be complex, multipaged, and visually oriented. Each subject will be broken down into many subset parts and then displayed in rubric form of differentiated levels of achievement. The report card will thus not only report but also diagnose achievement. As such, it will serve not as a single snapshot but as a working document for continuous dialogue between teachers, students, and parents. Initially, kids may have to explain its intricacies to their parents.

22. HOMEWORK

What teachers send home has to be reexamined in at least three ways. First, homework potentially turns each home into a homeschool. Second, homework needs to be differentiated to reflect the needs and growth of each student (the more diagnostic report card will help here). Third, parents need to become the teachers, coaches, and brokers of homework. But, sadly, teachers generally are not providing detailed instructions about homework, its uses, and its parental supporters. Generally, it was not part of their training in colleges of education. As a result they cannot provide the necessary guidance and training for parents to recognize their multiple supporting roles, which serve to link school and home. Teachers and parents should attend the same professional development workshop on homework.

23. RESEARCH AND EDUCATION

In general, educational research has been a mixed bag. At one extreme, much of it is unapplied. Often, the next step of translating findings into workable applications has not been taken or facilitated. At the other extreme, it is often ignored or underutilized. Educators go about reinventing the wheel. To ease and accommodate that process, books summarizing research have increasingly been appearing. But they are always at least two years behind current research.

Why are educators generally ignorant about or reluctant to use research? First, many do use research, but it is usually tied chronologically to when they received their degree. And that is true, sadly, of many professors of education. But the basic problem is that there is so much to know that it is overwhelming. Then, too, the findings of one study often are disputed by those of another study, frequently on grounds beyond the understanding of most educators.

Two solutions can be suggested. First, personalize the research. Encourage teachers to use classroom research as a way of reintroducing and affirming the practice and power of the research process itself. What is used and works is valued. Second, send teachers as a group to national conferences to learn about the state of the art and to discuss ways to make it happen in classrooms.

24. WORLD CITIZENRY

Schools all over world generally and rightly study the history of their country. But the increasing pervasiveness of global connectivity, economy, and ecology offers educators the opportunity to be advocates for the ideology of an interdependent world. Schools alone are in a position to offer a vision of one world and planet. It is a noble and proactive calling. It takes the high road of the future. In the process, interconnections can be studied, pen pal relationships all over the world can be developed, and, above all, the notion of dual citizenship—national and international—can be forged. By advocating such a future, education may rediscover and reaffirm its own.

POSTSCRIPT

Enough of me—now it's time for you to write some of your own solutions. If you wish to share them with me and perhaps see them incorporated into a second edition of this book, send them to me at ibuchen@msn.com.

References

Barth, R. 1999. *The Teacher Leader*. Providence, RI: Rhode Island Foundation.

Black, S. 2000. "Find Time to Lead." *ASBJM*, 1979.

Buchen, I. 2000. "Radical Vision of Education." *Futurist*. June.

———. 2002. "Convergence as Mega-Trend." *Foresight* 12, no. 3.

Carnegie Council on Adolescent Development. 1989. *Turning Points: Preparing American Youth for the 21st Century: The Report of the Task Force on Education of Young Adolescents*.

Chard, S. C. 1998. *The Project Approach*. New York: Scholastic.

Christian Science Monitor. 2002. May 22.

CNet. 2002. May 22.

Converse, J., and H. Schuman. 1974. *Conversations at Random*. New York: John Wiley.

Cummins, J. 1996. *Negotiating Identities*. Ontario, CA: Bilingual Education.

Curtis, D. 2002. "The Power of Projects." *Educational Leadership* 60, no. 1.

Dewey, J. 1899. In *Dewey on Education*, ed. M. Dworkin. Reprint, New York: Teachers College Press, 1959.

Douglas, J. 1985. *Creative Interviewing*. Beverly Hills, CA: Sage.

DuFour, E., and R. Eaker. 1998. *Professional Learning Community*. Bloomington, IN: National Education Service.

Education Week. 2002a. April 3.

———. 2002b. May 20.

———. 2002c. May 29.

———. 2002d. June 1.

———. 2002e. November 27.

———. 2003a. January 8.

———. 2003b. April 9.

——. 2003c. May 28.

Elmore, R. 2000. *Building a New Structure for School Leadership*. Washington, DC: Albert Shanker Institute.

——. 2002. "Hard Questions about Practice." *Educational Leadership* 59, no. 8.

Exemplars Project. 2002. At www.exemplars.com/differentiate.html.

Farber, H. S. 2003. "Job Loss in the U.S., 1981–2001." *Work Index* 24, no. 4.

Fink, E., and L. Resnick. 2001. "Developing Principals as Instructional Leaders." *PDK*, April.

Greenleaf, R. K. 1984. *Servant Leadership*. Mahwah, NJ: Paulist Press.

Hamel, G., and C. K. Pralahad. 1994. *Competing for the Future*. Cambridge, MA: Harvard Business School Press.

Hershberg, T. 2003. "Accountability, Adequacy, and Access." *Education Week*, March 3.

Hurley, J. C. 2001. "The Principalship: Less May Be More." *Education Week*, May 23.

Independent [London]. 2002. May 21.

Katz, L. G., and S. C. Chard. 1999. *Engaging Children's Minds*. Stanford: Ablex Publishing.

Kiuchi, T. 1998. "Lessons from the Rain Forest." Plenary address at World Future Society, San Francisco.

Kohm, B. 2002. "Opening Schools for Discussion." *Educational Leadership* 59, no. 8.

Lambert, L. 1995. *The Constructivist Leader*. New York: Teachers College Press.

——. 2002. "A Framework for Shared Leadership." *Educational Leadership* 59, no. 8.

Lieberman, G., and L. Hoody. 1998. *Closing the Achievement Gap*. San Diego: State Education Roundtable.

Maine, N. 1998. "Playing the Community Game." *New Directions for Youth Development* 14, no. 1.

Marx, R. W., P. C. Blumenfeld, J. S. Krajcik, and E. Soloway. 1997. "Enacting Project-Based Science." *Elementary School Journal* 97.

Mortimer, J. 2003. *Working and Growing Up in America*. Ann Arbor: University of Michigan Press.

Nagel, N. 1996. *Learning through Real-World Problem-Solving*. Thousand Oaks, CA: Corwin Press.

Neumann, F., and G. Wehlage. 1995. *Successful School Restructuring*. Madison, WI: Center on Organization and Restructuring of Schools.

Neuman, M., and W. Simmons. 2000. "Leadership for Student Learning." *PDK*, September. *New York Times*. 2003. July 11.

Ramsay, R. l999. *Lead, Follow, or Get Out of the Way*. Thousand Oaks, CA: Corwin Press.

Ratcliffe, J. 2002. "Scenario Planning: Strategic Interviews and Conversations." *Foresight* 4, no. 1.

Ringland, G. 1998. *Scenario Planning*. London: Wiley.

Silverman, D. 1997. *Qualitative Research*. London: Sage.

Simkins, M., K. Cole, F. Tavalin, and B. Means. 2002. *Increasing Student Learning through Multi-media Projects*. Alexandria, VA: ASCD.

Spillane, J., R. Halverson, and J. Diamond. 2001. "Investigating School Leadership Practice: A Distributed Perspective." *Educational Researcher* 30, no. 3.

Steinberg, L. 1984. *When Teenagers Work: The Social and Psychological Costs of Teenage Employment*. Philadelphia: Temple University Press.

Thomas, J. W. 2000. "A Review of Research on Project Based Learning." At http://www.k12reform.org/foundation/pbl/research/paper.pdf.

Tomlinson, C. A. 1999. *The Differentiated Classroom*. Alexandria, VA: ASCD.

van der Heijden, K. 1996. *Scenarios: the Art of Strategic Conversation*. London: Wiley.

Zucker, A., and R. Kozma. 2003. *The Virtual High School*. New York: Teachers College Press.

About the Author

Irving H. Buchen received his Ph.D. from Johns Hopkins University in Baltimore, Md., and has taught and served as an administrator at California State University, University of Wisconsin, and Penn State. He is currently vice president of academic affairs at Aspen University and a member of the doctoral faculty at Capella University, both distance education institutions. He is an active management and education consultant, a senior research associate with Comwell, HR Partners, and Ed/Visons, and CEO of his own training and coaching company, which offers parent success workshops both nationally and internationally. An experienced researcher, Dr. Buchen has published several books and over 150 articles. He can be reached at ibuchen@msn.com.